CHARLES DICKENS

THE TALE OF TWO CITIES

Charles Dickens

THE TALE OF TWO CITIES

[Edited with Summary and Analysis,
Study Questions and Criticism]

Mansi Sachdeva
B.A. English (Hons), Delhi University;
M.A., M. Phil. (English), IGNOU

ANMOL PUBLICATIONS PVT. LTD.
NEW DELHI - 110 002 (INDIA)

ANMOL PUBLICATIONS PVT. LTD.

H.O.: 4374/4B, Ansari Road, Darya Ganj,
New Delhi-110 002 (India)
Ph.: 23278000, 23261597

B.O.: No. 1015, Ist Main Road, BSK IIIrd Stage
IIIrd Phase, IIIrd Block
Bangalore - 560 085 (India)
Visit us at: www.anmolpublications.com

The Tale of Two Cities

First Published, 2009

PRINTED IN INDIA

Printed at Mehra Offset Press, Delhi.

Contents

Preface

A Tale of Two Cities (1859) is the second historical novel by Charles Dickens. The plot centres on the years leading up to the French Revolution and culminates in the Jacobin Reign of Terror. It starts with Dr. Alexandre Manette's 1757 imprisonment and concludes 36 years later with the execution of Sydney Carton. The first issue of Dickens's literary periodical All the Year Round appearing April 30, 1859, contained the first of thirty-one weekly instalments of the novel, which ran until November 26, 1859.

The opening – "It was the best of times, it was the worst of times..." – and closing – "It is a far, far better thing that I do, than I have ever done; it is a far, far better rest that I go to than I have ever known." – of the book are among the most famous lines in English literature.

The book tells, first and foremost, the story of Charles Darnay and Sydney Carton, who look similar but are very different in their personalities. The term for this is a doppelganger. A doppelganger is a character that physically looks like another character but there are other differences, like beliefs, values, personalities, etc. Darnay is a romantic French aristocrat; Carton is a cynical English barrister. Both fall deeply in love with the same woman, Lucie Manette.

Other major characters include Dr. Manette (Lucie's father), who was unjustly imprisoned in the infamous Bastille for many years under a lettre de cachet, and Madame Defarge, a female revolutionary with an implacable grudge against the aristocratic Evrémonde dynasty.

The title reflects the way in which the setting alternates between London and Paris. Two of the 45 chapters are set in both countries, nineteen in England and 24 in France. They tell of the shameless corruption, abuse and inhumanity of the French nobles towards the peasantry. The masses, oppressed for centuries, rise up at last and destroy their masters, becoming themselves just as evil and corrupt.

Author

Chapter 1

Introduction

Charles Dickens (1812-1870), English Victorian era author wrote numerous highly acclaimed novels including his most autobiographical *David Copperfield* (1848-1850).

"Whether I shall turn out to be the hero of my own life, or whether that station will be held by anybody else, these pages must show. To begin my life with the beginning of my life, I record that I was born (as I have been informed and believe) on a Friday, at twelve o'clock at night. It was remarked that the clock began to strike, and I began to cry, simultaneously."

As a prolific 19th Century author of short stories, plays, novellas, novels, fiction and non, during his lifetime Dickens became known the world over for his remarkable characters, his mastery of prose in the telling of their lives, and his depictions of the social classes, mores and values of his times. Some considered him the spokesman for the poor, for he definitely brought much awareness to their plight, the downtrodden and the have-nots. He had his share of critics like Virginia Woolf and Henry James, but also many admirers, even into the 21st Century.

Gilbert Keith Chesterton wrote numerous introductions to his works, collected in his Appreciations and Criticisms of the works of Charles Dickens (1911) and in his highly acclaimed biography Charles Dickens (1906) he writes: He was the voice in England of this humane intoxication and expansion, this encouraging of anybody to be anything. Critic John Forster (1812-1876) became his best friend, editor of many of his serialisations, and official biographer after his death, publishing The Life of Charles Dickens in 1874. Scottish poet and author Andrew Lang (1844-1912) included a letter to Dickens in his Letters to Dead Authors (1886).

Elbert Hubbard (1856-1915) in his Little Journeys (1916) series follows in the footsteps of Dickens through his old haunts in London. George Gissing (1857-1903) also respected his works and wrote several introductions for them, as well as his Charles Dickens: A Critical Study (1898) in which he writes: Humour is the soul of his work. Like the soul of man, it permeates a living fabric which, but for its creative breath, could never have existed. While George Orwell (1903-1950) was at times a critic of Dickens, in his 1939 essay Charles Dickens he, like many others before, again brought to light the author still relevant today and worthy of continued study: Nearly everyone, whatever his actual conduct may be, responds emotionally to the idea of human brotherhood. Dickens voiced a code which was and on the whole still is believed in, even by people who violate it. It is difficult otherwise to explain why he could be both read by working people (a thing that has happened to no other novelist of his stature) and buried in Westminster Abbey.

Charles John Huffman Dickens was born on 7 February, 1812 in Portsmouth, Hampshire, England (now the Dickens Birthplace Museum) the son of Elizabeth née Barrow (1789-1863) and John Dickens (c.1785-1851) a clerk in the Navy Pay Office. John was a congenial man, hospitable and generous to a fault which caused him financial difficulties throughout his life. He inspired the character Mr. Micawber in *David Copperfield* (1849-1850). Charles had an older brother Frances, known as Fanny, and younger siblings Alfred Allen, Letitia Mary, Harriet, Frederick William known as Fred, Alfred Lamert, and Augustus Newnham.

When Dickens' father was transferred to Chatham in Kent County, the family settled into the genteel surroundings of a larger home with two live-in servants—one being Mary Weller who was young Charles' nursemaid. Dickens was a voracious reader of such authors as Henry Fielding, Daniel Defoe, and Oliver Goldsmith. When he was not attending the school of William Giles where he was an apt pupil, he and his siblings played games of make-believe, gave recitations of poetry, sang songs, and created theatrical productions that would spark a lifelong love of the theatre in Dickens. But household expenses were rising and in 1824, John Dickens was imprisoned for debt in the Marshalsea Prison. All of the family went with him except for Charles who, at the age of twelve, was sent off to work at Warren's Shoe Blacking Factory to help support the family, pasting labels on boxes. He lived in a boarding house in Camden Town and walked to work everyday and visited his father on Sundays.

It was one of the pivotal points in Dickens' education from the University of Hard Knocks and would stay with him forever. The idyllic days of his childhood were over and he was rudely introduced to the world of the working poor, where child labour was rampant and few if any adults spared a kind word for many abandoned or orphaned children. Many of his future characters like Oliver Twist, David Copperfield, and Philip Pirrip would be based on his own experiences. The appalling working conditions, long hours and poor pay typical of the time were harsh, but the worst part of the experience was that when his father was released his mother insisted he continue to work there. While he felt betrayed by and resented her for many years to come, his father arranged for him to attend the Wellington House Academy in London as a day pupil from 1824-1827, perhaps saving him from a life of factory work and setting him on the road to becoming a writer.

In 1827 the Dickens were evicted from their home in Somers Town for unpaid rent dues and Charles had to leave school. He obtained a job as a clerk in the law firm of Ellis and Blackmore. He soon learned shorthand and became a court reporter for the Doctors Commons. He spent much of his spare time reading in the British Museum's library and studying acting. In 1830 he met and fell in love with Maria Beadnell, though her father sent her to finishing school in Paris a few years later. In 1833, his first story of many, "A Dinner at Poplar Walk" was published in the *Monthly Magazine*. He also had some sketches published in the *Morning Chronicle* which in 1834 he began reporting for and adopted the pseudonym 'Boz'. At this time Dickens moved out on his own to live as a bachelor at Furnival's Inn, Holborn. His father was arrested again for debts and Charles bailed him out, and for many years later both his parents and some of his siblings turned to him for financial assistance.

Dickens' first book, a collection of stories titled *Sketches by Boz* was published in 1836, a fruitful year for him. He married Catherine Hogarth, daughter of the editor of the *Evening Chronicle* on 2 April, 1836, at St. Luke's in Chelsea. A year later they moved into 48 Doughty Street, London, now a museum. The couple would have ten children: Charles Culliford Boz (b.1837), Mary (Mamie) (1838-1838), Kate Macready (b.1839), Walter Landor (b.1841), Francis (Frank) Jeffrey (b.1844), Alfred Tennyson (b.1845), Sydney Smith (b.1847), Henry Fielding (b.1849), Dora Annie (1850-1851), Edward Bulwer Lytton (b.1852). Also in the same year, 1836, Dickens became editor for *Bentley's Miscellany* of which *Pickwick Papers* (1836-1837) was first serialised.

Thus began a prolific and commercially successful period of Dickens' life as a writer. Most of his novels were first serialised in monthly magazines as was a common practice of the time. *Oliver Twist* between 1837 and 1839 was followed by *Nicholas Nickleby* (1838-1839), *The Old Curiosity Shop* (1840-1841), and *Barnaby Rudge* (1841). Dickens' series of five Christmas Books were soon to follow; *A Christmas Carol* (1843), *The Chimes* (1844), *The Cricket on the Hearth* (1845), *The Battle of Life* (1846), and *The Haunted Man* (1848). Dickens had found a readership who eagerly anticipated his next installments.

After the death of Catherine's sister Mary in 1837 the couple holidayed in various parts of England. After Dickens resigned from *Bentley's* in 1839, they moved to 1 Devonshire Terrace, Regent's Park. Further travels to the United States and

Canada in 1842 led to his controversial *American Notes* (1842). *Martin Chuzzlewit* was first serialised in 1843. The next year the Dickens traveled through Italy and settled in Genoa for a year of which his *Pictures From Italy* (1846) was written.

Dombey and Son (1846) was his next publication, followed by *David Copperfield* (1849). In 1850 he started his own weekly journal *Household Words* which would be in circulation for the next nine years. From 1851 to 1860 the Dickens lived at Tavistock House where Charles became heavily involved in amateur theatre. He wrote, directed, and acted in many productions at home with his children and friends, often donating the money raised from ticket sales to those in need. He collaborated with Wilkie Collins on the drama *No Thoroughfare* (1867). Novels to follow were *Bleak House* (1852-1853), *Hard Times* (1854), and *Little Dorrit* (1855-1857). In 1856 Dickens purchased Gad's Hill, his last place of residence near Rochester in Kent County. He continued in the theatre as well, acting in Wilkie Collins' *The Frozen Deep* in 1857 with actress Ellen Ternan (1839-1914) playing opposite him. The two fell in love and Dickens would leave Catherine a year later.

By now Dickens was widely read in Europe and in 1858 he set off on a tour of public readings. A year later he founded his second weekly journal All the Year Round, the same year A Tale of Two Cities (1859) was first serialised. Great Expectations (1860-1861) was followed by Our Mutual Friend (1864-1865). In 1865, traveling back from Paris with Ellen and her mother, they were involved in the disastrous Staplehurst train crash, of which Dickens sustained minor injuries, but never fully recovered from the post-traumatic shock of it. Two years later he traveled to America for a reading tour. His 'farewell readings' took place in London's St. James Hall. Charles Dickens died from a cerebral hemorrhage on 9 June 1870 at his home, Gad's Hill. He is buried in Poet's Corner of Westminster Abbey, London, his tomb inscribed thus: "He was a sympathiser to the poor, the suffering, and the oppressed; and by his death, one of England's greatest writers is lost to the world." Thomas Carlyle (1795-1881), Scottish historian and author, upon hearing of his death said: The good, the gentle, high-gifted, ever-friendly, noble Dickens—every inch of him an honest man. Unfinished at his death, The Mystery of Edwin Drood was published in 1870.

My father had left a small collection of books in a little room upstairs, to which I had access (for it adjoined my own) and which nobody else in our house ever troubled. From that blessed little room, Roderick Random, Peregrine Pickle, Humphrey Clinker, Tom Jones, the Vicar of Wakefield, Don Quixote, Gil Blas, and Robinson Crusoe, came out, a glorious host, to keep me company. They kept alive my fancy, and my hope of something beyond that place and time, - they, and the Arabian Nights, and the Tales of the Genii, - and did me no harm; for whatever harm was in some of them was not there for me; I knew nothing of it. It is astonishing to me now, how I found time, in the midst of my porings and blunderings over heavier themes, to read those books as I did

Chapter 2

Charles Dickens: Biography

THE LIFE OF CHARLES DICKENS

From a very early age Charles Dickens knew he wanted to be gentleman. Unfortunately the odds weren't in his favour.

His family was constantly on the edge of financial and social disaster. However they did have some limited funds put aside to send one of their children to a university or academy. Mr. and Mrs. John Dickens considered the talents and qualifications of all their children. They wanted to use the money earmarked for education where it would do the most good. It was as if they were placing all their bets on one child.

Charles was not that child. His parents chose to send their daughter, Fanny, to school. She had a talent for music and was sent to an academy. Not long after that Charles was sent to work at the blacking factory.

It seemed as if everything was against him. However he had talent, and more importantly he had desire, drive and a strong belief in himself. He worked hard to make his dream life into a reality.

Charles Dickens wasn't perfect. He was stubborn and sometimes quick tempered. He often blamed others for the problems that he himself caused. The force of will that enabled him to succeed prevented him from taking an honest look at his own life.

While he was unable to learn from the lessons of his own life perhaps we, his readers, can be more fortunate. A study of his life reveals that perfection is not a qualification for success and that no one really defines us but ourselves.

The Childhood of Charles Dickens

Charles Dickens was born on February 7, 1812 in Portsmouth. His parents were John and Elizabeth Dickens. Charles was the second of their eight children.

John was a clerk in a payroll office of the navy. He and Elizabeth were an outgoing, social couple. They loved parties, dinners and family functions. In fact, Elizabeth attended a ball on the night that she gave birth to Charles.

Finances were a constant concern for the family. The costs of entertaining along with the expenses of having a large family were too much for John's salary. In fact, when Charles was just four months old the family moved to a smaller home to cut expenses.

Mary Weller was an early influence on Charles. She was hired to care for the Dickens children. Her bedtime stories, stories she swore were quite true, featured people like Captain Murder who would make pies of out his wives.

The young woman who brought me acquainted with Captain Murderer had a fiendish enjoyment of my terrors, and used to begin, I remember - as a sort of introductory overture - by clawing the air with both hands, and uttering a long low hollow groan. So acutely did I suffer from this ceremony in combination with this infernal Captain, that I sometimes used to plead I thought I was hardly strong enough and old enough to hear the story again just yet. — *The Uncommercial Traveller - Nurse's Stories*

From a very young age Charles dreamed of becoming a gentleman. He wanted an education. His parents did have some limited funds put aside to send one of their children to a university or academy. Mr. and Mrs. John Dickens considered the talents and qualifications of all their children.

They wanted to use the money earmarked for education where it would do the most good. It was as if they were placing all their bets on one child. Charles was not that child.

His parents chose to send their daughter, Fanny, to school. She had a talent for music and was sent to an academy.

Then came the darkest hours in the life of Charles Dickens. When he was 12 it looked like his dreams would never come true. John Dickens was arrested and sent to jail for failure to pay a debt. At that time the family sent Charles to work in a blacking or shoe-polish factory. (While employed there he met Bob Fagin. Charles later used the name in *Oliver Twist*.) Charles was deeply marked by these experiences. He rarely spoke of this time of his life.

Luckily the situation improved within a year. Charles was released from his duties at the factory and his father was released from jail.

Law Clerk to Journalist

The start of 1827 found Charles Dickens enrolled as a student at Wellington House Academy. In May, through connections made by his mother, he obtained a position at the law firm of Ellis and Blackmore.

Dickens was a law clerk. His duties included keeping the petty cash fund, delivering documents, running errands and other sundry tasks.

In November of 1828 Dickens took a similar position for the law firm of Charles Molley. However Dickens remained with the firm for only a few months.

The law didn't appeal to him as a career. He found the work of a law clerk tedious. Actually becoming a lawyer didn't appeal to him either. So he left to find another way to make a living.

His next job was as a court stenographer. To qualify for that position Dickens had to learn the Gurney system of shorthand writing. It took most people about three years to master the system. Dickens, no doubt aided by his excellent memory, learned it in about three months. Consequently in 1829 he began work as a freelance court stenographer.

In 1831 he became a shorthand reporter with the *Mirror of Parliament.* The publication gave accounts of the activity in the House of Commons and the House of Lords. Dickens became known for his quick and accurate courtroom reporting.

During this time he also considered becoming an actor. He was so serious about the matter that he arranged for an audition at the Lyceum Theater. However he was ill on the day of his audition and could not go. He did have acting skills as proven later by his readings and performances in benefit productions. His life might have been dramatically different if it weren't for his illness on that day.

In 1833 he began writing "sketches" or essays. His sketches continued to grow in popularity. They eventually led to the publication of the *The Pickwick Papers* in 1836.

"Vell," said Mr. Weller, "Now I s'pose he'll want to call some witnesses to speak to his character, or p'raps to prove a alleybi. I've been a turnin' the bis'ness over in my mind, and he may make his-self easy, Sammy. I've got some friends as'll do either for him, but my adwice 'ud be this here—never mind the character, and stick to the alleybi. Nothing like a alleybi, Sammy, nothing." - *The Pickwick Papers*

I have tamed that savage stenographic mystery. I make a respectable income by it. I am in high repute for my accomplishment in all pertaining to the art, and am joined with eleven others in reporting the debates in Parliament for a Morning Newspaper. Night after night, I record predictions that never come to pass, professions that are never fulfilled, explanations that are only meant to mystify. I wallow in words. Britannia, that unfortunate female, is always before me, like a trussed fowl: skewered through and through with office-pens, and bound hand and foot with red tape. I am sufficiently behind the scenes to know the worth of political life. I am quite an Infidel about it, and shall never be converted. - *David Copperfield.*

Maria Beadnell

Maria Beadnell was the first love of Charles Dickens. They met in 1830 and he fell madly in love with her. For Charles it was love at first sight. His mind was quickly filled with thoughts of ever-lasting romance and marriage.

However her parents did not approve of the relationship. Mr. Beadnell was a banker. He felt that Charles was too young and lacking in prospects to be considered a serious suitor.

During these years Dickens worked as a court stenographer and shorthand reporter. His own dissatisfaction with his career and a desire to make a more favourable impression with the Beadnells lead him to consider becoming an actor. He even went so far as to schedule an audition. However he was sick on that day and missed his appointment.

The youthful Maria later inspired the character of Dora in *David Copperfield:*

I don't remember who was there, except Dora. I have not the least idea what we had for dinner, besides Dora. My impression is, that I dined off Dora, entirely, and sent away half-a-dozen plates untouched. I sat next to her. I talked to her. She had the most delightful little voice, the gayest little laugh, the pleasantest and most fascinating little ways, that ever led a lost youth into hopeless slavery. She was rather diminutive altogether. So much the more precious, I thought. - *David Copperfield*

We'll never know the nature of Maria's feelings for Charles. She sometimes treated him with indifference and sometimes seemed to encourage his affections. Later in life she claimed that she truly cared for him.

In early 1833, when Charles became twenty one, he threw himself a coming-of-age party. The Beadnells were invited and accepted the invitation. During the evening Dickens was able to speak privately to Maria. He spoke of his feelings for her. She insulted him badly by referring to him as a "boy".

Their relationship ended later that year. Maria Beadnell went on to become Mrs. Henry Winter.

After a twenty-four year separation Maria contacted Dickens. They were both married and Dickens, the man who had been lacking in prospects, had become a famous author.

Dickens was thrilled upon receiving her letter. The letter from Maria brought back the memories of his intense love for her and perhaps fantasies of what might have been.

In 1855 they agreed to a secret meeting without their spouses. Maria warned Dickens that she was not the same young woman that he remembered. Despite her warnings he apparently was surprised at the changes he saw in his first love. His feelings inspired him to base the character of of Flora Finching in *Little Dorrit* on Maria.

Flora, always tall, had grown to be very broad too, and short of breath; but that was not much. Flora, whom he had left a lily, had become a peony; but that was not much. Flora, who had seemed enchanting in all she said and thought, was diffuse and silly. That was much. Flora, who had been spoiled and artless long ago, was determined to be spoiled and artless now. That was a fatal blow. - *Little Dorrit*

They met once more for a dinner with their spouses. However after that, despite Maria's wishes for further contact, Dickens avoided her.

The Marriage of Charles Dickens

Catherine Hogarth was the eldest daughter of George and Georgina Hogarth. Catherine was born in Scotland. In 1834 she and her family moved to England where her father had taken a job as a music critic for the *Morning Chronicle*.

Charles Dickens, young and unattached, was also employed by the *Morning Chronicle*. His first romantic relationship, with Maria Beadnell, had ended badly. However he was quite recovered and was quickly taken with Catherine.

They met in 1834, became engaged in 1835 and were married in April of 1836. In January of 1837 the first of their ten children was born.

The early years of their marriage were apparently quite happy. Dickens was in love with his young wife and she was very proud of her famous husband. In 1841 the couple traveled to Scotland. In 1842 they traveled to America together.

After the 1842 trip to America, Catherine's sister Georgina came to live with the couple. Catherine was becoming overwhelmed the the duties of being the wife of a famous man and mother of ten children. Georgina stepped in to fill the gaps and eventually ran the Dickens household.

Dickens grew unhappy with Catherine and his marriage. He resented the fact that he had so many children to support. (Somehow he saw this as Catherine's fault.) He did not approve of Catherine's lack of energy. He began to indicate that she was not nor had ever been his intellectual equal.

In 1855 his discontent lead him to accept an invitation to meet with his former girlfriend, Maria Beadnell. Maria had married and had become Mrs. Henry Winter. However Mrs. Henry Winter did not live up to Dickens' romantic memories and nothing ever came of the reunion.

In 1857 Dickens met the woman who was to be his companion until his death, Ellen Ternan. Ellen, her mother and her sister were hired to act in a benefit presentation of *The Frozen Deep*. The event was sponsored by their co-star, Charles Dickens.

Dickens' life with Catherine seemed even more insufferable after meeting Ellen. Dickens wrote to his friend John Forster, "Poor Catherine and I are not made for each other, and there is no help for it. It is not only that she makes me uneasy and unhappy, but that I make her so too—and much more so."

In 1857 Charles and Catherine took separate bedrooms.

In the spring of 1858 a bracelet that Dickens bought as a present for Ellen was accidentally delivered to the Dickens household. Catherine discovered the bracelet and accused Dickens of having an affair. Dickens denied the accusation and said it was his custom to give small gifts to people that acted in his plays.

In June of 1858 Catherine and Charles were legally separated. Days later Dickens published a notice in the *London Times* and *Household Words* that tried to explain the separation to the public. In the notice he stated, "Some domestic trouble of mine, of long-standing, on which I will make no further remark than that it claims to be respected, as being of a sacredly private nature, has lately been brought to an arrangement, which involves no anger or ill-will of any kind, and the whole origin, progress, and surrounding circumstances of which have been, throughout, within the knowledge of my children. It is amicably composed, and its details have now to be forgotten by those concerned in it."

While an announcement of this sort seems extreme Dickens was motivated to do so by some of the rumors circulating about the breakup. There was some gossip about an actress and some stories even suggested that Dickens was having an affair with his sister-in-law, Georgina. The second rumor was particularly upsetting because in those times such a relationship would have been viewed as incestuous.

Despite assurances that things were "amicably composed" Dickens and Catherine were never again on pleasant terms. Catherine was given a house. Their oldest son, Charley, moved in with her. Dickens retained custody of the rest of the children. While the children were not forbidden to visit their mother they were not encouraged to do so.

Catherine lived for another twenty years after the separation. Deprived of both the role of wife and mother, she never seemed to recover from the breakup of her marriage.

Gad's Hill Place

When he was a boy Charles Dickens and his father took a walk through Kent. On Gravesend Road they passed a house called Gad's Hill Place. Young Charles was very impressed.

His family was plagued with financial problems. However this imposing structure seemed to be part of a different world. His father noted his interest and told Charles that if he "were to be very persevering and work very hard" he might one day live there.

He did. He bought the house in 1856 and lived there until his death in 1870.

"Bless you, sir," said the very queer small boy, "when I was not more than half as old as nine, it used to be a treat for me to be brought to look at it. And now, I am nine, I come by myself to look at it. And ever since I can recollect, my father, seeing me so fond of it, has often said to me, 'If you were to be very persevering and were to work hard, you might some day come to live in it.' Though that's impossible!" said the very queer small boy, drawing a low breath, and now staring at the house out of window with all his might. - *The Uncommercial Traveller - Travelling Abroad*

Charles Dickens and Mesmerism

In 1849 John Leech, a friend of Charles Dickens, was injured. The accident left Leech with concussion-like symptoms that wouldn't disappear despite all the work of his doctors. Leech was in a great deal of pain and unable to rest. Dickens heard of the incident and rushed to his friend's aid. Within a few days Leech's condition had significantly improved. What could Dickens do that the doctors couldn't? Dickens helped his friend via the use of mesmerism.

Mesmerism was developed by Franz Anton Mesmer. It used hypnotic trances to heal people. In 1838 Dickens attended several lectures on the subject including some by John Elliotson. Elliotson was the professor of clinical medicine who introduced the stethoscope to England. He also had campaigned against corrupt medical practices. Despite his many accomplishments Elliotson was forced to resign his teaching position in 1839 because of a scandal regarding mesmerism.

Despite the controversy Dickens was a believer in mesmerism. Elliotson taught Dickens the technique and it quickly became apparent that Dickens was skilled in this area. Initially he mesmerized family and friends just for fun or to help with minor illnesses. However in late 1844 he took on a more serious case, that of Madame de la Rue.

Augusta de la Rue suffered from extreme anxiety. It was so profound that it caused noticeable facial tics or spasms. Dickens was eager to help and during the next few months he treated her frequently. The treatments were effective. After a month Madame de la Rue showed much improvement. She was able to sleep and night and visibly looked more relaxed.

Once the physical symptoms of Madame de la Rue eased Dickens became interested in their underlying causes. The sessions began to focus more on Madame de la Rue's dreams, hallucinations and thoughts. She spoke of being pursued by a "phantom". Their sessions became almost like those of a therapist and a patient.

How exactly did mesmerism work? Perhaps it acted as a tranquilizer and promoted rest. At this point it's hard to say. However the health of Leech and de la Rue did seem to improve after being treated by Dickens.

Bonfire at Gad's Hill Place

In September of 1860, behind his home at Gad's Hill Place, Charles Dickens tried to cover his tracks. He gathered "the accumulated letters and papers of twenty years" and set them ablaze in his backyard.

What moved him to such drastic action? There seem to be two factors in his life that drove him to make a bonfire of his correspondence.

The first is fear of the press. He was concerned that his personal letters would be published and details of his life would become public knowledge. What did he have to hide?

In 1858 he had a very public separation from his wife, but it was not widely known that he had a mistress. Ellen Ternan, his mistress, was an actress who was much younger than Dickens. If his relationship with Ellen were public knowledge it would have created a scandal.

In 1843 he'd written about workhouses and prisons in *A Christmas Carol*. However very few people knew that Dickens's father had been sent to Marshalsea prison for failure to pay a debt and that Charles Dickens, then only twelve years old, was sent to work in a shoe-polish factory. Dickens was deeply scarred by these incidents and rarely spoke of them.

A second inspiration for the bonfire at Gad's Hill Place could have been that Dickens was at a turning point in his life. The destruction of his private papers might have been his way of coming to terms with his past.

In 1860 he was still coming to terms with the separation from his wife and his relationship with Ellen. Also in July of that year his favourite daughter, Katie, married and left Gad's Hill Place. Ten days after the wedding Dickens's brother, Alfred, died. Additionally Dickens's mother had become senile and needed constant care. All of these items could have motivated Dickens, at least on a subconscious level, to try to free himself from the demons of his past.

Whatever his motivations we can only imagine the things we might have learned about the era, Dickens's life and the lives of famous Victorians. Burned on that day were letters from authors like Wilkie Collins, George Eliot and William Makepeace Thackeray.

Dickens's two youngest sons, Henry and Plorn, carried out baskets and baskets of letters to feed into the fire. His daughter Mamie begged him to reconsider and save some of the letters. However Dickens was determined that the task be completed. As they were finishing it began to rain. Dickens said, "... I suspect my correspondence of having overcast the face of the Heavens."

The Staplehurst Railway Accident

In June of 1865 Charles Dickens was involved in the Staplehurst railway accident. Dickens was returning from a trip to Paris. In the coach with him were Ellen Ternan and her mother.

The train track was being repaired near Staplehurst. Workmen did not signal to oncoming trains that there was a gap, 42 feet long, in the tracks over a bridge. The train's engineer spotted the problem at the last minute, but it was too late. Momentum carried the engine and the first part of the train across the breach. However the coaches in the centre and the rear of the train fell into the river bed below. All but one of the first-class coaches went into the ravine. That was the coach that carried Dickens, Ellen Ternan and Mrs. Ternan.

While their carriage did not fall into gap, it was hanging off the bridge at a steep angle. Dickens and Mrs. Ternan were uninjured. Ellen had only minor injuries. Others weren't as lucky. Ten people were killed and about fifty were injured.

Once Dickens helped the Ternans from the coach he went about the work of assisting his fellow passengers. He retrieved a flask of brandy from the train as well as his top hat. He filled the hat with water and then did what he could to aid and comfort the injured. Later he said that the scene was unimaginable.

One poor man was visible to the rescuers, but there was no way to help him escape. The man later died, still pinned under the train. At one point Dickens gave an injured lady who was resting under a tree a sip of brandy. The next time he passed her she was dead. For three long hours Dickens did what he could to lessen people's pain and suffering.

When help finally arrived and the accident scene was being evacuated Dickens remembered something. There was still something in his train compartment that he needed. He made his way back into the wrecked train one last time to retrieve the latest installment of *Our Mutual Friend,* the novel he was writing at the time.

For years afterward Dickens would sometimes suffer from sudden feelings of anxiety when he was traveling by rail.

In the postscript for *Our Mutual Friend* Dickens wrote:

On Friday the Ninth of June in the present year, Mr. and Mrs. Boffin (in their manuscript dress of receiving Mr. and Mrs.

Lammle at breakfast) were on the South Eastern Railway with me, in a terribly destructive accident. When I had done what I could to help others, I climbed back into my carriage—nearly turned over a viaduct, and caught aslant upon the turn—to extricate the worthy couple. They were much soiled, but otherwise unhurt. The same happy result attended Miss Bella Wilfer on her wedding day, and Mr. Riderhood inspecting Bradley Headstone's red neckerchief as he lay asleep. I remember with devout thankfulness that I can never be much nearer parting company with my readers for ever, than I was then, until there shall be written against my life, the two words with which I have this day closed this book:—THE END.

The Children of Charles Dickens

Charles and Catherine Dickens had ten children. There is circumstantial evidence that Dickens and Ellen Ternan had a child that died shortly after being born. However this has never been proven.

Charles Culliford Boz Dickens (1837-1896) - Charles was known as Charley within the family. Charley married Bessie Evans despite the fact that his father had disagreements with Bessie's father. Charley was involved in banking and business. In 1868 he went into bankruptcy and was then hired by his father to work at All The Year Round. He bought Gad's Hill Place after his father died, but later gave it up because of his own failing health.

Mary Dickens (1838-1896) - Mary was named after her mother's sister who died in 1837. After her father's death she lived with her aunt, Georgina. Mary went on to write *My Father as I Recall Him*.

Kate Macready Dickens (1839-1929) - When Dickens and Catherine separated Kate was the only child to stand up to Dickens and side with Catherine. That shouldn't have been a surprise to Dickens as Kate had been called "Lucifer Box" within the family because of her fiery temper. She married Charles Allston Collins and after his death she married Carlo Perugini.

Walter Landor Dickens (1841-1863) - Walter achieved the rank of lieutenant in the East India Company. It looked like he had a bright future, but sadly things started to fall apart for Walter. Like many of his family members he fell into debt. At about this time he also became ill. He passed away of an aortic aneurysm and left many unpaid bills to his father.

Francis Jeffrey Dickens (1844-1886) - Francis considered many careers including medicine, farming and journalism. He ended up joining the Bengal Mounted Police. Later he joined Canada's Northwest Mounted Police. In 1886 he resigned his commission and passed away within the year.

Alfred D'Orsay Tennyson Dickens (1845-1912) - When he was 20 Alfred left England, as well as many unpaid bills, and went to Australia. There he married the "Belle of Melbourne", Jessie Devlin. Sadly she died in a carriage accident four years later leaving Alfred alone with their two girls. After his father's death Alfred gave lectures on his father's life and work.

Sydney Smith Haldimand Dickens (1847-1872) - Charles Dickens was very proud of Sydney's naval career. However later he was very displeased about Sydney's financial troubles. Sydney passed away when he was only twenty five. He died while trying to return home for sick leave.

Henry Fielding Dickens (1849-1933) - Henry was nicknamed Harry and is often called the most successful of Dickens' children. He was a sportsman and had a very successful career in law. In 1922 he was knighted. Henry was the grandfather of Monica Dickens who became an author like her great grandfather. Among her works is One Pair of Hands.

Dora Annie Dickens (1850-1851) - Dora was named after a character from one of her father's novels, Dora from David Copperfield. Dora was never a strong baby and died when she was only eight months old.

Edward Bulwer Lytton Dickens (1852-1902) - Edward was nicknamed Plorn. He left England to join his brother Alfred in Australia. Edward became a Member of Parliament in New South Wales.

The Friends of Charles Dickens

Ellen Ternan - In 1857 Ellen, her mother and her sister were hired to act in a benefit presentation of *The Frozen Deep*. The event was sponsored by their co-star, Charles Dickens. This first meeting lead to an affair that would last until his death in 1870.

Wilkie Collins - Although twelve years younger than Dickens, Wilkie Collins became one of Dickens best friends. Collins was a popular novelist who helped to develop the mystery novel genre. *The Moonstone* is one of his best. He and Dickens wrote *The Frozen Deep*.

John Forster - John Forster was a biographer and historian. His close friendship with Dickens began when Forster critiqued his work. Later Forster wrote a book about his famous friend, *Life of Dickens*.

William Makepeace Thackeray - This author wrote *Vanity Fair*. He was also a friend of Charles Dickens.

Quotes by William Makepeace Thackeray

- "No, you are not worthy of the love which I have devoted to you. I knew all along that the prize I had set my life on was not worth the winning; that I was a fool, with fond fancies, too, bartering away my all of truth and ardour against your little feeble remnant of love. I will bargain no more: I withdraw."
- A woman with fair opportunities, and without an absolute hump, may marry whom she likes.
- The world is a looking-glass, and gives back to every man the reflection of his own face. Frown at it, and it will in turn look sourly upon you; laugh at it and with it, and it is a jolly kind companion; and so let all young persons take their choice
- Mother is the name for God in the lips and hearts of little children.
- The true pleasure of life is to live with your inferiors.

- The wicked are wicked, no doubt, and they go astray and they fall, and they come by their deserts: but who can tell the mischief which the very virtuous do?
- "'Tis not the dying for a faith that's so hard, Master Harry—every man of every nation has done that—'tis the living up to it that is difficult... "
- 'Tis strange what a man may do, and a woman yet think him an angel
- 'tis misfortune that awakens ingenuity, or fortitude, or endurance, in hearts where these qualities had never come to life but for the circumstance which gave them a being.
- He had placed himself at her feet so long that the poor little woman had been accustomed to trample upon him. She didn't wish to marry him, but she wished to keep him. She wished to give him nothing, but that he should give her all. It is a bargain not unfrequently levied in love.

Edgar Allan Poe - Poe was an American author best known for his poems and short fiction. *The Fall of the House of Usher* and *The Murders in the Rue Morgue* are two of his most popular works.

Dickens met Edgar Allan Poe in Philadelphia while Dickens was on his first tour of the United States. They talked about literature and seemed to enjoy one another's company. However two years later Poe broke off the relationship because he was angry about an article on American poetry. The article was written by Thackarey, but Poe believed that Dickens was behind the article.

Quotes by Edgar Allan Poe

- The best chess-player in Christendom may be little more than the best player of chess; but proficiency in whist implies capacity for success in all those more important undertakings where mind struggles with mind

- By undue profundity we perplex and enfeeble thought; and it is possible to make even Venus herself vanish from the firmament by a scrutiny too sustained, too concentrated, or too direct.
- A valet, of stealthy step, thence conducted me, in silence, through many dark and intricate passages in my progress to the studio of his master.
- I have, indeed, no abhorrence of danger, except in its absolute effect - in terror.
- Deep into that darkness peering, long I stood there wondering, fearing, Doubting, dreaming dreams no mortals ever dared to dream before;
- Once upon a midnight dreary, while I pondered, weak and weary, Over many a quaint and curious volume of forgotten lore.

Chapter 3

Major Works by Charles Dickens

THE WORKS OF CHARLES DICKENS

Barnaby Rudge

Barnaby Rudge was the 5th novel by Charles Dickens. The novel was published in installments during 1841.

Dickens's Life At The Time

- Dickens first gets the idea for the plot of *Barnaby Rudge* in 1836.
- Dickens begins to write *Barnaby Rudge* in 1839.
- 1840 marks the publication of *The Old Curiosity Shop*.
- In June and July of 1841 Dickens and Catherine tour Scotland. Also that year their son, Walter, is born and *Barnaby Rudge* is published.
- In 1842 Charles and Catherine travel to America.

Reviews

Barnaby Rudge was actually the first novel that Dickens planned on writing. In 1836 he was going to call it *Gabriel Vardon, the Locksmith of London*. Circumstances forced him to put off writing it until later. When the novel was eventually published it wasn't very well received. John Forrester, a good friend of Dickens, said the novel was structurally flawed. Norrie Espstein, author of *The Friendly Dickens*, states, "*Barnaby*

Rudge must be the least-read — and least-attractive — novel in the Dickens canon."

Grip

One of the people who read *Barnaby Rudge* and seemed to like it was Edgar Allan Poe. However Poe did have a few suggestions about Grip, Barnaby's pet raven. He didn't think that the raven should be so playful. A few years later Poe wrote about a very solemn raven in his famous poem *The Raven.* Was Grip the inspiration for the poem? We'll never know, but some historians believe so.

Gordon Riots

Barnaby Rudge is an historical novel that deals with the Gordon Riots of 1780.

In 1778 the British parliament passed the Catholic Relief Act. The act replaced anti-Catholic legislation. However it was not a universally popular change. On June 2nd of 1780 Lord George Gordon lead a group of like-minded people to parliament. They wanted the Catholic Relief Act repealed. Violence broke out and spread. Peace wasn't restored until June 9th. By that time Catholic chapels had been broken into, Newgate Prison was burned and hundreds of people were killed.

Dickens only wrote one other historical novel. *A Tale of Two Cities* deals with the French revolution.

Theme

Dickens first developed the plot for *Barnaby Rudge* when he was in his early twenties. He was coming into his own and developing a life apart from his family. It was a life without the constant brushes with poverty and disaster that were his father's hallmarks. Perhaps this is why the novel is filled with disastrous relationships between fathers and sons.

Both Barnaby and Maypole Hugh are abandoned by their fathers. Maypole's brother, Edward, is not abandoned by their father, Sir John Chester. However their relationship is not a good one as Sir John firmly discourages Edward from pursuing a relationship with Emma Haredale. Another troubled relationship between father and son can be found between John Willet and his son Joe. John refuses to see Joe as an adult.

Bleak House

Bleak House was the 9th novel of Charles Dickens. The novel was published in installments from March 1852 through September 1853.

Dickens's Life at the Time

- In 1851 Catherine Dickens, Charles Dickens's wife, suffers a nervous collapse. Later Dora Dickens, the youngest daughter of Charles and Catherine, dies when she is only eight months old. The father of Charles Dickens also dies in 1851.
- The publication of *Bleak House* begins in 1852. That year also sees the birth of the youngest child of Charles Dickens, Edward known as "Plorn".
- In 1853 George Lewes complains about the manner of death for a *Bleak House* character.

What's in a Name

Bleak House had several working titles. Some of these included:

- East Wind
- Tom-All-Alone's
- Bleak House and the East Wind
- The Solitary House that was Always Shut Up

Spontaneous Combustion

In *Bleak House* a character dies via an unusual method – spontaneous combustion. The unfortunate character to meet this fate is Krook, the brother of Mrs. Smallweed.

George Henry Lewes, a writer for the Leader, complained in his February 1853 column that people just didn't suddenly burst into flame. Dickens responded by writing a coroner's inquest into the next segment of *Bleak House.* In the book Krook's death was investigated and authorities on spontaneous combustion were cited to prove that the the phenomena really did exist.

Spontaneous combustion was a good literary device to demonstrate that passionate forces can lie within us. However, despite the fact that a *Bleak House* inquest "proved" that people can spontaneously combust, this idea is not taken seriously today.

Theme

Bleak House dramatizes the flaws in the British Court of Chancery. In Dickens's time there were two main types of courts. Courts of Common Law dealt with crimes like murder or theft. In this type of case someone was accused and tried. The outcome of the trial was based on principles of common law.

The other court system was the Court of Chancery. The Chancery handled items like property disputes. Each case was to be decided on the principles of Equity. In other words, each case was to be considered on its own merits. This was thought to be an improvement over trying this type of case in the Courts of Common Law.

However the Chancery became as bad as the system it replaced. The Chancery was commonly looked upon as an ineffective, expensive and technically difficult system.

The litigants were charged fees at every step of the legal process. These fees went directly to the court officials. More steps in the justice process meant that there would be more opportunities to collect fees. As a consequence the system became a bureaucratic nightmare.

Sometimes it took years for cases to even come to trail. From that point it could be years before a decision on the case was reached. In the preface of a non-serialized volume of *Bleak House* Dickens writes:

At the present moment (August, 1853) there is a suit before the court which was commenced nearly twenty years ago, in which from thirty to forty counsel have been known to appear at one time, in which costs have been incurred to the amount of seventy thousand pounds, which is A Friendly Suit, and which is (I am assured) no nearer to its termination now than when it was begun.

Dickens was very familiar with the court system from this time spent as a law clerk. He also had a bad experience with the court in 1844. Dickens brought a case to Chancery that dealt with the copyright to *A Christmas Carol*. Dickens did win the case, however his opponents declared bankruptcy. Instead of collecting damages Dickens found himself paying court costs — on the case that he won.

A Christmas Carol

A Christmas Carol, probably the most popular piece of fiction that Dickens ever wrote, was published in 1843.

Dickens's Life At The Time

- Late in 1842 or early in 1843 Dickens begins work on *Martin Chuzzlewit.*
- Dickens begins work on *A Christmas Carol* in October of 1843. It is published during the holiday season of that year.
- On January 15, 1844 Francis Jeffery (Frank) Dickens, the third son of Charles Dickens, is born.

Popularity of the Book

A Christmas Carol was the most successful book of the 1843 holiday season. By Christmas it sold six thousand copies and it continued to be popular into the new year. Eight stage adaptations were in production within two months of the book's publication.

The book is as popular today as it was over 150 years ago. Charles Dickens, through the voice of Scrooge, continues to urge us to honour Christmas in our hearts and try to keep it all the year.

Ragged Schools

Dickens was involved in charities and social issues throughout his entire life. At the time that he wrote *A. Christmas Carol* he was very concerned with impoverished children who turned to crime and delinquency in order to survive.

"This boy is Ignorance. This girl is Want."

Dickens, as well as others, thought that education could provide a way to a better life for these children. The Ragged School movement put these ideas into action. The schools provided free education for children in the inner-city. The movement got its name from the way the children attending the school were dressed. They often wore tattered or ragged clothing.

Themes

Scrooge's transformation is legendary. At the beginning of the story he's a greedy, selfish person.

"... every idiot who goes about with 'Merry Christmas' on his lips, should be boiled with his own pudding, and buried with a stake of holly through his heart." to the man who "knew how to keep Christmas well"

Initially Scrooge is a miser who shows a decided lack of concern for the rest of mankind. However after a ghostly night, Scrooge sees life in a whole new way.

He became as good a friend, as good a master, and as good a man, as the good old city knew, or any other good old city, town, or borough, in the good old world.

Beyond merely urging his readers to not be miserly Dickens seems to be reminding us of the importance in taking notice of the lives of those around us.

"It is required of every man," the ghost returned, "that the spirit within him should walk abroad among his fellow-men, and travel far and wide; and, if that spirit goes not forth in life, it is condemned to do so after death."

Dickens had this to say about *A Christmas Carol*:

I have endeavoured in this Ghostly little book, to raise the Ghost of an Idea, which shall not put my readers out of humour with themselves, with each other, with the season, or with me. May it haunt their houses pleasantly, and no one wish to lay it.

Their faithful Friend and Servant,
C. D.
December,

David Copperfield

David Copperfield was Dickens's eighth novel. It was first published in 1849.

Dickens's Life At The Time

- In July of 1848 Dickens's sister, Fanny, is terminally ill.
- Fanny dies in September of 1848
- *The Haunted Man,* his last Christmas book is published in December of 1848.
- In January of 1849 Dickens begins to write *David Copperfield* and his son Henry Fielding Dickens is born.
- In August of 1850 daughter, Dora Annie Dickens is born. She is named after Dora in *David Copperfield*.

Death in the Family

In 1848 Dickens's beloved sister, Fanny was terminally ill. She had been his childhood companion, the model for Fan in *A Christmas Carol* and now she was dying of consumption.

Her death was painful and lingering. She finally passed away in September of 1848. After her death Dickens and some of his friends went on a walking tour of some of Dickens's childhood haunts. His thoughts naturally turned to Fanny and to their childhood.

It seems natural that in early 1849 he began to write what he later called his favourite child, the novel David Copperfield.

Autobiographical Elements

David Copperfield contains many autobiographical elements. At a surface level it is easy to notice that even the name of the main character, David Copperfield, has the inverted initials of its author, Charles Dickens.

David's employment at Murdstone and Grinby's is drawn from Dickens's own painful experiences at Warren's Blacking Factory. Even their careers, reporter and then novelist are similar. David's love for Dora Spenlow is modeled after Dickens's youthful fascination for Maria Beadnell.

Various versions of Dickens's parents surface in the novel. Both his father and Mr. Micawber were imprisoned for debt. Mr. Dick, good hearted but unable to deal with the world, may represent another incarnation of Dickens's father.

David's pretty young mother, was inspired by Dickens's mother, who attended a ball on the very night she gave birth to her son Charles. Perhaps also the death of David's mother represented the change Dickens felt toward his mother when she was eager for him to work at Warren's Blacking Factory.

Themes

Dickens, through the voice of David Copperfield, shares with us some of the values that he believed lead to his success in life:

My meaning simply is, that whatever I have tried to do in life, I have tried with all my heart to do well; that whatever I have devoted myself to, I have devoted myself to completely;

that in great aims and in small, I have always been thoroughly in earnest.

I have been very fortunate in worldly matters; many men have worked much harder, and not succeeded half so well; but I never could have done what I have done, without the habits of punctuality, order, and diligence, without the determination to concentrate myself on one object at a time, no matter how quickly its successor should come upon its heels, which I then formed.

Some happy talent, and some fortunate opportunity, may form the two sides of the ladder on which some men mount, but the rounds of that ladder must be made of stuff to stand wear and tear; and there is no substitute for thorough-going, ardent, and sincere earnestness.

Dombey and Son

Dombey and Son was Dickens' seventh novel. It was first published in installments that began in 1846 and ran through 1848.

Dickens' Life At The Time

- 1844 - His son Francis Jeffrey (Frank) is born. Dickens and family travel to Italy. Treated Madame de la Rue with mesmerism.
- 1845 - Alfred, his sixth child, is born.
- 1846 - Dickens and his family travel to Lausanne, Switzerland. Publication of *Dombey and Son* begins. In November the Dickens family leaves Lausanne and travels to Paris.
- 1847 - In February the Dickens family leaves Paris ahead of schedule and return to England because Charley Dickens has scarlet fever. On April 18 Sydney Dickens is born to Charles and Kate.
- 1848 - Dickens' sister, Fanny, dies in September. *The Haunted Man*, his last Christmas book is published.

The Beginning of Public Readings

While Dickens was in Lausanne he gave a reading of the first installment of Dombey to some of his friends. It went so well that the later wrote to his friend John Forster, "a great deal of money might possibly be made (if it were not infra dig) by one's having Readings of one's own books." This germ of an idea became Dickens' public readings.

In 1853 Dickens gave the first public reading of one of his works. He read *A Christmas Carol* for a charity event. The readings were a combination of oratory and passionate acting. They were very popular. In 1858 he began giving professional readings and continued to do so throughout his life.

Dickens was an electrifying performer. One of his most popular performances was *Sikes and Nancy* from *Oliver Twist.* It was an exceptionally dramatic selection in which Dickens acted out Nancy's murder.

When Dickens was performing he threw himself into the characters heart and soul. So much so that the performances began to endanger his health. In 1869 his doctor advised him against giving further readings. The strain to his system was too great. Dickens arranged a farewell tour and gave his last reading in March of 1870. It is thought that the effects of the readings was one of the factors leading to his death.

Mems

Dombey and Son is the earliest novel of Dickens for which a complete set of working notes survives. Dickens called these notes "mems" witch is short for memoranda. The mems allowed him to keep track of complicated plot lines and the many characters that populate his novels.

These working notes for *Dombey and Son* reveal that young Paul Dombey was doomed to die from the first moment that Dickens created him. Although he did live for one chapter longer than Dickens originally intended. Walter Gay was originally intended to go bad was saved from that fate. Edith, the second Mrs. Dombey, was bound for adultery and death, but Dickens spared her character at the urgings of his friend Lord Jeffrey.

Themes

In her book, *The Friendly Dickens,* Norrie Epstein states that "*Dombey and Son* is the closest Dickens ever came to writing a feminist novel."

In the eyes of Mr. Dombey, marriage wasn't about romance. It was more like a business arrangement:

Mr. Dombey would have reasoned: That a matrimonial alliance with himself must, in the nature of things, be gratifying and honourable to any woman of common sense. That the hope of giving birth to a new partner in such a house, could not fail to awaken a glorious and stirring ambition in the breast of the least ambitious of her sex.

Mrs. Dombey dies shortly after giving birth to her second child, a long-awaited son. The eldest Dombey child was a girl and Mr. Dombey didn't see much use in daughters:

But what was a girl to Dombey and Son! In the capital of the House's name and dignity, such a child was merely a piece of base coin that couldn't be invested—a bad Boy—nothing more.

Throughout the novel Florence represents the virtues of love, understanding and tenderness. While Mr. Dombey represents business and logic. At the end of the novel Mr. Dombey finally turns to the love and affection that his daughter has been offering him all along.

"And so Dombey and Son, as I observed upon a certain sad occasion," said Miss Tox, winding up a host of recollections, "is indeed a daughter, Polly, after all."

Great Expectations

Great Expectations was the thirteenth novel of Charles Dickens. He began writing it in October of 1860. The novel was initially published in weekly installments in *All the Year Round* from December of 1860 until August 1861.

Dickens' Life At The Time

- In September of 1860 Gad's Hill Place becomes Dickens' permanent residence.
- Dickens and Wilkie Collins travel to North Devon on November of 1860 to gather materials for "A Message from the Sea".
- Dickens begins a series of readings at St. James's Hall in March of 1861.
- In October of 1861 Dickens begins another series of readings.

The Ending

Originally Dickens planned a different ending for *Great Expectations*. However he was persuaded by his friend, Bulwer-Lytton, to change the ending to a happier one.

The original ending had Estella remarrying after the death of her first husband. She and Pip had a brief meeting in London and then parted forever. The rewritten ending hints at a reconciliation for Pip and Estella:

I took her hand in mine, and we went out of the ruined place; and, as the morning mists had risen long ago when I first left the forge, so, the evening mists were rising now, and in all the broad expanse of tranquil light they showed to me, I saw no shadow of another parting from her.

All the Year Round

Charles Dickens founded the weekly publication *All the Year Round*. Its first issue was printed on April 30, 1859. Dickens served as editor and publisher. One feature of the publication was its serialization of novels. The first novel serialized in *All the Year Round* was *A Tale of Two Cities*.

In October of 1860 sales of *All the Year Round* were dropping because the featured novel, *A Day's Ride* by Charles

Lever, wasn't very popular. Dickens was originally going to have *Great Expectations* published in another format, however to increase sales of *All the Year Round* he adapted it to the weekly format. His plan worked and sales for the publication increased.

At the time of Dickens' death circulation of the publication was 300,000.

Themes

Pip, like Dickens himself, dreams of becoming a gentleman. However during the course of the novel Pip comes to realise that there is more to life than wealth and station.

Pip is raised by his sister and her husband, Joe. Joe is an honest, hard-working man. However as Pip ascends in society he is embarrassed by Joe and his simple ways.

Another example of this theme is Pip's relationship with Magwitch. Initially Pip is horrified to learn that his benefactor is not Miss Havisham, but instead Magwitch the convict. At the end of the story Pip has different feelings toward Magwitch. He is very fond of him and is at his side when he dies.

Magwitch himself experiences how highly society values the appearance of gentility. Here Magwitch describes how differently he and his partner in crime, the supposed gentleman Compeyson, are treated during their trial:

"... And when it come to character, warn't it Compeyson as had been to the school, and warn't it his schoolfellows as was in this position and in that, and warn't it him as had been know'd by witnesses in such clubs and societies, and nowt to his disadvantage? And warn't it me as had been tried afore, and as had been know'd up hill and down dale in Bridewells and Lock-Ups? And when it come to speech-making, warn't it Compeyson as could speak to 'em wi' his face dropping every now and then into his white pocket-handkercher - ah! and wi' verses in his speech, too - and warn't it me as could only say, 'Gentlemen, this man at my side is a most precious rascal'? And when the verdict come, warn't it Compeyson as was recommended to mercy on account of good character and bad company, and giving up all the information he could agen me, and warn't it me as got never a word but Guilty?... "

Another theme that runs through *Great Expectations*, as it does through *Our Mutual Friend*, is the ease with which wealth can corrupt people. Pip describes his spending habits:

We spent as much money as we could, and got as little for it as people could make up their minds to give us. We were always more or less miserable, and most of our acquaintance were in the same condition. There was a gay fiction among us that we were constantly enjoying ourselves, and a skeleton truth that we never did. To the best of my belief, our case was in the last aspect a rather common one.

In the end Pip, like Estella, has undergone some serious interior transformations. Estella states:

"...suffering has been stronger than all other teaching, and has taught me to understand what your heart used to be. I have been bent and broken, but - I hope - into a better shape."

Hard Times

Hard Times was Dickens' tenth novel. It was first published in installments that began in April of 1854 and ran through August of that year

Themes

Hard Times takes a hard, unsympathetic look at Utilitarianism. This philosophy was also called Philosophical Radicalism or Benthamism and was influential in the mid-Victorian period. The goal of Utilitarianism was "the greatest happiness of the greatest number." This no-nonsense movement relied heavily on statistics, rules and regulations. Individualism and imagination are not highly valued in this philosophy.

Thomas Gradgrind represents Utilitarianism within the novel. As he raises his children he stresses facts over imagination and function over feelings.

Herein lay the spring of the mechanical art and mystery of educating the reason without stooping to the cultivation of the sentiments and affections. Never wonder. By means of addition, subtraction, multiplication, and division, settle everything somehow, and never wonder. - Hard Times by Charles Dickens

Divorce is also dealt with in *Hard Times*. (Dickens would face this dilemma himself in just a few years.) Stephen Blackpool is caught in a loveless marriage. He is unable to obtain a divorce and marry the woman he really loves.

... and he knew very well that if he were free to ask her, she would take him. He thought of the home he might at that moment have been seeking with pleasure and pride; of the different man he might have been that night; of the lightness then in his now heavy-laden breast; of the then restored honour, self-respect, and tranquillity all torn to pieces. He thought of the waste of the best part of his life, of the change it made in his character for the worse every day, of the dreadful nature of his existence, bound hand and foot, to a dead woman, and tormented by a demon in her shape. - Hard Times by Charles Dickens.

Household Words

Hard Times was originally published in the weekly magazine, *Household Words*. The magazine was edited by Dickens from March of 1850 until May of 1859.

The original format for *Household Words* did not include serialized fiction. However Dickens reconsidered his plan after the magazine's circulation dropped. Hoping for increased magazine sales, he serialized *Hard Times* in *Household Words*. His new plan worked. The circulation of *Household Words* more than doubled.

Just as the novel had an effect on the magazine, the magazine had an effect on the novel. *Household Words* was a magazine with limited space. Dickens wrote to his friend Forster, "The difficulty of space is Crushing." In order to make *Hard Times* fit within the magazine Dickens made *Hard Times* his shortest novel. It does not feature the prolonged humourous or sentimental scenes that are in many of his novels.

Little Dorrit

Little Dorrit was the 11th novel of Charles Dickens. The novel was published in installments from December of 1855 through June of 1857.

Dickens's Life at the Time

- In 1855 Dickens has a disappointing reunion with Maria Winter (Maria Beadnell). This incident was dramatized to become the reunion of Arthur Clennam and Flora Finching in *Little Dorrit*.
- The next year Dickens purchases Gad's Hill Place.
- In 1857 Dickens meets Ellen Ternan. He would eventually separate from his wife, Catherine, and would be involved with Ellen for the rest of his life.

Maria Beadnell and Flora Finching

In *Little Dorrit* Arthur Clennam becomes reacquainted with Flora Finching. She was the love of his youth. However time had not been kind to Flora:

> Flora, always tall, had grown to be very broad too, and short of breath; but that was not much. Flora, whom he had left a lily, had become a peony; but that was not much. Flora, who had seemed enchanting in all she said and thought, was diffuse and silly. That was much. Flora, who had been spoiled and artless long ago, was determined to be spoiled and artless now. That was a fatal blow.

This scene was based on an incident in the life of Charles Dickens. The first love of Charles Dickens was the delightful Maria Beadnell. The relationship was a troubled one. At that time Dickens was a young man with few prospects and Maria's parents did not approve of the match. Additionally Maria and Charles had a falling out at his 21st birthday party. They did not speak for twenty four years after that argument.

In 1855 Maria, who had become Mrs. Henry Winter, contacted Dickens. Although she warned him that she was no longer as he remembered, he was shocked by her appearance and personality. That experience found its way into *Little Dorrit*.

Marshalsea

The Marshalsea debtor's prison plays a large part in *Little Dorrit*. The novel opens there. The Dorrits live there and eventually Arthur is imprisoned there.

It was a common practice for the entire family to move into debtor's prison, not just the family member declared insolvent. The family members that were not convicted of insolvency could leave the prison during the day. Some prisoners even had regular maid service during their incarceration.

During Dickens's lifetime very few people knew that Dickens's father had been sent to Marshalsea for three months. While his father was in prison Charles, then only twelve years old, was sent to work in a shoe-polish factory. Dickens was deeply scarred by these incidents and rarely spoke of them.

Theme

The main theme of Little Dorrit is imprisonment. The novel begins in a prison. Mrs. Clennam is confined to her wheelchair. Even the city echoes this theme:

Melancholy streets, in a penitential garb of soot, steeped the souls of the people who were condemned to look at them out of windows, in dire despondency.

The theme echoes throughout this dark novel. There are loveless marriages, incompetent government offices and the stifling influence of society.

However at the end of the novel some characters find freedom. Some through the truth, some through death and some through love.

They all gave place when the signing was done, and Little Dorrit and her husband walked out of the church alone. They paused for a moment on the steps of the portico, looking at the fresh perspective of the street in the autumn morning sun's bright rays, and then went down.

Martin Chuzzlewit

Martin Chuzzlewit was Dickens's sixth novel. It was first published in installments that began in January of 1843 and ran through July of 1844.

Dickens's Life At The Time

- In January of 1842 Dickens and his wife, Catherine, sail for America. They return to England in July of that year.
- *American Notes* is published in October of 1842.
- Late in 1842 or early in 1843 Dickens begins work on *Martin Chuzzlewit.* The first installment is printed in January of 1843.
- Dickens begins work on *A Christmas Carol* in October of 1843. It is published during the holiday season of that year.
- On January 15, 1844 Francis Jeffery (Frank) Dickens, the third son of Charles Dickens, is born.
- In July of 1844 the final installment of *Martin Chuzzlewit* is printed.
- In 1867 Dickens returned to the United States for an extensive reading tour.

Themes

The overriding theme of *Martin Chuzzlewit* is selfishness, selfishness of all types.

The elder Martin Chuzzlewit is a very rich man. When he appears to be near death the worst comes out in those around him. Pecksniff tries to scheme his way to the Chuzzlewit fortune. The vulture-like Chuzzlewits and

Spottletoes sweep in to wait for the old man's death. All of them hoping for an inheritance.

However there are other types of selfishness. Young Martin Chuzzlewit is arrogant and oblivious to the feelings of others. He takes Tom Pinch and Mark Tapley for granted. Later in the book, continued exposure to Mark Tapley and a change of fortune in America bring out the better side of his character.

At the end of the novel the elder Chuzzlewit states:

"The curse of our house," said the old man, looking kindly down upon her, "has been the love of self; has ever been the love of self. How often have I said so, when I never knew that I had wrought it upon others."

America

Martin Chuzzlewit was written after Dickens traveled to America in 1842. The United States left quite an impression on Dickens, a very unfavourable impression.

Dickens was horrified by slavery, appalled by the common use of spitting tobacco and indignant about his treatment by the press. Like any good author he used his life experience in his work. His dissatisfaction with America came out in *American Notes* and later in *Martin Chuzzlewit*.

As Washington may be called the head-quarters of tobacco-tinctured saliva, the time is come when I must confess, without any disguise, that the prevalence of those two odious practices of chewing and expectorating began about this time to be anything but agreeable, and soon became most offensive and sickening. In all the public places of America, this filthy custom is recognised. In the courts of law, the judge has his spittoon, the crier his, the witness his, and the prisoner his; while the jurymen and spectators are provided for, as so many men who in the course of nature must desire to spit incessantly. - *American Notes*

Schools may be erected, East, West, North, and South; pupils be taught, and masters reared, by scores upon scores of thousands; colleges may thrive, churches may be crammed, temperance may be diffused, and advancing knowledge in all other forms walk through the land with giant strides: but while the newspaper press of America is in, or near, its present abject state, high moral improvement in that country is hopeless. - *American Notes*

An American gentleman ... likewise stuck his hands deep into his pockets, and walked the deck with his nostrils dilated, as already inhaling the air of Freedom which carries death to all tyrants, and can never (under any circumstances worth mentioning) be breathed by slaves. - *Martin Chuzzlewit*

Dickens returned to America in 1867 for an extensive reading tour. He found the conditions in America greatly improved from his first visit. In a postscript added to later printings of *Martin Chuzzlewit* Dickens shared a portion of a speech that he gave in New York in April of 1868:

"... how astounded I have been by the amazing changes I have seen around me on every side—changes moral, changes physical, changes in the amount of land subdued and peopled, changes in the rise of vast new cities, changes in the growth of older cities almost out of recognition, changes in the graces and amenities of life, changes in the Press, without whose advancement no advancement can take place anywhere."

The Mystery of Edwin Drood

The Mystery of Edwin Drood was the fifteenth novel of Charles Dickens. Dickens was only halfway finished with the book when he died.

Dickens' Life At The Time

- During October of 1869, at Gad's Hill Place, Dickens begins work on *The Mystery of Edwin Drood*.
- On March 15, 1870 Dickens gives his final public reading.
- In April of 1870 publication of Drood begins.

- On June 8, 1870 Dickens spends the day working on *The Mystery of Edwin Drood*. During dinner he collapses.
- On June 9, 1870 Dickens dies at Gad's Hill Place.

Public Readings

In 1853 Dickens gave the first public reading of one of his works. He read *A Christmas Carol* for a charity event. The readings were a combination of oratory and passionate acting. They were very popular. In 1858 he began giving professional readings and continued to do so throughout his life.

Dickens was an electrifying performer. One of his most popular performances was *Sikes and Nancy* from *Oliver Twist*. It was an exceptionally dramatic selection in which Dickens acted out Nancy's murder.

When Dickens was performing he threw himself into the characters heart and soul. So much so that the performances began to endanger his health. In 1869 his doctor advised him against giving further readings. The strain to his system was too great. Dickens arranged a farewell tour and gave his last reading in March of 1870. It is thought that the effects of the readings was one of the factors leading to his death.

Possible Endings

There is a lot of speculation about how T*he Mystery of Edwin Drood* was to have ended. Dickens didn't leave any notes outlining the plot so no one will ever really know what he intended.

One of the most popular beliefs is that John Jasper, Edwin's uncle, is the murderer. Jasper lead the double life of a choirmaster and opium addict. He was also in love with Rosa Bud, the woman his nephew was to marry. Conversations Dickens had before he died seem to support this theory. John Forester, his good friend, said Dickens told him that Jasper had indeed murdered Drood. Dickens' son, Charley, also stated that his father told him Drood really was dead.

Some people speculate that Edwin Drood, like John Harmon in *Our Mutual Friend*, wasn't really dead. The fact that Edwin's body was never found adds weight to this theory.

Themes

As mentioned earlier, John Jasper lead a double life. "You are always training yourself to be, mind and body, as clear as crystal, and you always are, and never change; whereas I am a muddy, solitary, moping weed," he says to Mr. Crisparkle. Little did Mr. Crisparkle know the truth of that statement.

Dickens used this theme in Our Mutual Friend as well. In that novel the respectable Mr. Bradley Headstone is not all that he appears. To some extent the same could be said for Dickens himself. He was always careful to keep his relationship with Ellen Ternan a secret from the public.

Nicholas Nickleby

Nicholas Nickleby was the third novel of Charles Dickens. The first installment was published on March 31, 1838 and the last installment was published on October 1, 1839.

Dickens' Life At The Time

- In early 1838 Dickens and Hablot Browne, the illustrator for Nickleby, travel to Yorkshire to see the boarding schools for themselves.
- On March 6th of that year Dickens' daughter Mary is born.
- The first installment of *Nicholas Nickleby* is published on March 31, 1838.
- In January of 1839 Dickens begins writing *Barnaby Rudge.*
- On October 1, 1839 the final installment of Nickleby is published.
- On October 29th of that year Dickens' daughter Kate is born.

Yorkshire Boarding Schools

One of Dickens' goals in writing Nicholas Nickleby was to expose the ugly truth about Yorkshire boarding schools. In the preface to the novel Dickens has this to say about Yorkshire schoolmasters:

Traders in the avarice, indifference, or imbecility of parents, and the helplessness of children; ignorant, sordid, brutal men, to whom few considerate persons would have entrusted the board and lodging of a horse or a dog; they formed the worthy cornerstone of a structure, which, for absurdity and a magnificent high-minded *laissez-aller* neglect, has rarely been exceeded in the world.

In the novel Nicholas is sent to teach at Dotheboys Hall. It is a school where there are no holidays, no trips home for the abused and neglected pupils of Mr. Wackford Squeers.

Sadly schools like Dotheboys Hall really did exist. In early 1838 Dickens and Hablot Browne, the illustrator of Nicholas Nickleby, visited Yorkshire to get a first hand look at the situation. It was a very short visit, just two days, but it was enough to gather all the material they needed.

During their visit they called on William Shaw, the headmaster of Bowes Academy. In 1823 Shaw had been prosecuted for neglect after two pupils became blind because of beatings and poor nutrition. The situation improved somewhat after the investigation. However even after the investigation it was common for one pupil to die at Bowes Academy every year.

Dickens got the idea for Smike as he wandered through a churchyard near Bowes Academy. He read the engravings on the tombstones of the boys who died while attending Bowes and the idea sprang into his mind.

MRS. NICKLEBY

Dickens' own mother, Elizabeth Dickens, was the model for the always confused, comic Mrs. Nickleby. Luckily for Charles she didn't recognize herself in the character. In fact she asked someone if they "really believed there ever was such a woman".

Theme

An issue raised in Nicholas Nickleby deals with the definition of being a gentleman. What exactly does it take to be a true gentleman?

Is it a matter of breeding? Sir Mulberry Hawk, who was determined to ruin Kate Nickleby, was surely not a true gentleman despite his good breeding. Wackford Squeers, the headmaster at Dotheboys Hall, proved that it takes more than position to be a gentleman. Ralph Nickleby illustrated that money alone does not make a gentleman.

However in Nicholas Nickleby himself we see that a man is defined by his acts rather than breeding, money or position.

It was a harder day's journey than yesterday's, for there were long and weary hills to climb; and in journeys, as in life, it is a great deal easier to go down hill than up. However, they kept on, with unabated perseverance, and the hill has not yet lifted its face to heaven that perseverance will not gain the summit of at last.

The Old Curiosity Shop

The Old Curiosity Shop was the fourth novel of Charles Dickens. The novel was published in installments in the periodical "Master Humphrey's Clock". The first installment was printed in April of 1840 and the last was printed in February of 1841.

Dickens's Life At The Time

- 1837 - The first of Dickens's 10 children, Charles Culliford Boz Dickens, is born. Mary Hogarth, Catherine's sister, dies. The publication of *Oliver Twist* begins.
- 1838 - Mary Dickens is born. Publication of *Nicholas Nickleby* begins.

- 1839 - Kate Dickens is born.
- 1840 - Publication of *The Old Curiosity Shop* begins
- 1841 - *Barnaby Rudge* is published. Charles and Catherine tour Scotland. Their son, Walter, is born.
- 1842 - Charles and Catherine travel to America. Late in 1842 or early in the next year Dickens begins work on *Martin Chuzzlewit*.

Overly Sentimental ?

During the novel Little Nell's health begins to deteriorate. The journey to the countryside is a one-way trip for Nell and she dies at the end of the novel. At the time of its writing it's rumored that people waited on the docks of New York for the last installments of *The Old Curiosity Shop*. When the ship carrying the magazines arrived people in the crowd asked, "Is Little Nell dead?"

Many people have strong reactions to Nell's death in *The Old Curiosity Shop*. However that reaction varies widely from person to person. Some readers were greatly moved by her death. Some were not. Oscar Wilde, the author of *The Importance of Being Earnest* and *The Picture of Dorian Gray*, said of the novel, "One must have a heart of stone to read the death of Little Nell without laughing."

Little Nell and Mary Hogarth

Dickens was traumatized by the death of Little Nell. As he was writing it he felt as though he were experiencing the death of one of his children. It also brought back painful memories of the death of his sister-in-law, Mary Hogarth.

In 1837 Mary Hogarth was seventeen, pretty and living with her sister Catherine and Catherine's husband, Charles Dickens. Mary was a favourite with the couple and had become like a little sister to Charles.

On the evening of May 6th Mary went with the couple to the St. James Theatre. The group returned late in the evening and Mary retired for the night. Shortly after that Dickens heard a cry from Mary's room. She was ill. Despite her doctor's care Mary passed away in Dickens' s arms on May 7th.

He had her tombstone inscribed with these words, "Young, beautiful, and good, God in his mercy numbered her with His angles at the early age of seventeen."

Dickens wrote to his friend, John Forster, about Little Nell's death, "Old wounds bleed afresh when I think of this sad story."

Theme

In the preface to The Old Curiosity Shop Dickens wrote:

I had it always in my fancy to surround the lonely figure of the child with grotesque and wild, but not impossible companions, and to gather about her innocent face and pure intentions, associates as strange and uncongenial as the grim objects that are about her bed when her history is first foreshadowed.

Dickens indeed carried out his fancy with *The Old Curiosity Shop*. The book is a study in contrasts:

- Youthful Little Nell versus the old curios and her elderly grandfather at the Old Curiosity Shop
- The goodness and virtue of Little Nell as compared to the evil Quilp
- Little Nell acting like an adult when her grandfather can't cope
- The masculine qualities of Sally Brass as well as the feminine qualities of Sampson Brass
- The passivity of Nell versus the energy of Quilp

In *The Friendly Dickens* Norrie Epstein writes something that can help us all understand and digest this novel:

The trick to enjoying this remarkable work is to view it not as a syrupy period piece or a realistic novel but as a fairy tale for adults, filled with unsettling elements, startling, inexplicable symbols, and dark meanings just below the surface. Like all tales of enchantment, it transforms unspeakable and primal anxieties and taboos—such as incest, freaks, sadism, separation anxiety, and death—into something manageable and strangely compelling.

Oliver Twist

Oliver Twist was the second novel of Charles Dickens. It was initially published in monthly installments that began in February of 1837 and ended in April of 1839. The publication of *Oliver Twist* began before the monthly publication of *The Pickwick Papers* ended. The two novels overlapped for nine months. Additionally Dickens started *Nicholas Nickleby* (also issued in monthly installments) before Twist finished publication. Those two novels overlapped for nine months as well.

Fagin

Charles Dickens did not have a happy childhood. The low point came when he was twelve. His father, John Dickens, was arrested and sent to jail for failure to pay a debt. Worst of all, young Charles Dickens was sent to work in a blacking (shoe polish) factory.

It was at the blacking factory that Dickens met Bob Fagin. Bob was another employee at the factory. However unlike some of the others Bob never teased young Dickens. In fact, Fagin defended Dickens when the other boys taunted him. He also taught Dickens how to wrap and tie the bottles of polish. He even helped Dickens when he was ill at work.

Why would Dickens remember someone who had showed him such kindness by naming such villain after him? The time Dickens spent at the blacking factory was the worst time of his entire life. His shame over the incident made him keep it a secret from all but a few people. So perhaps it was just that Bob Fagin introduced him to the ways of the factory in the same way that the other Fagin showed Oliver the correct way to pick pockets. Maybe both men, the real Bob Fagin and the imaginary one, showed young boys, Charles Dickens and Oliver Twist, the darker side of life.

Once in a Lifetime

In June of 1837 something happed that only occurred once in Dickens's career. He missed a deadline. He was writing two serialized novels at once, The Pickwick Papers and Oliver Twist. However in June of 1837 there was no Pickwick. There was no Oliver Twist. Instead there was a funeral.

In 1837 Mary Hogarth was seventeen, pretty and living with her sister Catherine and Catherine's husband, Charles Dickens. Mary was a favourite with the couple and had become like a little sister to Charles.

On the evening of May 6th Mary went with the couple to the St. James Theatre. The group returned late in the evening and Mary retired for the night. Shortly after that Dickens heard a cry from Mary's room. She was ill. Despite her doctor's care Mary passed away in Dickens's arms on May 7th.

Charles was devastated. The June installments of Twist and Pickwick were not published due to "the sudden death of a very dear young relative to whom he was most affectionately attached and whose society had been for a long time the chief solace of his labours."

The character Rose Maylie in Oliver Twist was inspired by Mary Hogarth.

Themes

In *Oliver Twist* Dickens attacks the New Poor Law of 1834. The New Poor Law was really a series of measures that were enacted in 1834. Supposedly these laws were to provide aid and assistance to impoverished people. However the system had serious flaws.

People with no means of support were sent to workhouses. The system was designed with the idea that the workhouses would be unpleasant. It was thought that this would provide added incentive for people to be self sufficient.

As a result of that thinking the food in the workhouses was meager and meals were to be eaten in silence. Upon entering the workhouse families were separated and assigned to same-sex quarters. Also, the children were separated from the adults. Infants were sent to "baby farms".

Rather than finding this treatment motivational it broke the spirit of many people forced to live there. The adventures of young Oliver Twist make this point. Dickens also touches on this topic in other works. In *A Christmas Carol* Scrooge says that "those who are badly off" must got to workhouses or other places like them. The reply is, "Many can't go there; and many would rather die."

Charles Dickens used his novel to point out truths about Victorian England that polite society tried to ignore. After reading the novel Lord Melbourne protested, "It is all among workhouses and pickpockets and coffinmakers. I do not like those things: I wish to avoid them. I do not like them in reality and therefore do not like to see them represented

Our Mutual Friend

Our Mutual Friend was the fourteenth and last completed novel of Charles Dickens. He began writing it in 1863. It was initially published in monthly installments that began in May of 1864 and ended in November 1865.

Dickens's Life At The Time

- On September 12, 1863 his mother, Elizabeth dies.
- In November of 1863 Dickens begins to write *Our Mutual Friend*.
- Walter Dickens, his son, dies in India in January of 1864.
- The first installment of *Our Mutual Friend* is published in May of 1864.
- In June of 1865 Charles Dickens is involved in the Staplehurst railway accident.

- The final chapters of *Our Mutual Friend* are published in November of 1865.

We'll Never Know

In *Our Mutual Friend* one of the characters is thought to be dead, but really isn't. In *The Mystery of Edwin Drood,* Dickens's last novel, Edwin Drood disappears. Was Drood murdered? People believe so but no body is ever found.

Was Dickens planning to use the same plot twist that he'd used in *Our Mutual Friend*? Perhaps, just like the character in *Our Mutual Friend,* Edwin Drood wasn't really dead. We'll never know. Dickens died before *The Mystery of Edwin Drood* was completed.

Dust

The dust, or garbage, business plays a large part in *Our Mutual Friend*. The elder John Harmon made his fortune as a dust contractor. Noddy Boffin becomes the "Golden Dustman" while Silas Wegg finds something in a mound of garbage that he thinks could take away Noddy's wealth.

In the mid-nineteenth century garbage was collected by private contractors. The rubbish was piled into mounds and people sifted through the mounds looking for for things to sell. They might find jewelry or money that was accidentally thrown away. However most of the trash was sold as raw materials for other industries. Soap makers, road builder, paper manufacturers and others bought items from dust contractors.

Themes

One of the themes of the novel is the corruption that wealth can bring. Bella Wilfer undergoes great changes during the novel as she deals with this issue. Toward the beginning of the novel she makes a stunning declaration.

"I have made up my mind that I must have money, Pa. I feel that I can't beg it, borrow it, or steal it; and so I have resolved that I must marry it."

Later in the book her feelings change.

"O Mr. Rokesmith, before you go, if you could but make me poor again! O! Make me poor again, Somebody, I beg and pray, or my heart will break if this goes on! Pa, dear, make me poor again and take me home! I was bad enough there, but I have been so much worse here. Don't give me money, Mr. Boffin, I won't have money. Keep it away from me, and only let me speak to good little Pa, and lay my head upon his shoulder, and tell him all my griefs. Nobody else can understand me, nobody else can comfort me, nobody else knows how unworthy I am, and yet can love me like a little child. I am better with Pa than any one—more innocent, more sorry, more glad!"

The Pickwick Papers

The Pickwick Papers was the first novel of Charles Dickens. The novel was initially published in monthly installments from March of 1836 until November 1837.

Dickens' Life At The Time

- The first installment of *The Pickwick Papers* is published on March 30, 1836
- On April 2, 1836 Charles Dickens marries Catherine Hogarth
- Their first child is born on January 6, 1837
- Publication of *Oliver Twist* begins in *Bentley's* on January 31, 1837. Dickens writes Pickwick and Twist simultaneously until November of 1837 when Pickwick ends.

The First Novel of Charles Dickens

The publishing firm of Chapman and Hall faced a huge decision in April of 1836. The firm had just started a series of amusing stories dealing with "Cockney sporting scenes". The series was built around the illustrations of Robert Seymour. Publication began on March 30th and on April 20th Seymour committed suicide. Edward Chapman and William Hall had to decide if they were going to continue the series.

The author who wrote the text to accompany Seymour's illustrations had an idea. Why not increase the text and hire a less well-known artist? The series could continue, but the focus would change from the illustrations to the story.

The author's name was Charles Dickens and the series was *The Pickwick Papers*.

Chapman and Hall agreed with Dickens ideas and *The Pickwick Papers* became wildly popular.

The first installment of Pickwick sold about 500 copies while the last installment sold about 40,000 copies. There were theatrical adaptations before the series was even completed. Pickwick merchandise began to appear. People could buy Pickwick cigars, song books and china figurines.

Charles Dickens' first book was a hit.

Once in a Lifetime

In June of 1837 something happed that only occurred once in Dickens' career. He missed a deadline. He was writing two serialized novels at once, but there was no Pickwick that month. There was no Oliver Twist. Instead there was a funeral.

In 1837 Mary Hogarth was seventeen, pretty and living with her sister Catherine and Catherine's husband, Charles Dickens. Mary was a favourite with the couple and had become like a little sister to Charles.

On the evening of May 6th Mary went with the couple to the St. James Theatre. The group returned late in the evening and Mary retired for the night. Shortly after that Dickens heard a cry from Mary's room. She was ill. Despite her doctor's care Mary passed away in Dickens' arms on May 7th.

Charles was devastated. The June installments of Twist and Pickwick were not published due to "the sudden death of a very dear young relative to whom he was most affectionately attached and whose society had been for a long time the chief solace of his labours."

Themes

Dickens works a very serious subject into this comic novel, that of the injustice of the justice system.

Dickens had a first hand look at the legal system when he worked as a law clerk. His outrage over the inequities and incompetence of the system show up in more than one of his novels.

In a very funny scene Pickwick tries to talk his landlady, Mrs. Bardell, about Sam Weller moving into the house. She misunderstands and thinks he is proposing marriage. Later she sues for breach of promise.

The novel is full of humourous quotes dealing with the legal system:

"Why, I don't exactly know about perjury, my dear sir," replied the little gentleman. "Harsh word, my dear sir, very harsh word indeed. It's a legal fiction, my dear sir, nothing more."

"Battledore and shuttlecock's a wery good game, vhen you ain't the shuttlecock and two lawyers the battledores, in which case it gets too excitin' to be pleasant."

"Vell," said Mr. Weller, "Now I s'pose he'll want to call some witnesses to speak to his character, or p'raps to prove a alleybi. I've been a turnin' the bis'ness over in my mind, and he may make his-self easy, Sammy. I've got some friends as'll do either for him, but my adwice 'ud be this here—never mind the character, and stick to the alleybi. Nothing like a alleybi, Sammy, nothing."

A Tale of Two Cities

A Tale of Two Cities was the twelfth novel of Charles Dickens. The first chapters of the book appeared in print in April of 1859. The last chapter was printed in November of that same year.

Dickens' Life At The Time

- In January of 1857 the first performances of *The Frozen Deep* are given. Dickens plays the role of Richard Wardour. This play gives Dickens the idea for *A Tale of Two Cities*.
- In August of 1857 Dickens meets Ellen Ternan, an actress hired to act in benefit performances of *The Frozen Deep*. Ellen later becomes his mistress.
- Dickens separates from his wife Catherine in 1858.
- In March of 1859 Dickens begins writing *A Tale of Two Cities*.

"Let them eat cake."

The novel takes place during the French Revolution. The revolution began in 1789. The French people were tired of the social and economic inequalities enforced by the ruling monarchy. The aristocracy and clergy lived a life of luxury while people in the Third Estate (peasants, artisans, merchants and professional men) paid most of the taxes and didn't have as many rights. Legend has it that when the queen of France, Marie Antoinette, was told that the poor people didn't have any bread to eat she responded, "Let them eat cake."

On September 22, 1792 France was declared a republic. In an effort to preserve the newly-founded republic many people were put on trial for crimes against the state. Thousands of people were sentenced to death in unfair trials and many more people were imprisoned. The time from September 1793 to July 1794 is known as The Reign of Terror.

It was the best of times, it was the worst of times, it was the age of wisdom, it was the age of foolishness, it was the epoch of belief, it was the epoch of incredulity, it was the season of light, it was the season of darkness, it was the spring of hope, it was the winter of despair, we had everything before us, we had nothing before us, we were all going direct to heaven, we were all going direct the other way—in short, the period was so. far like the present period, that some of its noisiest authorities insisted on its being received, for good or for evil, in the superlative degree of comparison only. - *A Tale of Two Cities*

The Frozen Deep

The Frozen Deep was the inspiration for *A Tale of Two Cities*. In 1857 Dickens acted in the play and portrayed the character of Richard Wardour. In the play Wardour decides that he's going to kill Frank Aldersley because Frank stole his true love, Clara Burnham. Instead Wardour ends up saving Aldersley's life at the cost of his own. Wardour dies in Clara's arms and earns her eternal gratitude for saving the life of the man that she loves.

In addition to giving him the idea for *A Tale of Two Cites,* the play brought about lasting changes to Dickens' life. In 1857 Dickens was not happy in his marriage. The once happy couple had grown apart.

Professional actresses were hired to act in a benefit production of *The Frozen Deep*. One of them was Ellen Ternan. She became Dickens' mistress. Their affair lasted until Dickens' death in 1870.

Themes

In the story Doctor Manette is imprisoned for many years. He is kept in solitary confinement for years. His only activity is making shoes and when asked his name he answers, "One Hundred and Five, North Tower." So harsh are his circumstances that it as if he were buried alive.

Sydney Carton is another character who is "buried alive" only in this case the burial is of his own choosing.

Sadly, sadly, the sun rose; it rose upon no sadder sight than the man of good abilities and good emotions, incapable of their directed exercise, incapable of his own help and his own happiness, sensible of the blight on him, and resigning him-self to let it eat him away.

Carton is skilled at his profession, but he dislikes himself and sees nothing of value in life. However when Carton meets Lucie Manette that changes.

"... I wish you to know that you have been the last dream of my soul. In my degradation I have not been so degraded but that the sight of you with your father, and of this home made such a home by you, has stirred old shadows that I thought had died out of me. Since I knew you, I have been troubled by a remorse that I thought would never reproach me again, and have heard whispers from old voices impelling me upward, that I thought were silent for ever. I have had unformed ideas of striving afresh, beginning anew, shaking off sloth and sensuality, and fighting out the abandoned fight. A dream, all a dream, that ends in nothing, and leaves the sleeper where he lay down, but I wish you to know that you inspired it."

Chapter 4

Introduction to Industrial Revolution

THE INDUSTRIAL REVOLUTION

by Joseph A. Montagna

Introduction

The era known as the Industrial Revolution was a period in which fundamental changes occurred in agriculture, textile and metal manufacture, transportation, economic policies and the social structure in England. This period is appropriately labeled "revolution," for it thoroughly destroyed the old manner of doing things; yet the term is simultaneously inappropriate, for it connotes abrupt change. The changes that occurred during this period (1760-1850), in fact, occurred gradually. The year 1760 is generally accepted as the "eve" of the Industrial Revolution. In reality, this eve began more than two centuries before this date. The late 18th century and the early 19th century brought to fruition the ideas and discoveries of those who had long passed on, such as, Galileo, Bacon, Descartes and others.

Advances in agricultural techniques and practices resulted in an increased supply of food and raw materials, changes in industrial organization and new technology resulted in increased production, efficiency and profits, and the increase in commerce, foreign and domestic, were all conditions which promoted the advent of the Industrial Revolution. Many of these conditions were so closely interrelated that increased activity in one spurred an increase in activity in another. Further, this interdependence of conditions creates a problem when one attempts to delineate them for the purpose of analysis in the classroom. Therefore, it is imperative that the reader be acutely aware of this when reading the following material.

The narrative portion of this unit is intended for the teacher's use as a guide to teaching about this subject. It does not purport to include all that is needed to teach about the Industrial Revolution. It does provide a basis for teaching about the subject, leaving room for the teacher to maneuver as his/her style of teaching permits. One manner of capitalizing on any shortcomings in this material is to design individual or small group student activities which will enhance their study skills (reference materials, library use, research reports, etc.), while at the same time locating specific information. Also included are suggestions for utilizing this material in class. In the final analysis it is the teacher who will determine the manner in which this material is used, so it is his/her's to modify as deemed necessary.

Agricultural Changes

Agriculture occupied a prominent position in the English way of life of this period. Not only was its importance rooted in the subsistence of the population, but agriculture was an indispensable source of raw materials for the textile industry. Wool and cotton production for the manufacture of cloth increased in each successive year, as did the yield of food crops.

The improved yield of the agricultural sector can be attributed to the enclosure movement and to improved techniques and practices developed during this period. A common practice in early agriculture was to allow the land to lie fallow after it had been exhausted through cultivation. Later it was discovered that the cultivation of clover and other legumes would help to restore the fertility of the soil. The improved yields also increased the amount of food available to sustain livestock through the winter. This increased the size of herds for meat on the table and allowed farmers to begin with larger herds in the spring than they had previously.

Other advances in agriculture included the use of sturdier farm implements fashioned from metal. Up until this period most farming implements were made entirely out of wood. We do not find much technical innovation beyond the slight improvements made on existing implements. We do find increased energy being placed into the breeding of livestock, control of insects, improved irrigation and farming methods, developing new crops and the use of horsepower in the fields to replace oxen as a source of power.

These changes which have occurred in agriculture made it possible to feed all of the people that were attracted to the industrial centres as factory workers. By providing enough food to sustain an adequate work force, England was preparing the way for expansion of the economy and industry.

A strategy which may be employed to promote the students' understanding of the changes that have occurred in agriculture during the period of this unit, and from this period to today's modern farms, is to start with the present and work back in time to the period we are studying. Students may participate in an informative and interesting discussion centred around today's farming methods and machinery. Classroom activities could also centre about constructing a chart which lists farming methods in pre-industrial revolution times, during the industrial revolution and today. Also, activities could be centred around having students write letters to manufacturers of farm machinery, the U.S. Department of Agriculture, or other farm-related concerns (e.g., farm museums).

In 18th century England, the enclosure of common village fields into individual landholdings, or the division of unproductive land into private property was the first significant change to occur. This concentrated the ownership of the land into the hands of a few, and made it possible to institute improved farming techniques on a wider scale. Students may engage in a debate over the question of enclosure, concerning its effect on the rural poor. Historians are not in complete agreement on the effects of enclosure on the poor, some arguing that it contributed to swelling the numbers of poor, while others argue that their plight was only marginally related to the enclosure movement. An excellent resource for the teacher's use in this section is Chapter Seven of E. P. Thompson's book, *The Making of the English Working Class*.

Textiles

Prior to 1760 the manufacture of textiles occurred in the homes, by people who gave part of their time to it. It was a tedious process from raw material to finished product. In the case of woolen cloth, the wool had to be sorted, cleaned and dyed. Then the wool was carded and combed. Next, it was spun into thread which was woven into cloth. Subsequent processes were performed upon the cloth to change the texture or the colour of the woolen cloth. Many of these stages of production were performed by women and children. The supply of raw material for the woolen industry was obtained domestically. In the cases of silk and cotton, the raw materials were obtained from foreign sources, such as, China, the West Indies, North American and Africa.

The organization of the textile industry was complicated and grossly inefficient before the age of mechanization. Differences existed from one locality to another; generally, a merchant employed putters-out to distribute the raw materials to spinners and weavers who were scattered throughout the countryside.

Changes in the textile industry were already occurring in the early 1700s; however, these changes were not easily accepted as evidenced by the workers' riots which broke out in response to these new machines. John Kay's flying-shuttle, which enabled one weaver to do the work of two, and Lewis Paul's roller spinner, which was to make spinning more efficient (later to be perfected by Richard Arkwright), were the precursors of the inventive spirit and the application of new technology to the textile industry.

In the mid-1760s the textile industry began to experience rapid change. James Hargreaves' jenny, a device which enabled the operator to simultaneously spin dozens of threads, was readily adopted. By 1788 nearly 20,000 of them were being employed in England. Arkwright and others developed the water frame. This device performed similarly to Paul's roller spinner, though its use demanded greater power than could be applied by muscle.

Arkwright enlisted the financial support of Samuel Need and Jedidiah Strutt to set up a water-powered factory that utilized his invention. This factory, located in Cromford, employed more than 600 workers, many of whom were women and children. The adage "necessity is the mother of invention" is quite appropriate here, for this machine spun the cotton thread faster than human hands could supply the carded and combed raw material. This led to Arkwright's development of a machine which would perform that function.

The changes that took place in the textile industry must certainly centre about the inventions and their inventors, though not necessarily be limited to them. These inventions that were perfected and employed led to tremendous change in the world of work. Gone were the days of the Domestic System, yielding to the new ways of the Factory System. These factories which were to spring up throughout the countryside were large, dusty, poorly illuminated and ventilated and dangerous. The employment of women and children was commonplace and desired, for they were paid lower wages than their male counterparts. Working conditions in these factories were not subject to much regulation.

A strategy similar to the one that was suggested in the previous section may easily be employed here also.

Discussions may centre around today's textile industry, before moving on to the methods of preindustrial and industrialized England. Today, blue jeans are often referred to as "America's national dress." Some interesting discussions may develop around the manufacture of blue jeans, from the cotton fields to the finished product.

By comparing and contrasting conditions of work today and in days gone by, the students should begin to grasp the magnitude of impact that technological change has had on societies. The modern-day factory bears very little resemblance to Arkwright's factory at Cromford. Students may be assigned to write letters to the U.S. Department of Labour and its related agencies to request materials on factories today. Letters may also be written to representatives of the textile industry, as well as to labour unions within the industry. Students may also gather information concerning governmental regulation related to work in the textile industry. An excellent resource which should be used by the teacher is E. Royston Pike's, *Hard Times: Human Documents of the Industrial Revolution*.

Coal Mining

One finds the working conditions and practices of coal mining in the 18th and 19th centuries to be risky, at best, and suicidal at worst. This industry, even today, provokes thoughts of hazards at every turn. During the 18th and 19th centuries one even finds specific jobs in mining which required the employee to have a "death wish" of sorts. For example, a fireman employed in a colliery had the duty of ridding a mine tunnel of dangerous, flammable gases. His job entailed crawling through the tunnel holding a long stick. Attached to the end of the stick was a lighted candle which exploded any gases that might be accumulated ahead of him. All of the jobs that existed in coal mining were not as dangerous as the fireman's,; however, every one of them could be termed hazardous.

Different methods of mining coal were employed in various locales throughout England. All coal mining had one trait in common; the movement of coal was accomplished solely by muscle power—animal, man, woman and child, the latter being the most desirable for their size. The process of removing the coal was obviously as slow as it was dirty. Coal was moved along horizontal tunnels by the basketful and hauled up a vertical shaft to the surface. Later, the underground movement of coal was speeded up by the utilization of ponies and carts on rail. The production of coal increased steadily, from 2 1/2 million to more than 15 million tons by 1829.

Improvements in coal mining came in the form of improved tunnel ventilation, improved underground and surface transportation, the use of gunpowder to blast away at the coal seams, and improved tunnel illumination through the use of safety lamps.

Coal mining today continues to be a hazardous job, though modern machinery and safety equipment have made the industry more efficient and safe. Students should better understand the difficulties of mining coal in the 19th century by studying modern-day coal mining. Several modern-day issues related to the use of coal (strip-mining, air pollution, etc.) should make for some lively discussions in class. Discussions may also touch upon the question of health-related problems of this industry (black lung disease).

It was not uncommon in the 19th century for women to be employed in the mining of coal. Entire families could be found working side by side in the mines. Several sections of Pike's book, *Hard Times,* are an excellent teacher resource for material related to women and children working in England's coal mines. All of these short stories, as well as the illustrations, should be sufficient to help the students to understand the harsh conditions that were endured by these people.

Iron

Improvements in the iron industry came in the early l8th century. Abraham Darby successfully produced pig iron smelted with coke. This was a significant breakthrough, for prior to this discovery pig iron was smelted with the use of charcoal. Charcoal, derived from the charring of wood in a kiln, was an excellent source of energy to smelt the iron; however, its widespread use caused a serious depletion of England's forests. Darby's technique was gaining popularity within the industry, though problems still existed due to its use. Iron produced through this method was impure and brittle, making it unsuitable for the forgemaster to be able to fashion in into implements, so its use was limited to castings. Later, improvements would occur which produced high quality material and improved techniques in fashioning it.

Transportation

As an integral part of determining the cost and availability of manufactured products and as a means of improved communications, and as an industry unto itself, the improvement of transportation stimulated the course of the Industrial Revolution. Finished products, raw materials, food and people needed a reliable, quicker and less costly system of transportation. Canals and rivers had long been used as a means of internal transportation.

The mid-1700s began the first construction of canals between industrial districts. The construction of trunk lines opened the central industrial districts in the 1770s. The major thurst of financial backing came from the merchants and industrialists, who had a great stake in their construction. The problem of moving bulk goods overland was addressed, at least for the time being, by canals. However, their days were numbered, for the coming of the railroads was imminent.

The principles of rail transport were already in use in the late 1700s. Tramways, using cast iron rails, were being employed in a number of mines in England. By 1800 more than 200 miles of tramway served coal mines. It is not surprising, then, to find a number of engineers connected with coal mines searching for a way to apply the steam engine to railways.

A number of men were involved in experimentation concerning the development of railroads in England. Between

1804 and 1820 we find a few partially successful attempts at developing a practical means of rail transport: Richard Trevithick's "New Castle," a steam locomotive that proved to be too heavy for the rails, John Blenkinsop's locomotive, which employed a toothed, gear-like wheel, and William Hedley's "Puffing Billy," which was used for hauling coal wagons from the mines.

A pioneer in railroads that bears mentioning here is George Stephenson. Stephenson was invited by the Stockton and Darlington Railway to build the railroad between those two towns. The Stockton to Darlington line was the first public railroad to use locomotive traction and carry passengers, as well as freight. The equipment on this line proved to be too expensive to maintain. This was not the last to be heard from Stephenson.

In 1829 the Liverpool and Manchester Railway sponsored a competition to determine the best type of locomotive. This contest took place on the Rainhill level at Lancashire from October 6 to 14, 1829. Three steam locomotives participated in the Rainhill Trials; Timothy Hackworth's "Sans Pareil," John Braithwaite and John Ericsson's "Novelty," and Stephenson's "Rocket." The "Rocket" won the Rainhill Trials. It is interesting and ironic to note here that the first railroad accident death occurred at these trials.

Railroads dominated the transportation scene in England for nearly a century. Railroads proliferated in England, from 1,000 miles in 1836 to more than 7,000 miles built by 1852. Here again is another example of economic necessity producing innovation. The development of reliable, efficient rail service was crucial to the growth of specific industries and the overall economy.

By researching the railroad industry in the United States, students will find them to have been neglected over the years. Railroads have been superceded by modern forms of transport and superhighways. Perhaps a renaissance is due for the railroads in this country. Students will also find that the railroads are a reliable means of transportation for passengers and freight in Europe. Some interesting discussions may evolve around the railroads' role in mass transit in an energy-conscious world.

Steam

The development and subsequent application of steam power was undoubtedly the greatest technical achievement of the Industrial Revolution. A number of industries needed the ability to apply the enormous power produced by the steam engine, in order to continue their advancement in production. James Watt is credited with the invention of the steam engine. In fact, Watt improved upon a design which was developed by Thomas Savery and Thomas Newcomen. Watt's engine improved the efficiency of Newcomen's engine fourfold, and he utilized the latest technology in gunmaking, where precision was absolutely necessary. The transfer of one technology to another is evident here, in that Watt used John Wilkinson's device for boring cannon to accurately bore the large cylinder for his engine.

The development of a practical, efficient steam engine and its application to industry and transportation caused a great leap for industrialization. Its application was virtually limitless, and it was responsible for lifting industries from infancy to adolescence. Obviously, the study of steam power can be a course of study unto itself, and it is included in various sections within this unit. H. W. Dickinson and H. P. Vowles book, *James Watt and the Industrial Revolution,* is an excellent teacher resource for use in the classroom. This book contains a number of drawings of early designs of steam engines, as well as a complete history of the search for the practical design.

The Human Aspect

In the 18th century the population grew at a faster rate than ever before. There are four primary reasons which may be cited for this growth: a decline in the death rate, an increase in the birth rate, the virtual elimination of the dreaded plagues and an increase in the availability of food. The latter is probably the most significant of these reasons, for English people were consuming a much healthier diet.

One can find a myriad of reasons for the growth of the population, in addition to those above. Industry provided higher wages to individuals than was being offered in the villages. This allowed young people to marry earlier in life, and to produce children earlier. The old system of apprenticeship did not allow an apprentice to marry. City life provided young people with a greater choice of prospective partners, in contrast to the limited choices in some isolated village. Finally, industry provided people with improved clothing and housing, though it took a long time for housing conditions to improve.

With the adoption of the factory system, we find a shift in population. Settlements grew around the factories. In some cases, housing was provided to workers by their employers, thus giving the factory owners greater control over the lives of his workers. In some cases factories started in existing towns, which was desirable because a labour pool was readily available. The prime consideration for locating a factory was the availability of power. The early form of power was derived directly from moving water. Thus, we find factories cropping up in the hills near streams and rivers. Later, when steam power was developed, factories could be located near any source of water. Other factories, such as those involved in the manufacture of iron, had considerations of a different kind involving their location. Due to the great difficulty in moving bulk materials, such as iron ore, these mills had to be located close to the mineral source. In such situations, large communities grew directly above the seams of ore in the earth.

The development of the steam engine to drive machinery freed the mill owners from being locked into a site that was close to swiftly moving water. The steam powered mill still had to be located near a source of water, though the field of choice was much wider. Also, factories could be located closer to existing population centres or seaports, fulfilling the need for labour and transportation of materials.

The towns that grew in the North were crowded, dirty and unregulated. They grew so rapidly that no one took the time to consider the consequence of such conditions. In the areas of public sanitation and public health, ignorance reigned. No one understood the effects of these unsanitary conditions upon humans. Conditions in these densely populated areas worsened to the point of the reappearance of outbreaks of disease. In the mid-1800s there were several outbreaks of typhoid and cholera. Some attention to these conditions was accorded by Parliament in the form of Public Health Acts. These acts did improve conditions, though they were largely ineffective, for they did not grant local Boards of Health the powers to compel improvements.

E. Royston Pike's *Hard Times* is literally a treasure chest brimming with short stories that document living and working conditions during the Industrial Revolution. These stories may be utilized in the classroom in a variety of ways, and they should be quite effective in conveying the reality of life during this period.

Capital

Prior to industrialization in England, land was the primary source of wealth. The landed aristocracy held enormous powers the feudal system. However, a new source of great wealth grew from the Industrial Revolution, that which was derived from the ownership of factories and machinery. Those who invested in factories and machinery cannot be identified as belonging to any single class of people (landed aristocracy, industrialists, merchants). Their backgrounds were quite diverse, yet they had one thing in common: the daring to seize the opportunity to invest in new ventures. It was these capitalists who gave the necessary impetus to the speedy growth of the Industrial Revolution.

In the early years of this period we find most investments being made in a field closely related to one's original source of capital. Manufacturers took a substantial portion of their profits to "plough back" into their business, or they invested capital in ventures that were related to their primary business. Eventually, as opportunities to realise great profits proliferated, it was not uncommon to find these entrepreneurs investing substantially in concerns about which they knew very little.

Two kinds of capital were needed by these industrialists; long-term capital to expand present operations, and short-term capital to purchase raw materials, maintain inventories and to pay wages to their employees. The long-term capital needs were met by mortgaging factory buildings and machinery. It was the need for short-term capital which presented some problems. The need for short-term capital for raw materials and maintaining stock was accommodated by extending credit to the manufacturers by the producers or dealers. Often, a supplier of raw materials waited from 6 to 12 months for payment of his goods, after the manufacturer was paid for the finished product.

The payment of wages was not an easily solved problem, one which taxed the creativity of employers. The problem was in finding a sufficient amount of small value legal tender to pay the wages. Some employers staggered the days on which they paid their employees, while others paid them in script. Some paid a portion of their work force early in the day, allowing them to shop for household needs. When the money had circulated through the shopkeepers back to the employer, another portion of the work force was paid. All of these methods proved to be unacceptable.

The root of the problem was the lack.of an adequate banking system in these remote industrial centres. The Bank of England, established in the late 1690s, did not accommodate the needs of the manufacturers. It concentrated its interest on the financial affairs of state and those of the trading companies and merchants of London.

The early 1700s brought with it the first country banks. These private banks were founded by those who were involved in a variety of endeavors (goldsmith, merchant, manufacturer). Many industrialists favoured establishing their own banks as an outlet for the capital accumulated by their business and as a means for obtaining cash for wages. When the Bank of England tightened credit because of government demands, many of these banks failed. A great number of them had a large proportion of their assets tied up in long-term mortgages, thus leaving them vulnerable when demands for cash were presented by their depositors. From 1772 to 1825, a large number of these banks failed. Their limited resources were inadequate to meet the demands of the factory economy. A banking system was eventually set up to distribute capital to areas where it was needed, drawing it from areas where there was a surplus.

Labour

If the conditions in which people lived in these factory towns were considered bad, then the conditions in which they worked can be appropriately characterized as being horrendous. Inside these factories one would find poorly ventilated, noisy, dirty, damp and poorly lighted working areas. These factories were unhealthy and dangerous places in which to work. Normally, workers put in twelve to fourteen hours daily. Factory Acts that were later enacted by Parliament regulated the number of hours that men, women and children worked.

The factory system changed the manner in which work was performed. Unlike the domestic system the work was away from home, in large, impersonal settings. Workers were viewed by their employers merely as "hands."

Slowly, workers began to realise the strength they could possess if they were a unified force. It was a long, uphill battle for workers to be able to have the right to organize into officially recognized unions. Their lot was one of having no political influence in a land where the government followed a laissez-faire policy.

This hands off policy changed as the pressure from growing trade unions increased. A movement was beginning to free workers from the injustices of the factory system.

Political leaders called for reform legislation which would address these injustices

Lesson Outline

The outline which follows does not include a time frame for the use of Dickens' *Hard Times* and *Oliver Twist*. The frequency of use and depth of study concerning these works is best left up to the teacher. Instead, notes on these two books are included at the end of this section.

A "study set," consisting of maps, drawings and other resources is also available to supplement the unit. Copies of this set are available through the Yale-New Haven Teachers Institute. This material may be used in a variety of ways.

Geography: Spend as much time as is necessary to acquaint students with major geographical features of England. This knowledge will be helpful to the student later in the unit to make the connection between the location of industry and geographical features.

Agriculture: Construct a chart which outlines the major changes from pre-industrialization to the present.

Enclosure

Techniques and Inventions:

- Metal implements
- Crop rotation—Lord Townshend
- Stock breeding—Robert Bakewell
- Writer who popularized agricultural techniques—Arthur Young
- Seed drill cultivation, use of horsepower—Jethro Tull

Letters to:

- Deere & Co. Farm Equipment Manufacturers
- 1400 3rd Avenue
- Moline, Illinois 61265
- Locate agricultural improvements (see map)

Textiles: Construct a chart similar to the one used for agriculture. Trace development in textiles to the present, Domestic to Factory System.

Inventors:

- John Kay—flying shuttle
- James Hargreaves—spinning jenny
- Richard Arkwright—water frame, first factory
- Samuel Crompton—spinning mule
- Edward Cartwright—power loom
- Pages 31-34, Pike's *Hard Times*
- Factory and working conditions (see study set)
- Locate textile centres (see map)

Mining:

- Locate mining centres
- Present improvements in coal and iron mining Stories from Pike's *Hard Times* (see study set)
- *Transportation*—discuss improvements
- Canals Assign individual students the task of
- Roads locating the addresses of museums re-
- Railroads lated to these forms of transportation
- Steamboats Write letters to museums.

Prominent figures in transportation revolution:

- John Ericsson and Robert Fulton—steamboat
- John Macadan—road building
- George Stephenson—locomotive

Steam power: This topic may be adequately covered in the section on transportation. Certainly, it may be studied in depth by small groups or individual students.

Living conditions: A number of class periods may be spent on this topic. Discussions may centre around: Has the quality of life improved since the 18th century? What have we learned about public health? What is the importance of providing for local Boards of Health in modern-day cities?

Present material covered in the narrative.

A number of stories from Pike's *Hard Times* are appropriate here (see study set).

Working conditions: Also Pike's *Hard Times*.

Capital and labour: These two sectors of our system are purposely blended into one. The employers and employees, though seemingly at odds with one another, are very much dependent on each other. It is as important to the employer to have a healthy and adequate labour force, as it is for jobs to be available to the workers.

DISCUSS THE MAJOR POINTS OF CAPITALISM

Research labour legislation: From the early 1800s to the early 1900s, a number of laws pertaining to factory work were enacted in England:

- Pauper Apprentice Act 1802
- Cotton Factory Act 1819
- Factory Act 1833
- Mines Act 1842
- Ten Hour Act 1847
- Safety Code 1855
- Factory Code 1878, 1902
- Discuss the rise of the labour movement.
- Discuss the major "weapons" of unions and employers:
- Workers' Weapons Employers'

Weapons: Strike, Lockout, Boycott, Injunction,

Collective bargaining, Blacklist, Legislative lobbying, Individual bargaining, Political action, Open shop, Picketing Right-to-work, Legislation Closed, Shop Union shop etc.

Future: Discussions may be initiated which speculate about the future. Are we in the midst of an industrial revolution today? How is society changed by technological advances? How has faster transportation and global communications made the world smaller?

At the level for which this unit is intended, seventh grade, it is important for the students to be exposed to some classic pieces of literature as part of their assigned reading. Thus, the work of Dickens is made to order.

Dickens' writings selected for use in this unit should prove to be entertaining to the students, while bringing the material contained in the narrative to life. The imagery that Dickens creates should be adequate to convey to the students the real "flavour" of life in England during this period, and his social criticisms that are evident in them should aid the students in their understanding of the issues of the times.

The teacher should select the best method for utilizing Dickens in his/her classroom. Readings may be assigned to individuals, or to small or large groups. It was very common in the Victorian period for members of a family to read to others in the early evening. The teacher may choose to read aloud to the class, or even have individual students read to the rest of the class.

Notes on Oliver Twist

Oliver Twist was born to an unknown young woman in the parish workhouse. He worked on a parish farm until he was nine years old. An offer was made to pay five pounds to whomever would take Oliver as an apprentice. He was taken in by Mr. Sowerberry, an undertaker, who put him to work as a "mute."

Oliver was treated very well by Mr. Sowerberry, though he was mistreated by several other characters in the story. One morning Oliver decides to run away.

Upon his arrival at the outskirts of London, Oliver meets a young boy named Artful Dodger. Dodger takes Oliver to meet Fagin, a master criminal. Oliver gets involved with the law when he is with two thieves who rob an old gentleman. Oliver is saved from jail by Mr. Brownlow. Later, Oliver is kidnapped by two of Fagin's cohorts and made to participate in a burglary, during which Oliver is shot.

The plot thickens when the reader learns that Oliver's half-brother made a pact with Fagin to make Oliver a criminal, thus disinheriting him from their father's will.

Suggested questions for discussion:

What social injustices is Dickens attacking in *Oliver Twist*?

Which characters in *Oliver Twist* struck you as being comical?

What were some of their qualities which gave you this impression of them?

Charles Dickens criticized crime and poverty in many of his writings. What kind of man do you think Dickens was?

Notes on Hard Times

Much of Dickens' writing provides commentary and criticism of social issues of the period and descriptions of settings that make it impossible for the reader to distinguish fact from fiction. *Hard Times* is no exception. In this social protest novel, the working class, know as "Hands," as well as the other classes, experience some 'hard times.'

The utilization of this book in the classroom can best be determined by the teacher. This may be the book that teacher chooses to read aloud to the class. Dickens' descriptions of Coketown and some of its inhabitants are quite graphic and are examples of his best writings.

Chapter 5

French Revolution and Tale of Two Cities

In 1859, Charles Dickens wrote the book A Tale of Two Cities. In A Tale, Dickens writes about the French Revolution, and relates the events in the lives of two families, one French and one English. In addition to writing about a very interesting fiction plot, Dickens also tied in a wide variety of important themes and sub plots that keep the reader interested as well as portraying very valuable lessons for us even today. He chose very archetypical characters for the book, all strengthening or portraying one of the themes. The main themes are revenge, courage and sacrifice, and resurrection.

One theme involves revenge; the evil effects of revenge bring out one's bad side. Although it occurs many times in A Tale, Madame Defarge is the main character representing this theme. Her sister and mother were assaulted by the brothers Evrémonde. After this, she vows to herself that all members of the Evrémonde family will die. She turns into a ruthless killer because she must get revenge. When her husband tells her to stop, she replies, "tell the wind and fire to stop, not me". We now see that she is a person teeming with hatred. Revenge is so powerful. When she found out Charles Darnay is an Evrémonde and is planning to marry Lucie Manette, she began to knit his name into the shroud she was making, symbolizing his impending death. Also, she tried to kill Lucie and her daughter, just because they were related to an Evrémonde, even though Darnay (Evrémonde) denounced his heritage and disconnected all relationships to them. Lucie was in a state of mourning so Defarge jumped on the situation.

"She will be at home, awaiting the moment of his death. She will be mourning and grieving. She will be in a state of mind to impeach the justice of the Republic. She will be full of sympathy with its enemies. I will go to her."

She had no mercy, her main goal was to kill all descendants of the Evrémonde family, women and children included and even non-blood relatives. At the end of the novel, she receives an end fitting her ways; she was killed by Ms. Pross, who is the epitome of love and kindness. It is evident from here that Dickens believed that good would always win over bad. Madame Defarge was going to kill out of hate and revenge, but she got killed because of the love Ms. Pross had for her friend Lucie.

Another key theme in the novel has to do with courage and sacrifice. There were many sacrifices in this novel by many different characters. Charles Darnay went back into the war-torn France from his safe house and family in England to save his former servant Gabelle from the hands of the rebels. He did this, for the simple reason that he gave his promise, many months ago. Also, Dr Manette 'sacrifices' his love for her for her love to Darnay. After the wedding, we see how much Lucie means to Dr Manette in his return to cobbling shoes.

Sydney Carton made the ultimate sacrifice. Because of his love for Lucie and his friendship with Darnay, Carton's actions portray one of the most important themes implied in this book. Carton helps others, and does not think so much of himself. As we first see Sydney Carton, he is a lazy man, who drinks his life away. However there is more to him as he said "I cause no harm to any man on earth, and no man on earth cares for me". He does not like the other people's view of him, and he wants to change it. When Darnay was sent to the guillotine, Carton could have let him go, and possibly have Lucie for himself. However, he ended up being the true hero, and sacrificed his life for the life of another, in the name of love. Right before going to the guillotine, Carton visualizes a better life, a life where he gave to others, not thinking of himself. It shows the complete turn-a-round in his view of life for the better. Sydney Carton is really a courageous, loving man.

The final main theme in the book is the idea of resurrection. Book one of A Tale is entitled 'Recalled to Life'. This shows resurrection being a major theme. An example of this is Dr Manette's resurrection after being in prison for nearly eighteen years of mental torment, and when he got out; he was asked the question, "you know that you are recalled to life". We know that he has been, as he no longer refers to himself as "105 North Tower". He is spiritually resurrected with his daughter when they first meet. Lucie forms a relationship with him, which gives Dr. Manette a sense of pride.

"The Doctor was in his best condition, and looked especially young. The resemblance between him and Lucie was very strong at such times, and as they sat side by side, she leaning on his shoulder, and he resting his arm on the back of her chair, it was very agreeable to trace the likeness".

Throughout the novel, Dr. Manette has gone through several mentally tragic episodes. Every time he goes into a relapse, Lucie is the only one that can help him regain normalcy. Darnay also took a part in this theme of resurrection. Charles Darnay's soul had been spiritually resurrected and saved from being killed. Due to being an Evrémonde and for portraying his own family, he was tried and sentenced to death by the guillotine. Dr Manette tried to save Darnay many times, though Barsad would always seem to find a way to get him back to prison and succeeded in sentencing him to death. When the final day of Darnay's life came, it turned out a happy one for him, "The door was quickly opened and closed, and there stood before him face to face, quiet, intent, upon him, with the light of a smile on his features, and a cautionary finger on his lip, Sydney Carton". Sydney Carton, who resembled Darnay very closely, exchanged places with him. Feigning illness, Darnay was thus snuck out of prison, and physically resurrected.

Often when reading a book, the individual tends to draw parallels in the literature. One parallel often used is the difference between the beginning and ending of the book. A Tale of Two Cities began and ended with a journey. In the second chapter of the novel, Jarvis Lorry travels to recall Dr Manette to life. In the end of the book, Sydney Carton is taken to his death, because of Defarge's revenge. He saved his friends life. Lorry began with the theme of resurrection, and Carton finished off with the theme of sacrifice, dying because of revenge.

Critical Reception

The novel's events begin in Paris, roughly fourteen years prior to the French Revolution. Dr. Alexandre Manette has been released from the Bastille after having been unjustly imprisoned for eighteen years for trying to bring two members of the noble St. Evrémonde family to trial for their crimes. His daughter, Lucie, whom he has not seen since she was a small child, has traveled to Paris from London with Jarvis Lorry, a family friend, to bring him home. Lucie and Lorry arrive in Paris at the wineshop of Monsieur and Madame Defarge, who are both active in the movement to incite a peasant revolution. Dr. Manette, now old, feeble, and too mentally impaired to recognize his daughter, has been staying in a room above the shop, where he works at a shoemaker's bench in the belief that he is a cobbler.

Five years later in London, the Manettes are called to testify in the treason trial of Charles Darnay, whom they had met during their return from France. Darnay, a French language tutor who is the nephew of the Marquis St. Evrémonde, has been accused of spying for the French. Darnay is acquitted when his attorney, C. J. Stryver, confuses a witness by presenting his law partner, Sydney Carton, who so closely resembles Darnay that the witness is unable to make a positive identification. Carton, who has a brilliant legal mind but suffers from alcoholism, becomes attracted to Lucie and through his feelings for her finds new direction in his life. Darnay, Carton, and Stryver, all of whom seek Lucie's hand in marriage, become frequent visitors at the Manette household, which is governed by Miss Pross. In the interim, the situation in France worsens as its citizens grow more angry and dissatisfied with the French aristocracy. Though Darnay has taken his mother's maiden name in an effort to shed his connection with his noble family, he feels compelled to return to France when his uncle runs down a peasant child with his carriage. Darnay pleads with his uncle to make amends for the past deeds committed by the family, but the Marquis refuses. Later that night, the Marquis is killed in his sleep by Gaspard, the father of the child he killed.

Darnay returns to England and asks Manette for his daughter's hand in marriage. He tries to reveal his true name to the old man, but Manette tells him to wait until the morning of his wedding day. Carton is also in love with Lucie, but she refuses his proposal of marriage. Carton tells her never to forget that he will do anything he can to help her and those she loves. Six years later, the Bastille is stormed and the French Revolution begins. Darnay again returns to France, this time in an effort to save a loyal family servant from the revolutionaries. When his true identity is discovered, Darnay is arrested and put on trial. Lucie and Dr. Manette come to Paris on his behalf, and Manette's sympathetic testimony at Darnay's trial succeeds; Darnay is released, but under condition that he remain in France. Shortly thereafter, Darnay is arrested again, accused of crimes against the people by Defarge and an unknown party. In an effort to help, Carton, Miss Pross, and Jerry Cruncher, an employee of Lorry's, arrive in Paris, where they encounter Miss Pross's long-lost brother, Solomon, whom Cruncher recognizes as John Barsad, the man who accused Darnay of being a spy almost fourteen years before. At Darnay's trial, Defarge testifies against him, claiming that Dr. Manette is the second accuser, presenting papers he recovered from Manette's cell in the Bastille in which Manette chronicled the various crimes of the St. Evrémonde family and showed how they were responsible for his imprisonment. Darnay is found guilty and sentenced to death. Carton blackmails Barsad, a prison turnkey, and gains access to Darnay's cell. He then drugs Darnay and has him taken away so that he may pose as the Frenchman and take his place. While attempting to prevent the Manettes from leaving Paris,

Madame Defarge is shot and killed during a struggle with Miss Pross. Lucie and Darnay escape to England, and Carton sacrifices himself, taking Darnay's place at the guillotine.

For Dickens, prisons are symbolic of the grave—a comparison he makes throughout his works. Critics note that the prevalence of this theme may be related to Dickens's father's incarceration in debtors' prison. Coupled with this notion in *A Tale of Two Cities* is the possibility of resurrection: Manette is "resurrected" upon his release from the Bastille, and Carton, who serves as a Christ-figure in his act of self-sacrifice, essentially lives on in the form of his double, Darnay. Additionally, Dickens uses memory as a driving force in the novel, whether as an instrument of destruction or of hope. While it is the memory of the rape and deaths of her siblings that prompts Madame Defarge's hatred of the aristocrats, it is the memory of Manette's dead wife that begins the process of his resurrection from the grave of his prison and insanity. Carton, in fact, is referred to by Stryver as "Memory Carton" for his brilliant legal mind; Carton renounces the memory of his former life when he dies with the words, "It is a far; far better thing that I do, than I have ever done."

Though *A Tale of Two Cities* was immensely popular with general readers, many of Dickens's contemporary critics found fault with the novel. These critical attacks essentially focused on three fronts: that the novel is flawed as history, mechanical and unrealistic in its construction, and uncharacteristic of Dickens. It is perhaps upon this last point that most critics choose to base their criticisms; many argue that the novel lacks the characteristic humour usually present in Dickens's work, and that the events with which it concerns itself are too far removed from the Victorian issues that Dickens typically chose to address. Rather than examine the novel on its own merits, these critics often fall into comparisons of *A Tale of Two Cities* with Dickens's other works. Regardless of the initial criticisms leveled at the novel, *A Tale of Two Cities* has come to receive a great deal of praise from modern critics, and it continues to be included on high school and college reading lists.

Chapter 6

Social Realities of Victorian Era

VICTORIAN AGE

Workers of the Industrial Era

During the whole Victorian age, most people hade to work inhumanly much. In 1833, the average man working in factories had to spend fifteen of the twenty four hours in the day working for their employees. They had two hours of eating time per day, and all they ate was potatoes and bread, which didn't give them much energy and encouragement to proceed with their work. For the average Englishman it was a working day, and a very hard one indeed.

Their Working Conditions

Because of the extreme amount of time spent working, many workers got very tired and exhausted. They made to little money to get some really good, proper food which could have given them some more energy.

The places they worked weren't clean either. The worksites were dirty and brought much noise and pollution to the workers. They worked on dangerous machines which could easily cut a mans hand off, and this sort of working accidents happened a lot. It was no good to ask your boss for some hours off, because if you gave any sign of discomfort or being tired, he would fire you at once without any warnings. No one dared to strike, because they had too much respect and fear for their bosses.

A Difficult Life

The workers in the big cities had a very tough and challenging life. Their day at work started at four in the morning and didn't end until eleven in the evening, nineteen hours later. They had very little to come home to, because most workers lived with their families in dirty, small houses. They had four or five days of holidays throughout the whole year. To escape from their problems, many workers drank very large amounts of alcohol the few hours they were not at work. As in any job, the workers could be unfortunate enough to break something. Then their employees would beat them up, so that they would think twice before breaking something again.

A Better Society

One courageous industrial was Robert Owen. The goals he worked very hard to achieve was getting better houses for the workers and providing them with a better salary so their children could have a good education. The workers who were rich received help at once when they had accidents or were sick, while no one would do anything to help the poor workers who didn't have any money. But people had sympathy for the poor workers, and in the middle of the nineteenth century, broke workers received money and assistance from sensitive people, just trying to help. They were creating a better society. After this, work went easier because machines took over most of the work, and people didn't have to work as hard as they had done earlier.

Inventions

The Victorian age (1837-1901) was a period of enormous technological progress in communications, transport and many other areas of life.

The vivid picture of the Victorian age unfolds as inventions from the ground-breaking such as aspirin, dynamite, and the telephone to everyday things like blue jeans and tiddlywinks are revealed decade by decade. Together they provide a vivid picture of Victorian life.

The lives of the inventors and their circumstances provide entertaining insights into this world. For example, Almon Strowger invented the automatic telephone exchange as he was convinced that telephone operators were giving his business to a rival firm of undertakers.

The Ritty brothers designed a cash register to prevent the bartenders they employed from cheating them. And Adalbert Kwiatkowski, among many Victorians preoccupied with the risk of premature burial, invented a coffin that would sound an alarm upon the slightest movement of an apparently dead body.

Charles Dickens and the Brontë Sisters

Charles Dickens was born in Landport, Hampshire, during the new industrial age, which gave birth to theories of Karl Marx. Dickens's father was a clerk in the navy pay office. He was well paid but often ended in financial troubles. In 1814 Dickens moved to London, and then to Chatham, where he received some education. The schoolmaster William Giles gave special attention to Dickens, who made rapid progress. In 1824, at the age of 12, Dickens was sent to work for some months at a blacking factory, Hungerford Market, London, while his father John was in Marshalea debtor's prison. "My father and mother were quite satisfied," Dickens later recalled bitterly. "They could hardly have been more so, if I had been twenty years of age, distinguished at a grammar-school, and going to Cambridge." Later this period found its way to the novel Little Dorritt (1855-57). John Dickens paid his £40 debt with the money he inherited from his mother; she died at the age of seventy-nine when he was still in prison.

Dickens and the women

Dickens's relationship with Maria Beadnell, the daughter of a banker, whom he had courted for four years, ended in 1833. Three years later Dickens married Catherine Hogart, the daughter of his friend George Hogarth, who edited the newly established *Evening Chronicle*. With Catherine he had 10 children. They separated in 1858. Some biographers have suspected that Dickens was more fond of Catherine's sister, Mary, who moved into their house and died in 1837 at the age of 17 in Dickens's arms. Eventually she became the model for Dora Copperfield. Dickens also wanted to be buried next to her and wore Mary's ring all his life. Another of Catherine's sisters, Georgiana, moved in with the Dickens's, and the novelist fell in love with her. Dickens also had a long liaison with the actress Ellen Ternan, whom he had met by the late 1850s.

Life Ends...

Dickens lived in 1844-45 in Italy, Switzerland and Paris, and from 1860 one his address was at Gadshill Place, near Rochester, Kent, where he lived with his two daughters and sister-in-law. He had also other establishments - Gad's Hill, and Windsor Lodge, Peckham, which he had rented for Ellen Ternan. His wife Catherine lived at the London house. In 1858-68 Dickens gave lecturing tours in Britain and the United States. By the end of his last American tour, Dickens could hardly manage solid food, subsisting on champagne and eggs beaten in sherry.

In an opium den in Shadwell, Dickens saw an elderly pusher known as Opium Sal, who then featured in his mystery novel The Mystery of Edwin Drood. He collapsed at Preston, in April 1869, after which his doctors put a stop to his public performances. Dickens died at Gadshill on suddenly of a stroke on June 8, 1870. Some of his friends later thought the readings killed him. Dickens had asked that he should be buried "in an inexpensive, unostentatious, and strictly private manner".

Chapter 7

Historical Context

CONTEXT

Charles John Huffam Dickens was born on February 7, 1812, in Portsmouth, England. He moved with his family to London and later to Chatham, Kent, where he had many happy childhood experiences. His father was a well-paid clerk in the Navy pay office, but was extravagant and wasteful with his money. He eventually landed in a debtor's prison, and Charles was forced to quit school and work in a factory, an experience that scarred him. Though he detested his brief foray into the working class, the experience acquainted him with the struggles and poverty of the lower classes, and he gained a sympathy for them that appeared in his later works. After his father's release from prison, he re-entered school briefly but left at age 15. After briefly working for two legal firms, he learned shorthand and became a court reporter, which gave him the legal knowledge he later used in his novels. He became romantically involved with Maria Beadnell, a woman who would haunt him for years after their affair cooled because she deemed his family and his prospects unsatisfactory. She briefly reentered his life years later, an experience that proved disappointing and disillusioning to Dickens.

After acting on the London stage and seriously considering a career in the theater, Dickens became a parliamentary reporter for the *Mirror of Parliament* and the *True Sun*. His experiences as a reporter left him with a life-long affection for journalism and a suspicion of law and parliament. He published his first sketch, "A Dinner at Poplar Walk," in the *Monthly Magazine* in 1833. In 1836 he married Catherine Hogarth, became editor of *Bentley's Miscellany*, and published *Sketches by "Boz."* A year later, "Oliver Twist" began to appear as a serialization in *Bentley's Miscellany*. A year later, "Nicholas Nickelby" began to appear, and the first of his nine children was born. After the publication of "Barnaby Rudge," he visited the United States. Though he was warmly welcomed, the experience left him disillusioned with the country. Following the publication of "Martin Chuzzlewit," and "A Christmas Carol" and the births of several more children, he served briefly as the editor of the *Daily News*. In 1849, he began serialization of "David Copperfield," probably his most successful novel.

As a personality, Dickens was popular and engaging; he was considered to be one of the best after-dinner speakers in London and was popular in his circle of sophisticated and illustrious friends. Dickens relished his public popularity and long maintained a deep affection for his public. He was convivial, yet complicated; his creative process was marked by a deep commitment to punctuality and organization, along with the long walks through the London streets that became essential to his creativity. He was devoted to his children and prided himself on maintaining a happy home and family life. This happiness eventually deteriorated, however, in later years. Tragedy struck when several of his children died. He also fell out of love with his wife, and some of his other children proved to be disappointing to him.

In 1856, he collaborated with Wilkie Collins, a close friend, on a play, "The Frozen Deep." When the play was produced a year later, Dickens fell in love with one if the actresses, Ellen Ternan. His scandalous affair led to his separation from Catherine in 1858, but it did nothing to dim his immense public popularity. His romance with Ternan continued until his death. After his separation from Catherine, he began to perform public readings, an act he greatly enjoyed and would continue for many years. Also that year, he began to publish installments of *A Tale of Two Cities.*

A Tale of Two Cities was one of Dickens' final novels and a departure from his usual style. It was a dense narrative that relied less on humour, dialogue, and characterization than usual. Though it remains a staple on high school reading lists, it is not generally regarded from a critical standpoint as one of his major works. While many readers, and Dickens himself, found Sydney Carton's self-sacrifice to be extremely moving, many critics are now more impressed with Dr. Manette as an achievement in characterization. The following year, he published *Great Expectations,* which is considered to be less ambitious than earlier novels but still his finest literary achievement. In 1864, he published *Our Mutual Friend,* another novel of social criticism. Though his health was by now deteriorating, he nonetheless embarked on a second reading tour of America. During this time, critics became more hostile to him, and he struck friends as being sadder than before. His sons continued to cause him worry and disappointment, though he still loved the country house, Gad's Hill, which became his permanent home until his death.

In 1865, he was injured in a railway accident; an experience that left him badly shaken and that proved to be the beginning of a descent into poor health. He collapsed in 1869 during a farewell reading tour. He gave one more short series of readings in London and began writing his last novel, *Edwin Drood.* The novel was never completed; Dickens suffered a stroke and died at Gad's Hill on June 9, 1870, at age 58. He was buried at Westminster Abbey.

Despite the critical hostility he faced in his later years, he is now considered to be ranked second only to Shakespeare in the canon of English authors.

Plot Summary

It is the year 1775, and England and France are undergoing a period of social upheaval and turmoil. The forces that are leading to revolution in France are colliding with a circle of people in England, causing their destinies to be irrevocably intertwined.

Lucie Manette, a young woman who has been raised as an orphan and a ward of Tellson's bank, learns that her father is alive and has recently been released from prison after eighteen years of unjust incarceration. She travels to the French suburb of Saint Antoine with Mr. Jarvis Lorry, a longtime Tellson's employee who had managed her father's affairs before his imprisonment. They find her father at the home of Ernest Defarge, a former domestic of Dr. Manette's who has housed the doctor since his release. Though her father is teetering on the brink of insanity, she solemnly vows that she will be true to him and devote her life to helping him recover himself. The family relocates to London, and Mr. Lorry becomes a friend of the family. After time, the doctor begins to recover and resumes his practice, and though he occasionally reverts back to his trance-like state, he slowly but surely returns to himself. Throughout the process, he and Lucie become extremely close.

After a period of five years, Lucie and her father are called to testify in the trial of Charles Darnay, a French citizen and London resident who has been accused of treason against England. Lucie testifies that she and her father saw Darnay on a ship bound for England the night she brought her father back home to London, and that he was conversing with other men and poring over documents. Though the testimony is damaging, Lucie notes that Darnay had been extremely kind and helpful to her in caring for her father on the ship, and she admits that she hopes her testimony has not doomed him. Darnay is ultimately saved when one witness' testimony hinges on the witness' certainty that he saw Darnay at a certain locale at a particular time.

When Sydney Carton, a member of Darnay's defence team, removes his wig in court, it is revealed that he bears a striking resemblance to Darnay, thereby eroding the witness' credibility in terms of his certainty of having seen Charles Darnay himself. Darnay is ultimately freed, and this circumstance draws everyone involved closer together. Darnay, along with Mr. Lorry, becomes a friend of the family, and Sydney Carton becomes a regular visitor, if not an entirely welcome one—he is frequently drunk, often sullen, and coarse in his manner.

Though the others complain of Carton's manner, one evening he confides in Lucie and tells her that while he has made nothing of his life and will not improve before he dies, he wants her to know that she has awakened feelings in him that he thought had been stamped out long ago. She asks if she can help him, and he says no, but that he wants her to know that he cares for her deeply. The group continues to visit regularly, and on one particular evening, Lucie notes that there is an ominous feeling in the air, as if she is able to forecast that grave danger and turmoil are in her future. But the family continues to be happy, and Lucie eventually marries Darnay, who tells her father that he has a secret that no one else knows. Dr. Manette asks Darnay to save the secret for the marriage morning, and Darnay does.

A year passes. Darnay returns to France to attend to the business that had gotten him into trouble in England in the first place. He pays a visit to his uncle, a corrupt aristocrat who is so cruel that when his carriage driver recklessly ran over and killed a peasant's child, he blamed the peasants for being in the way. After having dinner in his uncle's lavish chateau, Darnay wakes up to find that his uncle has been murdered.

He returns to England, and several more years pass. He and Lucie have two children, a son and a daughter. The son passes away as a young boy, but the family continues to be relatively happy despite this tragic circumstance. But the foreboding sense looms in the air, and Mr. Lorry notes that many of Tellson's Paris customers are frantically transferring their assets to the London branch, signaling some kind of danger in Paris. He notes that he will have to travel to Paris to help the office there handle the volume.

One day, Mr. Lorry remarks to Darnay that he has received a letter addressed to a Marquis St. Evrémonde in care of Tellson's. Darnay says that he knows the man and will deliver the letter; in truth, Darnay *is* the Marquis St. Evrémonde, a descendant of the corrupt rulers of France. The letter is from an old friend who has been put in prison unjustly and who fears that he will soon be executed. Darnay, who has so long avoided France for fear of what might happen to him there because of his heritage, realises that he must go.

He goes to intervene on his friend's behalf and quickly realises that the situation is worse than he could have imagined. A revolution has taken place; the peasants have overthrown the government and are murdering anyone who they feel represents the old guard. Darnay is immediately taken into custody, though he tries desperately to explain that unlike his uncle and father, he is on the peasants' side and wants to help them. They disregard his testimony, and none other than Ernest Defarge, who has since become a revolutionary, sends Darnay to prison. By this time, Lucie and her father have learned that Darnay has returned to France, aware that Darnay is probably in grave danger. The revolutionaries treat Dr. Manette as a hero, however, because he had so long suffered at the hands of the same government that oppressed them (and that they have since overthrown). Because of his newfound influence, he is able to learn where Darnay is, and he intervenes on his behalf.

When Darnay is tried for his life in front of a corrupt and farcical tribunal, only Dr. Manette's testimony saves him. He is freed, but before even one day passes, he is recaptured on the grounds that three French citizens have denounced him. He is forced to undergo another trial, at which it is learned that the citizens who denounced him are Ernest Defarge, Madame Defarge (Ernest's cruel and vengeful wife), and Dr. Manette. When Dr. Manette declares that he has never denounced Charles and that whoever accused him of doing so is lying, Defarge presents a paper to the tribunal to be read aloud.

The paper turns out to be a journal that Dr. Manette had written after ten years in prison and hidden in a chimney; Defarge discovered it when the peasants freed that particular prison. The account reveals that Dr. Manette had learned that a Marquis St. Evrémonde and his brother had cruelly murdered a peasant, and he learned this because the men retrieved him to give medical attention to their victims before they died. He saw how the brothers treated their victims so cruelly, and he had written a letter to the government informing them of what he saw. The brothers Evrémonde learned that Dr. Manette had written the letter. Shortly thereafter, he was taken prisoner, and his wife was never informed of what happened to him. For this, Dr. Manette wrote that he denounced the brothers Evrémonde and all their descendants.

After the letter is read, the court erupts into an uproar, and the tribunal votes unanimously to execute Darnay. Lucie and her father are beside themselves; by this time, Carton has traveled to London, and he and Mr. Lorry confer and try to decide what to do. During this time, Dr. Manette tries to save Darnay, but he relapses into his trance-like state and is unable to do anything. Through a series of coincidences, Carton discovers that one of the men who testified against Darnay at his trial several years earlier is working as a spy in France. He learns that the man is a spy in the prison where Darnay is held, and he blackmails the man into granting him access to Darnay. Mr. Lorry remarks solemnly that this will not help Darnay; Carton says he knows this, and Darnay's fate seems irrevocably sealed. Carton, however, has other plans. He goes to the prison on the day of Charles' execution on the pretense of visiting him one last time. But once he gets inside, he uses his physical resemblance to Darnay and his ability to manipulate the spy to pull off the ultimate sacrifice.

He drugs Darnay into a stupor, switches clothing with him, and has the spy smuggle Darnay out of the prison and into a waiting carriage that also includes Dr. Manette, Lucie, and Mr. Lorry. He tells no one of his plan, and not even the Manettes know it. They are waiting in their carriage for Carton, fully expecting that he will join them and that they will leave France in a hurry. The rest of the family is in danger because of Madame Defarge, who wants to denounce all of them. The peasant that the Evrémonde brothers murdered was her brother, and she wants revenge against Darnay and his entire family. The spy smuggles Charles to the waiting carriage, and the family escapes France. Carton, however, goes to the guillotine and dies for Lucie, fulfilling his promise to her that he would die "to keep a life you love beside you." Just before he dies, he thinks to himself that his final act is far better than anything else he has ever done.

Chapter 8

Analysis of the Title

A TALE OF TWO CITIES

As an example of Dickens's literary work, A Tale of Two Cities is not wrongly named. It is his most typical contact with the civic ideals of Europe. All his other tales have been tales of one city. He was in spirit a Cockney; though that title has been quite unreasonably twisted to mean a cad. By the old sound and proverbial test a Cockney was a man born within the sound of Bow bells. That is, he was a man born within the immediate appeal of high civilisation and of eternal religion. Shakespeare, in the heart of his fantastic forest, turns with a splendid suddenness to the Cockney ideal as being the true one after all. For a jest, for a reaction, for an idle summer love or still idler summer hatred, it is well to wander away into the bewildering forest of Arden. It is well that those who are sick with love or sick with the absence of love, those who weary of the folly of courts or weary yet more of their wisdom, it is natural that these should trail away into the twinkling twilight of the woods.

Yet it is here that Shakespeare makes one of his most arresting and startling assertions of the truth. Here is one of those rare and tremendous moments of which one may say that there is a stage direction, "Enter Shakespeare." He has admitted that for men weary of courts, for men sick of cities, the wood is the wisest place, and he has praised it with his purest lyric ecstasy. But when a man enters suddenly upon that celestial picnic, a man who is not sick of cities, but sick of hunger, a man who is not weary of courts, but weary of walking, then Shakespeare lets through his own voice with a shattering sincerity and cries the praise of practical human civilisation:

> If ever you have looked on better days,
> If ever you have sat at good men's feasts,
> If ever been where bells have knolled to church,
> If ever from your eyelids wiped a tear
> Or know what 't is to pity and be pitied.

There is nothing finer even in Shakespeare than that conception of the circle of rich men all pretending to rough it in the country, and the one really hungry man entering, sword in hand, and praising the city. "If ever been where bells have knolled to church"; if you have ever been within sound of Bow bells; if you have ever been happy and haughty enough to call yourself a Cockney.

We must remember this distinction always in the case of Dickens. Dickens is the great Cockney, at once tragic and comic, who enters abruptly upon the Arcadian banquet of the æsthetics and says, "Forbear and eat no more," and tells them that they shall not eat "until necessity be served." If there was one thing he would have favoured instinctively it would have been the spreading of the town as meaning the spreading of civilisation. And we should (I hope) all favour the spreading of the town if it did mean the spreading of civilisation.

The objection to the spreading of the modern Manchester or Birmingham suburb is simply that such a suburb is much more barbaric than any village in Europe could ever conceivably be. And again, if there is anything that Dickens would have definitely hated it is that general treatment of nature as a dramatic spectacle, a piece of scene-painting which has become the common mark of the culture of our wealthier classes. Despite many fine pictures of natural scenery, especially along the English roadsides, he was upon the whole emphatically on the side of the town. He was on the side of bricks and mortar. He was a citizen; and, after all, a citizen means a man of the city. His strength was, after all, in the fact that he was a man of the city. But, after all, his weakness, his calamitous weakness, was that he was a man of one city.

For all practical purposes he had never been outside such places as Chatham and London. He did indeed travel on the Continent; but surely no man's travel was ever so superficial as his. He was more superficial than the smallest and commonest tourist. He went about Europe on stilts; he never touched the ground. There is one good test and one only of whether a man has travelled to any profit in Europe.

An Englishman is, as such, a European, and as he approaches the central splendours of Europe he ought to feel that he is coming home. If he does not feel at home he had much better have stopped at home. England is a real home; London is a real home; and all the essential feelings of adventure or the picturesque can easily be gained by going out at night upon the fiats of Essex or the cloven hills of Surrey. Your visit to Europe is useless unless it gives you the sense of an exile returning. Your first sight of Rome is futile unless you feel that you have seen it before. Thus useless and thus futile were the foreign experiments and the continental raids of Dickens. He enjoyed them as he would have enjoyed, as a boy, a scamper out of Chatham into some strange meadows, as he would have enjoyed, when a grown man, a steam in a police boat out into the fens to the far east of London. But he was the Cockney venturing far; he was not the European coming home. He is still the splendid Cockney Orlando of whom I spoke above; he cannot but suppose that any strange men, being happy in some pastoral way, are mysterious foreign scoundrels. Dickens's real speech to the lazy and laughing civilisation of Southern Europe would really have run in the Shakespearean words:

> but whoe'er you be
> Who in this desert inaccessible,
> Under the shade of melancholy boughs
> Lose and neglect the creeping hours of time.
> If ever you have looked on better things,
> If ever been where bells have knolled to church.

If, in short, you have ever had the advantage of being born within the sound of Bow bells. Dickens could not really conceive that there was any other city but his own.

It is necessary thus to insist that Dickens never understood the Continent, because only thus can we appreciate the really remarkable thing he did in A Tale of Two Cities. It is necessary to feel, first of all, the fact that to him London was the centre of the universe. He did not understand at all the real sense in which Paris is the capital of Europe. He had never realised that all roads lead to Rome. He had never felt (as an Englishman can feel) that he was an Athenian before he was a Londoner. Yet with everything against him he did this astonishing thing. He wrote a book about two cities, one of which he understood; the other he did not understand. And his description of the city he did not know is almost better than his description of the city he did know.

This is the entrance of the unquestionable thing about Dickens; the thing called genius; the thing which every one has to talk about directly and distinctly because no one knows what it is. For a plain word (as for instance the word fool) always covers an infinite mystery.

A Tale of Two Cities is one of the more tragic tints of the later life of Dickens. It might be said that he grew sadder as he grew older; but this would be false, for two reasons. First, a man never or hardly ever does grow sad as he grows old; on the contrary, the most melancholy young lovers can be found forty years afterwards chuckling over their port wine. And second, Dickens never did grow old, even in a physical sense. What weariness did appear in him appeared in the prime of life; it was due not to age but to overwork, and his exaggerative way of doing everything. To call Dickens a victim of elderly disenchantment would be as absurd as to say the same of Keats. Such fatigue as there was, was due not to the slowing down of his blood, but rather to its unremitting rapidity. He was not wearied by his age; rather he was wearied by his youth. And though A Tale of Two Cities is full of sadness, it is full also of enthusiasm; that pathos is a young pathos rather than an old one. Yet there is one circumstance which does render important the fact that A Tale of Two Cities is one of the later works of Dickens.

This fact is the fact of his dependence upon another of the great writers of the Victorian era. And it is in connection with this that we can best see the truth of which I have been speaking; the truth that his actual ignorance of France went with amazing intuitive perception of the truth about it. It is here that he has most clearly the plain mark of the man of genius; that he can understand what he does not understand.

Dickens was inspired to the study of the French Revolution and to the writing of a romance about it by the example and influence of Carlyle. Thomas Carlyle undoubtedly rediscovered for Englishmen the revolution that was at the back of all their policies and reforms. It is an entertaining side joke that the French Revolution should have been discovered for Britons by the only British writer who did not really believe in it. Nevertheless, the most authoritative and the most recent critics on that great renaissance agree in considering Carlyle's work one of the most searching and detailed power. Carlyle had read a great deal about the French Revolution. Dickens had read nothing at all, except Carlyle. Carlyle was a man who collected his ideas by the careful collation of documents and the verification of references.

Dickens was a man who collected his ideas from loose hints in the streets, and those always the same streets; as I have said, he was the citizen of one city. Carlyle was in his way learned; Dickens was in every way ignorant. Dickens was an Englishman cut off from France; Carlyle was a Scotsman, historically connected with France. And yet, when all this is said and certified, Dickens is more right than Carlyle. Dickens's French Revolution is probably more like the real French Revolution than Carlyle's. It is difficult, if not impossible, to state the grounds of this strong conviction. One can only talk of it by employing that excellent method which Cardinal Newman employed when he spoke of the "notes" of Catholicism. There were certain "notes" of the Revolution.

One note of the Revolution was the thing which silly people call optimism, and sensible people call high spirits. Carlyle could never quite get it, because with all his spiritual energy he had no high spirits. That is why he preferred prose to poetry. He could understand rhetoric; for rhetoric means singing with an object. But he could not understand lyrics; for the lyric means singing without an object; as every one does when he is happy. Now for all its blood and its black guillotines, the French Revolution was full of mere high spirits. Nay, it was full of happiness.

This actual lilt and levity Carlyle never really found in the Revolution, because he could not find it in himself. Dickens knew less of the Revolution, but he had more of it. When Dickens attacked abuses, he battered them down with exactly that sort of cheery and quite one-sided satisfaction with which the French mob battered down the Bastille. Dickens utterly and innocently believed in certain things; he would, I think, have drawn the sword for them. Carlyle half believed in half a hundred things; he was at once more of a mystic and more of a sceptic. Carlyle was the perfect type of the grumbling servant; the old grumbling servant of the aristocratic comedies. He followed the aristocracy, but he growled as he followed. He was obedient without being servile, just as Caleb Balderstone was obedient without being servile. But Dickens was the type of the man who might really have rebelled instead of grumbling. He might have gone out into the street and fought, like the man who took the Bastille. It is somewhat nationally significant that when we talk of the man in the street it means a figure silent, slouching, and even feeble. When the French speak of the man in the street, it means danger in the street.

No one can fail to notice this deep difference between Dickens and the Carlyle whom he avowedly copied. Splendid and symbolic as are Carlyle's scenes of the French Revolution, we have in reading them a curious sense that everything is happening at night. In Dickens even massacre happens by daylight. Carlyle always assumes that because things were tragedies therefore the men who did them felt tragic. Dickens knows that the man who works the worst tragedies is the man who feels comic; as for example, Mr. Quilp.

The French Revolution was a much simpler world than Carlyle could understand; for Carlyle was subtle and not simple. Dickens could understand it, for he was simple and not subtle. He understood that plain rage against plain political injustice; he understood again that obvious vindictiveness and that obvious brutality which followed. "Cruelty and the abuse of absolute power," he told an American slave-owner, "are two of the bad passions of human nature." Carlyle was quite incapable of rising to the height of that uplifted common-sense. He must always find something mystical about the cruelty of the French Revolution. The effect was equally bad whether he found it mystically bad and called the thing anarchy, or whether he found it mystically good and called it the rule of the strong. In both cases he could not understand the common-sense justice or the common-sense vengeance of Dickens and the French Revolution.

Yet Dickens has in this book given a perfect and final touch to this whole conception of mere rebellion and mere human nature. Carlyle had written the story of the French Revolution and had made the story a mere tragedy. Dickens writes the story about the French Revolution, and does not make the Revolution itself the tragedy at all. Dickens knows that an outbreak is seldom a tragedy; generally it is the avoidance of a tragedy. All the real tragedies are silent. Men fight each other with furious cries, because men fight each other with chivalry and an unchangeable sense of brotherhood. But trees fight each other in utter stillness; because they fight each other cruelly and without quarter. In this book, as in history, the guillotine is not the calamity, but rather the solution of the calamity. The sin of Sydney Carton is a sin of habit, not of revolution. His gloom is the gloom of London, not the gloom of Paris.

by Gilbert Keith Chesterton

Chapter 9

Timeline of the Novel

TIMELINE OF THE LIFE OF CHARLES DICKENS

- 1812 - Born on February 7 to John and Elizabeth Dickens.
- 1824 - John Dickens arrested and sent to the Marshalsea prison. Charles Dickens worked at the Warren's Blacking Factory.
- 1827 - Rejoins the workforce as the clerk of an attorney.
- 1830 - Dickens meets Maria Beadnell, his first love interest.
- 1833 - The relationship with Maria Beadnell ends. *A Dinner at Poplar Walk* is published.
- 1834 - Began using the pseudonym "Boz". Meets his future wife, Catherine Hogarth.
- 1835 - Becomes engaged to Catherine.
- 1836 - The first chapters of *The Pickwick Papers* are published. Marries Catherine Hogarth.
- 1837 - The first of his 10 children, Charles Culliford Boz Dickens, is born. Mary Hogarth, Catherine's sister, dies. The publication of *Oliver Twist* begins.
- 1838 - Dickens and Hablot Browne travel to Yorkshire to see the boarding schools. His daughter, Mary, is born. Publication of *Nicholas Nickleby* begins.

- 1839 - His daughter, Kate, is born.
- 1840 - Publication of *The Old Curiosity Shop* begins
- 1841 - *Barnaby Rudge* is published. Charles and Catherine tour Scotland. Their son, Walter, is born.
- 1842 - Charles and Catherine travel to America. Late in 1842 or early in the next year Dickens begins work on *Martin Chuzzlewit.*
- 1843 - *A Christmas Carol* is published.
- 1844 - His son Francis Jeffrey (Frank) is born. Dickens and family travel to Italy. Treated Madame de la Rue with mesmerism.
- 1845 - Another son, Alfred, is born.
- 1846 - Dickens and his family travel to Switzerland. Publication of *Dombey and Son* begins.
- 1847 - His son, Sydney, is born.
- 1848 - Dickens' sister, Fanny, dies. *The Haunted Man,* his last Christmas book is published.
- 1849 - His son, Henry Fielding Dickens, is born. The publication of *David Copperfield* begins.
- 1850 - His daughter, Dora Annie Dickens, is born.
- 1851- Catherine Dickens suffers a nervous collapse. John Dickens, the father of Charles Dickens, dies. Dora Dickens dies when she is only eight months old. *What Shall we have for Dinner?*, a cookbook by Catherine Dickens is published.
- 1852 - The publication of *Bleak House* begins. His son, Edward or "Plorn", is born.
- 1853 - Dickens gives his first public reading of one of his works.
- 1854 - *Hard Times* is published.
- 1855 - Dickens has a disappointing reunion with Maria Winter (Maria Beadnell). Publication of *Little Dorrit* begins.

- 1856 - Dickens works with Wilkie Collins on *The Frozen Deep*. Dickens purchases Gad's Hill Place.
- 1857 - Hans Christian Anderson is entertained at Gad's Hill Place. Dickens meets Ellen Ternan.
- 1858 - Dickens separates from Catherine, his wife.
- 1859 - *A Tale of Two Cities* is published.
- 1860 - Publication of *Great Expectations* begins in *All the Year Round*. His daughter, Katie, marries and ten days later his brother, Alfred, dies. Dickens burns his personal papers.
- 1863 - Dickens' mother, Elizabeth, dies. Dickens begins work on *Our Mutual Friend*.
- 1864 - His son, Walter, dies in India. The first installment of *Our Mutual Friend* is printed.
- 1865 - Dickens is involved in the Staplehurst railway accident along with Ellen Ternan and her mother.
- 1867 - Dickens tours America for the second time.
- 1868 - He gives his first *Murder of Nancy* reading.
- 1869 - Dickens is ordered by doctors to discontinue readings. Dickens begins writing *The Mystery of Edwin Drood*.
- 1870 - Dickens gives his final public reading. Publication of *The Mystery of Edwin Drood* begins. Charles Dickens dies at Gad's Hill Place on June 9.

Chapter 10

Character Sketch

CHARACTERS OF CHARACTERS

Major Characters

Dr. Manette: Father of Lucie Manette. Wrongfully imprisoned in France for 18 years, he is brought back from the brink of madness by his adoring daughter, whom he treasures above all else. Though he is eventually freed and makes his home in England with his daughter, where he resumes his medical practice, he is still prone to occasional relapses of a trance-like state, in which he does not remember who he is and can only make shoes. It is the condition in which Lucie found him after his years of imprisonment, and the relapses occur when he is in a state of distress. His unjust imprisonment eventually works in his favour when he is held up as a hero by the revolutionaries, a status that enables him to get his son-in-law, Charles Darnay, freed from prison—but only once. When Darnay is re-imprisoned and the doctor's status cannot help him, Dr. Manette reverts back to his trance-like state.

Lucie Manette: Dr. Manatee's kind, loving and beautiful daughter, she helped bring him back from the brink of insanity after his unjust imprisonment. Lucie evokes a deep love from those around her, including her father, Charles Darnay (who eventually marries her), Mr. Stryver, Miss Pross, and, perhaps most of all, Sydney Carton. She cares deeply for her father and marries Charles only after she reassures her father that the marriage will not separate her from him at all. Her beauty and tenderness evoke the last sentiments of real love and emotion in Sydney Carton, as Lucie is one of the last people on earth to treat him with sympathy and kindness. His deep, unspoken love for her leads him to commit an extremely selfless and courageous act on her behalf.

Charles Darnay: The son of corrupt French aristocrats, Darnay flees France to escape the shame of his family's name and to forsake his role in the oppression of the French peasants. Settles in England, where he is unsuccessfully tried for treason. Returns to France at the most dangerous period of the Revolution in order to save a friend who is unjustly imprisoned; is eventually tried twice for crimes against the Republic after the Revolution. Marries Lucie Manette and has a daughter with her; he is deeply committed to both Lucie and her father. Remaining committed to his family and his passionate dislike of corrupt aristocracy, he is one of the most morally upright characters in the book.

Sydney Carton: A lawyer and assistant to 'The Lion,' Mr. Stryver. Carton is known as Stryver's less successful 'jackal.' He is crude, frequently drunk, and often melancholy, and he feels resigned to the disappointing course his once-promising life has taken. Still, he is capable of feeling deep, immense, and tragic love that others cannot see. His one moment of grace comes in a single selfless act that ultimately renders him the hero of the book.

Jarvis Lorry: A long-time banker at Tellson's and a fiercely loyal family friend to the Manette. Had overseen Dr. Manette's affairs before his imprisonment; was in charge of that account when Lucie became a ward of Tellson's when it was assumed as a child that she was an orphan. Told Lucie that her father was alive and brought her to meet him for the first time. An honest, trustworthy, and compassionate man, Mr. Lorry held the institution of Tellson's and the Manette family above all else in his life.

Madame Defarge: A cruel, vengeance-seeking agent of the revolution, Madame Defarge spends her days knitting a 'register' of names of people she has marked for death. Married to Ernest Defarge, owner of a wine shop in Saint Antoine, Madame Defarge is utterly devoid of human sympathy and is single-minded in her zeal to have Charles Darnay executed, despite his proven innocence of any crimes and despite her husband's loyalty to and compassion for Dr. Manette. Her desire for vengeance stems from the murders of her brother and brother-in-law and the torture of her family at the hands of the Marquis St. Evro›nde and his brother—Charles Darnay's uncle and father. She is so filled with hatred toward them that she wants to wipe out Darnay's entire family, including the Manettes. She is the book's clearest example of how the oppressed peasants became the oppressors during the Revolution.

Monseigneur the Marquis: Charles Darnay's cruel and corrupt uncle. A French aristocrat by birth, Monseigneur has no trace of pity and despises the peasants of France. Born into wealth, he believes that his family was meant to enjoy a higher station in life than the lower classes. He tells his nephew, Charles Darnay, that he plans to keep the oppressed masses in their place as long as he is alive. He is eventually assassinated by one of those peasants, the action that starts the Revolution.

Monsieur Defarge: Former domestic of Dr. Manette's prior to the doctor's imprisonment; cares for Dr. Manette immediately after the doctor's release; married to Madame Defarge. Though he is fond of Dr. Manette, he secretly fears his wife and does not object when she demands the denunciation of Darnay. He is also an important leader of the revolution who discovered Dr. Manette's letter hidden in the chimney of his old cell in the Bastille.

Minor Characters

Miss Pross: Woman who cared for Lucie from the time she was orphaned. Sassy and tart-tongued, she is fiercely protective and loving of Lucie.

Roger Cly: Former servant of Charles Darnay. He testified against Darnay in England and later faked his own death to avoid persecution in his home country before fleeing to France to work as a spy for England.

John Barsad (a.k.a. Solomon Pross): Miss Pross' no-account brother who testified against Charles Darnay in England before fleeing to France to avoid persecution in England. Worked as a spy for England in France and was blackmailed by Sydney Carton into aiding Carton in his final scheme.

Mr. Stryver: Lawyer known as 'The Lion.' A longtime friend of Sydney Carton, he successfully defended Charles Darnay at his treason trial in England. Stryver became a frequent visitor of the Manettes and announced his intention to marry Lucie.

Jerry Cruncher: Messenger for Tellson's and Mr. Lorry's assistant. Comical yet possesses a mean streak, such as when he beats his wife for praying, which irritates him. Supports his income from Tellson's with occasional work as a grave robber. His nocturnal activities eventually play a critical role in the book.

The woodcutter/mender of roads: A revolutionary who works with the Defarges.

Jacques Three: A member of the corrupt Tribunal that sentences Charles Darnay to execution, he is a bloodthirsty and vengeful sidekick to Madame Defarge and the Vengeance.

Lucie: Daughter of Charles Darnay and Lucie Manette.

The Vengeance: Friend of Madame Defarge and fellow revolutionary.

Monsieur Gabelle: Tax collector who is persecuted by the revolutionaries in France; makes an appeal to Darnay to help free him from prison. His letter brings Charles to France, where his life is immediately threatened.

Young Jerry: Jerry Cruncher's son.

Mrs. Cruncher: Jerry Cruncher's wife. Her incessant praying on Jerry's behalf enrages him, though he learns to appreciate it later.

Gaspard: His young son is run over by the Marquis' carriage as it speeds through town. In response, the Marquis flicks Gaspard a coin, showing a complete disregard for Gaspard's daughter's life. Gaspard later assassinates the Marquis, and is then captured and killed himself. Support for Gaspard grows throughout these events—these three deaths are the beginning of the French Revolution.

Objects/Places

London: One of the two cities where the book takes place and where the Manettes and Darnay make their home after they are persecuted in France.

Paris: The other city in the story, it is a scene of a violent and brutal revolution that wreaks havoc on the lives of the book's main characters.

The guillotine: The violent revolutionaries' executional method of choice. It is used in many unjust executions and lionized by the bloodthirsty revolutionaries as a national treasure.

One Hundred Five, North Tower: Cell where Dr. Manette was imprisoned. When he is first released from prison, he does not know his name and refers to himself by this address. Defarge, his old domestic, returns to the cell when the prison is liberated in the revolution and discovered a paper the doctor had written several years ago, a discovery that eventually comes back to haunt the doctor.

Shoemaker's bench & tools: The tools Dr. Manette uses to comfort himself when he reverts back to his trance-like state. During his imprisonment, Dr. Manette learned to make shoes, which was very comforting to him, as it enabled him to occupy his mind with thoughts other than his constant mental torture. The tools are eventually destroyed when Mr. Lorry believes it might be helpful in Dr. Manette's full recovery.

Madame Defarge's knitting: The knitted register into which Madame Defarge knits her victim's names. Everyone who winds up in the register is marked for execution, and Madame Defarge's knitting is constantly at her side.

The chateau: Home of Monseigneur the Marquis and scene of his assassination. It is symbolic of the corruption and gross disparity of wealth between the ruling class and the peasants. It is burned during the revolution.

Saint Antoine: Suburb of Paris where the Defarges live. Its residents are extremely poor, and it is a hotbed and central point of revolutionary activity.

Red caps: Worn by the revolutionaries, they are symbolic of the newfound freedom of the peasants.

La Force: Prison that the corrupt revolutionaries use to imprison anyone they deem a traitor to the new Republic. Most who enter La Force are executed, often unjustly.

The Tribunal: The court that hears the cases of prisoners. Very corrupt as most trials are shams.

Tellson's: The bank that employs Mr. Jarvis Lorry, Lucie was raised as a ward of this bank.

Chapter 11

Chapter Wise Summary

BOOK THE FIRST: RECALLED TO LIFE CHAPTERS 1–4

Summary: Chapter 1: The Period

> It was the best of times, it was the worst of times, it was the age of wisdom, it was the age of foolishness....

As its title promises, this brief chapter establishes the era in which the novel takes place: England and France in 1775. The age is marked by competing and contradictory attitudes—"It was the best of times, it was the worst of times"—but resembles the "present period" in which Dickens writes. In England, the public worries over religious prophecies, popular paranormal phenomena in the form of "the Cock-lane ghost," and the messages that a colony of British subjects in America has sent to King George III. France, on the other hand, witnesses excessive spending and extreme violence, a trend that anticipates the erection of the guillotine. Yet in terms of peace and order, English society cannot "justify much national boasting" either—crime and capital punishment abound.

Summary: Chapter 2: The Mail

On a Friday night in late November of 1775, a mail coach wends its way from London to Dover. The journey proves so treacherous that the three passengers must dismount from the carriage and hike alongside it as it climbs a steep hill. From out of the great mists, a messenger on horseback appears and asks to speak to Jarvis Lorry of Tellson's Bank. The travellers react warily, fearing that they have come upon a highwayman or robber. Mr. Lorry, however, recognizes the messenger's voice as that of Jerry Cruncher, the odd-job-man at Tellson's, and accepts his message. The note that Jerry passes him reads: "Wait at Dover for Mam'selle." Lorry instructs Jerry to return to Tellson's with this reply: "RECALLED TO LIFE." Confused and troubled by the "blazing strange message," Jerry rides on to deliver it.

Summary: Chapter 3: The Night Shadows

A wonderful fact to reflect upon, that every human creature is constituted to be that profound secret and mystery to every other....

The narrator ponders the secrets and mysteries that each human being poses to every other: Lorry, as he rides on in the mail coach with two strangers, constitutes a case in point. Dozing, he drifts in and out of dreams, most of which revolve around the workings of Tellson's bank. Still, there exists "another current of impression that never cease[s] to run" through Lorry's mind—the notion that he makes his way to dig someone out of a grave. He imagines repetitive conversations with a specter, who tells Lorry that his body has lain buried nearly eighteen years. Lorry informs his imaginary companion that he now has been "recalled to life" and asks him if he cares to live. He also asks, cryptically, "Shall I show her to you? Will you come and see her?" The ghost's reaction to this question varies, as he sometimes claims that he would die were he to see this woman too soon; at other times, he weeps and pleads to see her immediately.

Summary: Chapter 4: The Preparation

The next morning, Lorry descends from the coach at the Royal George Hotel in Dover. After shedding his travel clothes, he emerges as a well-dressed businessman of sixty. That afternoon, a waiter announces that Lucie Manette has arrived from London. Lorry meets the "short, slight, pretty figure" who has received word from the bank that "some intelligence—or discovery" has been made "respecting the small property of my poor father... so long dead." After reiterating his duties as a businessman, Lorry relates the real reason that Tellson's has summoned Lucie to Paris. Her father, once a reputed doctor, has been found alive. "Your father," Lorry reports to her, "has been taken to the house of an old servant in Paris, and we are going there: I, to identify him if I can: you, to restore him to life, love, duty, rest, comfort." Lucie goes into shock, and her lively and protective servant, Miss Pross, rushes in to attend to her.

Analysis: Chapters 1–4

The opening sentence of the novel makes clear, as the title itself does, the importance of doubles in the text:

"It was the best of times, it was the worst of times, it was the age of wisdom, it was the age of foolishness, it was the epoch of belief, it was the epoch of incredulity, it was the season of Light, it was the season of Darkness, it was the spring of hope, it was the winter of despair...."

Doubles prove essential to the novel's structure, plot, and dominant themes. The idea of resurrection, a theme that emerges in these early pages, would not be possible without some form of its opposite—death. In order to pave the way for the first such resurrection—the recalling to life of the long-imprisoned Doctor Manette—Dickens does much to establish a dark, ominous tone suggestive of death. From the mist-obscured route of the Dover mail coach to the darkly paneled room in which Lorry meets Lucie Manette, the opening chapters brim with gloomy corners and suggestive shadows.

These descriptions of darkness and secrets also contribute to the gothic atmosphere of the novel's opening. Gothic literature, a genre that establishes an uneasy, mysterious mood through the use of remote, desolate settings, supernatural or macabre events, and violence, dominated much of fiction from the late eighteenth century through the end of the nineteenth century. Such classics as *Frankenstein* (1818), by Mary Shelley, and *Wuthering Heights* (1847), by Emily Brontë, helped establish a strong tradition of gothic themes in British literature of this period. Jerry Cruncher's mysterious appearance during the treacherous nighttime journey, and Lorry's macabre visions of disinterring a body, hearken back to the eerie and supernatural feel of *A Tale of Two Cities'* gothic predecessors.

The obscurity that permeates these pages points to the "wonderful fact" that Dickens continuously ponders: every person in every room in every house that he passes possesses a secret, unknown to anyone—even closest friends, family, and lover. As the novel progresses, the reader witnesses Dickens digging—much as Lorry anticipates having to "dig" the doctor out of his ruinous prison experience—for the secrets that provide his characters with their essences and motivations.

In typical Dickensian manner, this project of discovery happens bit by bit: secrets emerge only very slowly. Although the horrible effects of Doctor Manette's incarceration become clear in the next few chapters, the reader doesn't learn the causes of these effects until the end of the novel. This narrative tactic owes much to the form in which Dickens wrote much of his work. *A Tale of Two Cities* was published as a serial piece—that is, in weekly installments from April 20 to November 26, 1859. The original serial format provides the reason for the novel's relatively short chapters and specific chapter subheadings, which, read in sequence, offer a skeletal outline of the plot. For example, the first three chapters of the second book bear the subheadings "Five Years Later," "A Sight," and "A Disappointment," respectively.

In addition to his plentiful literary talents, Dickens also possessed a shrewd businessman's sense. He remained keenly aware of what his reading public wanted and, unlike most artists of his caliber, unapologetically admitted to aiming for the largest possible readership. As he had done previously, with *A Tale of Two Cities,* Dickens set his sights on writing a so-called popular novel. One means of hooking readers into the story was to create a climate of suspense. Within the first four chapters, Dickens already leaves the reader with many questions that need to be answered, creating a sense of excitement and anticipation.

BOOK THE FIRST: RECALLED TO LIFE CHAPTERS 5–6

Summary: Chapter 5: The Wine-shop

"The wine was red wine, and had stained the ground of the narrow street...."

The setting shifts from Dover, England to Saint Antoine, a poor suburb of Paris. A wine cask falls to the pavement in the street and everyone rushes to it. Men kneel and scoop up the wine that has pooled in the paving stones, while women sop up the liquid with handkerchiefs and wring them into the mouths of their babies. One man dips his finger into the "muddy wine-lees" and scrawls the word BLOOD on a wall.

The wine shop is owned by Monsieur Defarge, a "bull-necked, martial-looking man of thirty." His wife, Madame Defarge, sits solemnly behind the counter, watchful of everything that goes on around her. She signals to her husband as he enters the wine-shop, alerting him to the presence of an elderly gentleman and a young lady. Defarge eyes the strangers (they are Lorry and Lucie) but pretends not to notice them, speaking instead with three familiar customers, each of whom refers to the other two as "Jacques" (a code name that identifies themselves to one another as revolutionaries). After Defarge directs the men to a chamber on the fifth floor and sends them out, Mr. Lorry approaches from the corner and begs a word with Defarge. The men have a brief conversation, and soon Defarge leads Lorry and Lucie up a steep, dangerous rise of stairs. They come to a filthy landing, where the three men from the wine-shop stand staring through chinks in the wall. Stating that he makes a show of Doctor Manette to a chosen few "to whom the sight is likely to do good," Defarge opens the door to reveal a white-haired man busily making shoes.

Summary Chapter 6

The Shoemaker

Manette reports, in a voice gone faint with "solitude and disuse," that he is making a lady's shoe in the "present mode," or fashion, even though he has never seen the present fashion. When asked his name, he responds, "One Hundred and Five, North Tower." Lucie approaches. Noticing her radiant golden hair, Manette opens a knot of rag that he wears around his neck, in which he keeps a strand of similarly golden curls.

At first, Manette mistakes Lucie for his wife and recalls that, on the first day of his imprisonment, he begged to be allowed to keep these few stray hairs of his wife's as a means of escaping his circumstances "in the spirit." Lucie delivers an impassioned speech, imploring her father to weep if her voice or her hair recalls a loved one whom he once knew. She hints to him of the home that awaits him and assures him that his "agony is over." Manette collapses under a storm of emotion; Lucie urges that arrangements be made for his immediate departure for England. Fearing for Manette's health, Lorry protests, but Lucie insists that travel guarantees more safety than a continued stay in Paris. Defarge agrees and ushers the group into a coach.

Analysis: Chapters 5–6

In Chapters 5 and 6, Dickens introduces the reader to the first of the novel's two principal cities: Paris. The scramble for the leaking wine that opens "The Wine-shop" remains one of the most remembered (and frequently referenced) passages in the novel. In it, Dickens prepares the sweeping historical backdrop against which the tale of Lucie and Doctor Manette plays out. Although the French Revolution will not erupt for another fourteen years, the broken wine cask conveys the suffering and rage that will lead the French peasantry to revolt. The scene surrounding the wine cask contains a nightmarish quality. In clambering to feed on the dregs, the members of the mob stain themselves with wine. The liquid smears the peasants' hands, feet, and faces, foreshadowing the approaching chaos during which the blood of aristocrats and political dissidents will run as freely. The ominous scrawling of the word "blood" on the wall similarly prefigures the violence.

Dickens here betrays his conflicted ideas regarding the revolution. While he acknowledges, throughout the novel, the horrible conditions that led the peasantry to violence, he never condones the peasants' actions. In his text the mob remains a frightening beast, manifesting a threat of danger rather than the promise of freedom: "Those who had been greedy with the staves of the cask, had acquired a tigerish smear about the mouth."

Dickens uses several techniques to criticize the corrupt circumstances of the peasants' oppression. He proves a master of irony and sarcasm, as becomes clear in his many biting commentaries; thus we read, "[France] entertained herself... with such humane achievements as sentencing a youth to have... his body burned alive"(Book the First, Chapter 1). Dickens also makes great use of anaphora, a rhetorical device wherein a word or phrase appears repeated in successive clauses or sentences. His meditation on hunger, which he cites as a defining impetus behind the peasants' imminent uprising, serves as a perfect example of how the author uses repetition to emphasize his point:

Hunger was pushed out of the tall houses... Hunger was patched into them with straw and rag and wood and paper; Hunger was repeated in every fragment of the small modicum of firewood that the man sawed off; Hunger stared down the smokeless chimneys... Hunger was the inscription on the baker's shelves... Hunger rattled its dry bones among the roasting chestnuts in the turned cylinder; Hunger was shred into atomies in every farthing porringer of husky chips of potato....

With this repetition, Dickens demonstrates that hunger dominates every aspect of these peasants' lives—they cannot do anything without being reminded of their hunger. The presence of the word "Hunger" at the opening of each clause reflects the fact that hunger is the peasants' first thought and first word—they have no means to escape it. Reading the passage aloud, we become paralleled with the poor. We encounter "Hunger" at each breath.

In addition to setting the stage for revolution—both the historical upheaval in France and the more private but no less momentous changes in his characters' lives—Dickens establishes the unabashedly sentimental tone that characterizes many of the relationships in the novel, especially that between Doctor Manette and Lucie. As she coaxes her father into consciousness of his previous life and identity, Lucie emerges as a caricature of an innocent, pure-hearted, and loving woman. Most modern readers find her speech and gestures rather saccharine: "And if... I have to kneel to my honoured father, and implore his pardon for having never for his sake striven all day and lain awake and wept all night... weep for it, weep for it!" Indeed, as a realistically imagined woman grieving over a family tragedy, Lucie proves unconvincing. Her emotions, her speech, and even her physical beauty belong to the realm of hyperbole. But Dickens does not aim for realism: he employs these sorts of exaggerations for the sake of emphasis and dramatic effect.

The Parisian revolutionaries first began addressing each of other as "Jacques" during the Jacquerie, a 1358 peasant uprising against French nobility. The nobles contemptuously referred to the peasants by the extremely common name of "Jacques" in order to accentuate their inferiority and deny their individuality. The peasants adopted the name as a war name. Just as the fourteenth-century peasants rallied around their shared low birth, so too do Dickens's revolutionaries fight as a unified machine of war. For example, at the storming of the Bastille in Book the Second, Chapter 21, Defarge cries out, "Work, comrades all, work! Work, Jacques One, Jacques Two, Jacques One Thousand, Jacques Two Thousand, Jacques Five-and-Twenty Thousand... work!"

BOOK THE SECOND: THE GOLDEN THREAD CHAPTERS 1–4

Summary: Chapter 1: Five Years Later

It is now 1780. Tellson's Bank in London prides itself on being "very small, very dark, very ugly, very incommodious." Were it more welcoming, the bank's partners believe, it would lose its status as a respectable business. It is located by Temple Bar, the spot where, until recently, the government displayed the heads of executed criminals. The narrator explains that at this time, "death was a recipe much in vogue," used against all manner of criminals, from forgers to horse thieves to counterfeiters.

Jerry Cruncher, employed by Tellson's as a runner and messenger, wakes up in his small apartment, located in an unsavory London neighbourhood. He begins the day by yelling at his wife for "praying against" him; he throws his muddy boot at her. Around nine o'clock, Cruncher and his young son camp outside Tellson's Bank, where they await the bankers' instructions. When an indoor messenger calls for a porter, Cruncher takes off to do the job. As young Jerry sits alone, he wonders why his father's fingers always have rust on them.

Summary: Chapter 2: A Sight

The bank clerk instructs Cruncher to go to the Old Bailey Courthouse and await orders from Jarvis Lorry. Cruncher arrives at the court, where Charles Darnay, a handsome, well-bred young man, stands trial for treason. Cruncher understands little of the legal jargon, but he gleans that Darnay has been charged with divulging secret information to the king of France (Louis XVI): namely, that England plans to send armed forces to fight in the American colonies. As Darnay looks to a young lady and her distinguished father, a whisper rushes through the courtroom, speculating on the identity of the two. Eventually, Cruncher discovers that they will serve as witnesses against the prisoner.

Summary: Chapter 3: A Disappointment

The Attorney-General prosecutes the case, demanding that the jury find Darnay guilty of passing English secrets into French hands. The Solicitor-General examines John Barsad, whose testimony supports the Attorney-General's case. The cross-examination, however, tarnishes Barsad's pure and righteous character. It reveals that he has served time in debtor's prison and has been involved in brawls over gambling. The prosecution calls its next witness, Roger Cly, whom the defence attorney, Mr. Stryver, also exposes as a dubious, untrustworthy witness. Mr. Lorry then takes the stand, and the prosecution asks him if, five years ago, he shared a Dover mail coach with the accused. Lorry contends that his fellow passengers sat so bundled up that their identities remained hidden. The prosecutors then ask similar questions of Lucie, the young woman Darnay had noticed earlier. She admits to meeting the prisoner on the ship back to England. When she recounts how he helped her to care for her sick father, however, she seems to help his case—yet she then inadvertently turns the court against Darnay by reporting his statement that George Washington's fame might one day match that of George III. Doctor Manette is also called to the stand, but he claims that he remembers nothing of the trip due to his illness.

Mr. Stryver is in the middle of cross-examining another witness "with no result" when his insolent young colleague, Sydney Carton, passes him a note. Stryver begins arguing the contents of the note, which draws the court's attention to Carton's own uncanny resemblance to the prisoner. The undeniable likeness foils the court's ability to identify Darnay as a spy beyond reasonable doubt. The jury retires to deliberate and eventually returns with an acquittal for Darnay.

Summary: Chapter 4: Congratulatory

Doctor Manette, Lucie, Mr. Lorry, Mr. Stryver, and Darnay exit the courtroom. The narrator relates that Manette has established himself as an upright and distinguished citizen, though the gloom of his terrible past descends on him from time to time. These clouds descend only rarely, however, and Lucie feels confident in her power as "the golden thread" that unites him to a past and present "beyond his misery." Darnay kisses Lucie's hand and then turns to Stryver to thank him for his work. Lucie, Manette, and Stryver depart, and a drunk Sydney Carton emerges from the shadows to join the men. Lorry chastises him for not being a serious man of business. Darnay and Carton make their way to a tavern, where Carton smugly asks, "Is it worth being tried for one's life, to be the object of [Lucie's] sympathy and compassion... ?" When Darnay comments that Carton has been drinking, Carton gives his reason for indulging himself so: "I am a disappointed drudge, sir. I care for no man on earth, and no man on earth cares for me." After Darnay leaves, Carton curses his own image in the mirror, as well as his look-alike, who reminds him of what he has "fallen away from."

Analysis: Chapters 1–4

The courtroom scenes that open the second book of the novel allow Dickens to use a wonderful range of language. He employs a technique known as free indirect style, which fuses third-person narration with an interior point of view. He reveals the charges for which Darnay is being tried while rooting the reader in the uneducated mind (and ear) of the spectators: "Charles Darnay had yesterday pleaded Not Guilty to an indictment denouncing him (with infinite jingle and jangle) for that he was a false traitor to our serene, illustrious, excellent, and so forth, prince...." The juxtaposition of formal ("our serene, illustrious, excellent") and informal ("and so forth") speech produces a comical effect by highlighting the unrefined crowd's zealous craving for the juicy details of the case, even as they recognize the decorum of their setting.

Dickens also uses these scenes to implement another of his favourite literary devices, parody. The Attorney-General's long, self-important, and bombastic speech at the opening of Chapter 3 offers a highly comical imitation of legalese and serves indirectly to ridicule the Attorney-General, as well as the entire legal system. Thus the Attorney-General's informs the jury:

> If statues were decreed in Britain, as in ancient Greece and Rome, to public benefactors, this shining citizen [his witness] would assuredly have one. That, as they were not so decreed, he probably would not have one.

The Attorney-General melodramatically touts the virtues of his witness, John Barsad, and absurdly deifies him, as though Barsad were a great figure from antiquity. When he explains that Barsad would not in fact have such a statue erected in his honour, as no such practice exists in England, his words again produce a comical effect. They draw attention to the fact that the attorney's first sentence glorified Barsad to the point of irrelevant hypotheticals. Moreover, the redundant nature of the Attorney-General's statement highlights his obliviousness to the emptiness of his words.

The passage makes clear how Dickens's comical characterizations have won him the admiration of generations of readers. *A Tale of Two Cities*, however, is far from a comic novel; and perhaps in withholding humour from the book, Dickens sacrificed some opportunity to put his greatest talents to work. Dickens's most "Dickensian" novels abound with hilariously grotesque characters, whose speech (usually vulgar) and appearance (usually freakish) are rendered with extreme exaggeration. With his impeded speech, violent temper, mysteriously rusty fingers and muddy boots, Jerry Cruncher comes as close as any other character to this sort of caricature. But with *A Tale of Two Cities*, Dickens was making a conscious decision to steer away from his trademark characters, in order to write a novel in shorter and more frequent installments than usual. He determined to strip the story of dialogue, upon which he often relied to flesh out his characters and further his narration, in favour of describing the story's action. By shifting his attention from character to plot, Dickens crafted *A Tale of Two Cities* into a rather un-Dickensian novel. His biographer, John Forster, doubted the benefits of such a move:

To rely less upon character than upon incident, and to resolve that his actors should be expressed by the story more than they should express themselves by dialogue, was for him a hazardous, and can hardly be called an entirely successful, experiment.

As Charles Darnay and Sydney Carton take the stage in this section, Forster's comment becomes particularly pertinent. Darnay makes as uninteresting a hero as Lucie does a heroine. Both characters prove rather one-dimensional in their goodness and virtue. Only the supposedly loveless Carton promises more depth. He descends into the darkness of alcoholism while others bask in the glow of Darnay's acquittal. Reading of this, one cannot help but suspect that elaborate secrets dim his past.

BOOK THE SECOND: THE GOLDEN THREAD CHAPTERS 5–6

Summary: Chapter 5: The Jackal

Sydney Carton, the "idlest and most unpromising of men," makes his way from the tavern to Mr. Stryver's apartment. The men drink together and discuss the day's court proceedings. Stryver, nicknamed "the lion," compliments his friend, "the jackal," for the "rare point" that he made regarding Darnay's identification. However, he laments Carton's moodiness. Ever since their days in school together, Stryver observes, Carton has fluctuated between highs and lows, "now in spirits and now in despondency!" Carton shrugs off Stryver's accusation that his life lacks a unified direction. Unable to match Stryver's vaulting ambition, Carton claims that he has no other choice but to live his life "in rust and repose." Attempting to change the subject, Stryver turns the conversation to Lucie, praising her beauty. Carton dismisses her as a "golden-haired doll," but Stryver wonders about Carton's true feelings for her.

Summary: Chapter 6: Hundreds of People

Four months later, Mr. Lorry, now a trusted friend of the Manette family, arrives at Doctor Manette's home. Finding

Manette and his daughter not at home, he converses with Miss Pross. They discuss why the doctor continues to keep his shoemaker's bench.

Their conversation also touches on the number of suitors who come to call on Lucie. Miss Pross complains that they come by the dozen, by the hundred—all "people who are not at all worthy of Ladybird." In Miss Pross's opinion, the only man worthy of Lucie is her own brother, Solomon Pross, who, she laments, disqualified himself by making a certain mistake. Lorry knows, however, that Solomon is a scoundrel who robbed Miss Pross of her possessions and left her in poverty. He goes on to ask if Manette ever returns to his shoemaking, and Pross assures him that the doctor no longer thinks about his dreadful imprisonment.

Lucie and Manette return, and soon Darnay joins them. Darnay relates that a workman, making alterations to a cell in the Tower of London, came upon a carving in the wall: "D I G." At first, the man mistook these for some prisoner's initials, but he soon enough realised that they spelled the word "dig." Upon digging, the man discovered the ashes of a scrap of paper on which the prisoner must have written a message. The story startles Manette, but he soon recovers.

Carton arrives and sits with the others near a window in the drawing room. The footsteps on the street below make a terrific echo. Lucie imagines that the footsteps belong to people that will eventually enter into their lives. Carton comments that if Lucie's speculation is true, then a great crowd must be on its way.

Analysis: Chapters 5–6

Dickens devotes Chapter 5 to the character of Sydney Carton, whom he nicknames "the jackal." Given the secondary meaning of the term—an accomplice in the commission of menial or disreputable acts—the name seems fitting. Alongside his colleague Stryver, Carton seems little more than an assistant. He lacks ambition; in the courtroom he spends his time staring at the ceiling; outside of it, he spends his time getting drunk. Carton accepts his pathetic state—he says to Stryver matter-of-factly, "you have fallen into your rank, and I have fallen into mine." Yet, for all of his supposed indifference, he betrays his desire for a better, more exalted life. Carton alludes several times to the respectable life that he might have lived. At the end of Chapter 4, he admits to hating Darnay because the man reminds him of what he could have been. He echoes this sentiment in Chapter 5, telling Stryver, "I thought I should have been much the same sort of fellow [as Darnay], if I had had any luck." These feelings evidence his resentful awareness of Darnay as his double—a successful and happy double, and thus a mocking one. Carton views Darnay as a concrete manifestation of a life he might have led, a life preferable to his own. The closing of the chapter alludes to the secret longings of a man who will not admit to having any:

> In the fair city of this vision, there were airy galleries from which the loves and graces looked upon him, gardens in which the fruits of life hung ripening, waters of Hope that sparkled in his sight. A moment, and it was gone. Climbing to a high chamber in a well of houses, he threw himself down in his clothes on a neglected bed, and its pillow was wet with wasted tears

A great gulf exists between the life that Carton leads and the life that he imagines for himself, between the type of man that he is and the type of man that he dreams of being. Carton's complex and conflicted inner life paves the way for his dramatic development, which eventually elevates him out of his jackal status.

Dickens employs masterful foreshadowing in Chapter 6, as he uses these scenes both to hint at Carton's eventual ascendance into glory and to anticipate two vital plot turns. The discovery of the mysterious letter in the Tower of London, and Manette's distress upon hearing of it, foreshadows the moment when, during a later trial, the prosecution will confront the doctor with a letter he wrote while imprisoned in the Bastille. As the second trial forms the dramatic core of the latter half of the novel, the discovery of this second letter forms a crucial part of the plot and dictates the course of the characters' lives. By introducing the story of a first and parallel letter, Dickens prepares the reader for the discovery of the second. As soon as the second letter surfaces, the reader will instantly recognize it as important. The second event that Dickens foreshadows is the French Revolution itself. The "hundreds of people" to which the title of Chapter 6 owes its name refers not to Lucie's suitors (whose numbers Miss Pross clearly exaggerates) but to the multitude of angry, mutinous revolutionaries who, as Lucie and Carton foretell, will soon march into the characters' lives.

BOOK THE SECOND: THE GOLDEN THREAD CHAPTERS 7–9

Summary: Chapter 7: Monseigneur in Town

Monseigneur, a great lord in the royal court, holds a reception in Paris. He surrounds himself with the greatest pomp and luxury. For example, he has four serving men help him drink his chocolate. The narrator tells us that Monseigneur's money corrupts everyone who touches it. Monseigneur parades around his guests briefly and then returns to his sanctuary. Miffed at Monseigneur's haughtiness, one guest, the Marquis Evrémonde, condemns Monseigneur as he leaves. The Marquis orders his carriage to be raced through the city streets, delighting to see the commoners nearly run down by his horses. Suddenly the carriage jolts to a stop. A child lies dead under its wheels. The Marquis tosses a few coins to the boy's father, a man named Gaspard, and to the wine-shop owner Defarge, who tries to comfort Gaspard. As the Marquis drives away, a coin comes flying back into the carriage, thrown in bitterness. He curses the commoners, saying that he would willingly ride over any of them. Madame Defarge watches the scene, knitting the entire time.

Chapter 8: Monseigneur in the Country

The Marquis arrives in the small village to which he serves as lord. There, too, the people live wretched lives, exploited, poor, and starving. As he looks over the submissive faces of the peasants, he singles out a road-mender whom he passed on his journey, a man whose fixed stare bothered him. He demands to know what the road-mender was staring at, and the man responds that someone was holding onto the bottom of the carriage. The Marquis continues on his way and soon comes upon a peasant woman, mourning at a rustic graveside. The woman stops him and begs that he provide her husband's grave with some stone or marker, lest he be forgotten, but the Marquis drives away, unmoved. He arrives at his chateau and, upon entering, asks if Monsieur Charles has arrived from England.

Chapter 9: The Gorgon's Head

Later that night, at the Marquis's chateau, Charles Darnay, the nephew of the Marquis, arrives by carriage. Darnay tells his uncle that he wants to renounce the title and property that he stands to inherit when the Marquis dies. The family's name, Darnay contends, is associated with "fear and slavery." He insists that the family has consistently acted shamefully, "injuring every human creature who came between us and our pleasure." The Marquis dismisses these protests, urging his nephew to accept his "natural destiny." The next morning, the Marquis is found dead with a knife through his heart. Attached to the knife is a note that reads: "Drive him fast to his tomb. "

Analysis: Chapters 7–9

In Chapter 5 of Book the First, we read a description of the French public squabbling over the spilled contents of a broken wine cask; this passage, in its indictment of the greed and viciousness of the mob, forms the backbone of Dickens's criticism against the impending revolution. In this section, in contrast, Dickens expresses an equal disapproval for the aristocracy whose vile mistreatment of the peasantry contributes to the revolution. Again, Dickens uses sarcasm to great effect as he describes the Monseigneur's ridiculous dependence on his serving men:

> It was impossible for Monseigneur to dispense with one of these attendants on the chocolate and hold his high place under the admiring Heavens. Deep would have been the blot upon his escutcheon if his chocolate had been ignobly waited on by only three men; he must have died of two.

Dickens' choice of the word "escutcheon," referring to a family coat-of-arms, is key to our understanding of Monseigneur. For this emblem represents what the he sees as a power inherent to his family's bloodline, an innate nobility that he thinks justifies his absurd lavishness. Dickens undercuts Monseigneur's reverence for this symbol of his own power by commenting on his ridiculous fear that he might damage his reputation should he prove insufficiently ostentatious in the frivolous act of drinking chocolate. Moreover, in noting Monseigneur's deep interest in the ritual of imbibing his little treat, Dickens contrasts him with the more loftily motivated characters in the novel. While the novel's worthy characters act according to selfless and righteous goals, the Monseigneur conducts himself according to base and earthly instincts.

Dickens uses the Marquis Evrémonde to give a similar portrait of the aristocracy as elitist. The Marquis displays no sympathy for Gaspard, the father of the boy whom his carriage crushes. Rather, he believes that his noble blood justifies his malicious treatment of his plebian subjects. In tossing the coins to Gaspard, he aims to buy his way out of the predicament and rid his own conscience of the nuisance of Gaspard's grief. He believes that it is the commoner's lot in life to struggle and suffer. Likewise, he has no doubt that his nephew's rightful station is to dominate commoners, referring to his nephew's noble blood as his "natural destiny."

Dickens sets up the Marquis as a representative of the French aristocracy and, as such, a direct cause of the imminent revolution. Using a device called personification, he creates human manifestations of such abstract concepts as greed, oppression, and hatred. The Marquis, so exaggeratedly cruel and flamboyant, hardly seems an actual human being—hardly a realistic character. Instead, the Marquis stands as a symbol or personification of the "inhuman abandonment of consideration" endemic to the French aristocracy during the eighteenth century.

Dickens advances this impression of the Marquis's character in the opening passage of Chapter 9, when he describes the nobleman's chateau:

It was a heavy mass of building, that chateau of Monsieur the Marquis, with a large stone court-yard before it, and two stone sweeps of staircase meeting in a stone terrace before the principal door. A stony business altogether with heavy stone balustrades... and stone faces of men, and stone heads of lions, in all directions. As if the Gorgon's head had surveyed it, when it was finished, two centuries ago.

The repetition of the word "stone" solidifies, as it were, our impression of the man who lives in the chateau. His heart, Dickens suggests, possesses the same severity as the castle's walls. The mention of the Gorgon—one of three Greek mythological sisters who had snakes for hair and turned anyone who looked at them to stone—foreshadows the death of the Marquis. For by the end of the chapter, the chateau has one more stone face added to its collection—the dead Marquis's face, which the narrator describes as "like a stone mask, suddenly startled, made angry, and petrified." Lying dead on his pillow, the Marquis serves as a warning of the violence and bloodshed to come, initiated by the masses who can no longer abide the aristocracy's heartless oppression of them.

BOOK THE SECOND: THE GOLDEN THREAD CHAPTERS 10–13

Summary: Chapter 10: Two Promises

A year later, Darnay makes a moderate living as a French teacher in London. He visits Doctor Manette and admits his love for Lucie. He honours Manette's special relationship with his daughter, assuring him that his own love for Lucie will in no way disturb that bond. Manette applauds Darnay for speaking so "feelingly and so manfully" and asks if he seeks a promise from him. Darnay asks Manette to promise to vouch for what he has said, for the true nature of his love, should Lucie ever ask. Manette promises as much. Wanting to be worthy of his confidence, Darnay attempts to tell Manette his real name, confessing that it is not Darnay. Manette stops him short, making him promise to reveal his name only if he proves successful in his courtship. He will hear Darnay's secret on his wedding day. Hours later, after Darnay has left, Lucie hears her father cobbling away at his shoemaker's bench. Frightened by his relapse, she watches him as he sleeps that night.

Summary: Chapter 11: A Companion Picture

Late that same night, Carton and Stryver work in Stryver's chambers. In his puffed-up and arrogant manner, Stryver announces that he intends to marry Lucie. Carton drinks heavily at the news, assuring Stryver that his words have not upset him. Stryver suggests that Carton himself find "some respectable woman with a little property," and marry her, lest he end up ill and penniless.

Summary: Chapter 12: The Fellow of Delicacy

The next day, Stryver plans to take Lucie to the Vauxhall Gardens to make his marriage proposal. On his way, he drops in at Tellson's Bank, where he informs Mr. Lorry of his intentions. Lorry persuades Stryver to postpone his proposal until he knows for certain that Lucie will accept. This admonition upsets Stryver. He almost insults Lucie as a "mincing Fool," but Lorry warns him against doing so. Lorry asks that Stryver hold off his proposal for a few hours to give him time to consult the family and see exactly where Stryver stands. Later that night, Lorry visits Stryver and reports that his fears have been confirmed. If Stryver were to propose, the Manettes would reject his offer. Stryver dismisses the entire affair as one of the "vanities" of "empty-headed girls" and begs Lorry to forget it.

Summary: Chapter 13: The Fellow of No Delicacy

Carton, who frequently wanders near the Manettes' house late at night, enters the house one August day and speaks to Lucie alone. She observes a change in his face. He laments his wasted life, despairing that he shall never live a better life than the one he now lives. Lucie assures him that he might become much worthier of himself. She believes that her tenderness can save him. Carton insists that he has declined beyond salvation but admits that he has always viewed Lucie as "the last dream of [his] soul." She has made him consider beginning his life again, though he no longer believes in the possibility of doing so. He feels happy to have admitted this much to Lucie and to know that something remains in him that still deserves pity. Carton ends his confession with a pledge that he would do anything for Lucie, including give his life.

Analysis: Chapters 10–13

In this section, Dickens develops the love triangle among Lucie, Carton, and Darnay. Rather than simply writing an encyclopedic account of the French Revolution, Dickens balances history with the more private struggles of his principal characters. He links the two sides of his novel thematically, as each raises questions about the possibilities of revolution and resurrection—Carton, for example, like France itself, strikes out for a new life.

It is in Chapter 13 that Dickens lays the foundation for Carton's eventual turnaround. Upon seeing Carton, Lucie observes a change in his demeanor. Much of this change owes to Carton's feelings for her. Just as Carton shares Darnay's physical countenance, he also shares Darnay's devotion to Lucie. Yet Carton's confession strikes the reader as more touching and profound than that of his counterpart. The reader certainly believes Darnay as he informs Manette, "Dear Doctor Manette, I love your daughter fondly, dearly, disinterestedly, devotedly. If ever there were love in the world, I love her," but this declaration, while direct, seems rather vapid and unimaginative. The alliteration of "dearly, disinterestedly, devotedly" highlights the flat—almost bored—tone of the declaration as it slogs through its sequence of adverbs. The closing sentence seems almost a parody of Romantic love poetry. Darnay touts his love as a great force of the universe but does so with the most mundane possible phrasing, and the repetition of the word "love" is dogged and uninspired.

Carton's words, on the other hand, betray a deep psychological and emotional struggle, suggesting the existence of feelings more complex, perhaps even more worthy of reciprocation, than Darnay's:

> In my degradation I have not been so degraded but that the sight of you with your father, and of this home made such a home by you, has stirred old shadows that I thought had died out of me.... I have had unformed ideas of striving afresh, beginning anew, shaking off sloth and sensuality, and fighting out the abandoned fight.

In his depiction of his love, Carton opens himself to the reader's sympathy in a way that Darnay does not. Whereas Darnay makes an objective, almost factual statement of his love for Lucie, Carton describes his emotions, tinged as they are by realistic insecurity ("my degradation") and uncertainty ("unformed ideas"). He also speaks poetically of "old shadows" and "the abandoned fight"; his use of metaphor seems to reflect his inability to grasp fully his profound feelings. Darnay, in contrast, categorizes his experience simply as "love," not pausing to ponder the emotions behind the word.

Lucie's conjecture on whether she can "recall [Carton]... to a better course" echoes the beginning of the novel, when

Lorry recalls Doctor Manette to life. Manette had to suffer a death of sorts—wasting nearly twenty years in prison—before being reborn into the life of love and devotion with Lucie. Now, Carton, too, shall have to undergo a sort of death or sacrifice in order to win the fight for love and meaning that he claims to have abandoned.

Dickens's characteristic humour, largely absent from *A Tale of Two Cities,* shines through in his depiction of Stryver in Chapter 12. Dickens uses Stryver's name to suggest the essential nature of his character. Coldly ambitious, the man ruthlessly strives to distinguish himself as a great businessman and here, in Chapter 12, endeavors to win the hand of Lucie Manette. Dickens ironically entitles the chapter "The Fellow of Delicacy," bringing Stryver's coarseness into greater relief. In Stryver's surly refusal to heed Lorry's gentle advice and postpone his courtship of Lucie, we see clearly one of Dickens's greatest talents—the ability to capture a character through dialogue.

"Were you going there [to Lucie's] now?" asked Mr. Lorry.

"Straight!" said Stryver, with a plump of his fist on the desk.

"Then I think I wouldn't, if I was you."

"Why?" said Stryver. "Now, I'll put you in a corner," forensically shaking a forefinger at him. "You are a man of business and bound to have a reason. State your reason. Why wouldn't you go?"

The directness of Stryver's response to Lorry ("Straight!") and the emphatic nature of his accompanying thump on the table demonstrate his blind and unshakeable ambition. His finger-wagging and blustery imperative demanding to hear Lorry's "reason" reveal his aggressive nature and refusal to be hindered in his pursuits. In his interrogating and intimidating mannerisms, Stryver acts as if he were arguing a legal point or cross-examining a witness. It is clear to the reader that he approaches the courtship as he would a case in court—as a way to gain money and stature—and not out of fondness for Lucie.

BOOK THE SECOND: THE GOLDEN THREAD CHAPTERS 14–17

Summary: Chapter 14: The Honest Tradesman

One morning outside Tellson's Bank, Jerry Cruncher sees a funeral pass by. Jerry asks a few questions and learns that the crowd is preparing to bury Roger Cly, a convicted spy and one of the men who testified against Darnay in his court case. Cruncher joins the motley procession, which includes a chimney-sweep, a bear-leader and his mangy bear, and a pieman. After much drinking and carousing, the mob buries Cly and, for sport, decides to accuse passers-by of espionage in order to wreak "vengeance on them." At home that night, Cruncher once again harangues his wife for her prayers. He then announces that he is going "fishing." In reality, he goes to dig up Cly's body in order to sell it to scientists. Unbeknownst to Cruncher, his son follows him to the cemetery, but runs away terrified, believing that the coffin is chasing him. The next day, he asks his father the definition of a "Resurrection-Man"—the term describes men like Cruncher, who dig up bodies to sell to science. He announces his intentions to have this job as an adult.

Summary: Chapter 15: Knitting

In Paris, Defarge enters his wine-shop with a mender of roads whom he calls "Jacques." Three men file out of the shop individually. Eventually, Defarge and the mender of roads climb up to the garret where Doctor Manette had been hidden. There they join the three men who recently exited the shop, and whom Defarge also calls "Jacques." The mender of roads reports that, a year ago, he saw a man hanging by a chain underneath the Marquis's carriage. Several months later, he says, he saw the man again, being marched along the road by soldiers. The soldiers led the man to prison, where he remained "in his iron cage" for several days. Accused of killing the Marquis, he stood to be executed as a parricide (one who murders a close relative). According to rumor, petitions soon arrived in Paris begging that the prisoner's life be spared.

However, workmen built a gallows in the middle of town, and soon the man was hanged.

When the mender of roads finishes his recollection, Defarge asks him to wait outside a moment. The other Jacques call for the extermination of the entire aristocracy. One points to the knitting-work of Madame Defarge, which, in its stitching, contains an elaborate registry of the names of those whom the revolutionaries aim to kill. He asks if the woman will always be able to decipher the names that appear there. Later that week, Defarge and his wife take the mender of roads to Versailles to see King Louis XVI and Queen Marie Antoinette. When the royal couple appears, the mender of roads cries "Long live the King!" and becomes so excited that Defarge must "restrain him from flying at the objects of his brief devotion and tearing them to pieces." This performance pleases the Defarges, who see that their efforts will prove easier if the aristocrats continue to believe in the peasantry's allegiance.

Summary: Chapter 16: Still Knitting

The Defarges return to Saint Antoine later that evening. A policeman friend warns Defarge that a spy by the name of John Barsad has been sent to their neighbourhood. Madame Defarge resolves to knit his name into the register. That night, Defarge admits his fear that the revolution will not come in his lifetime. Madame Defarge dismisses his impatience and compares the revolution to lightning and an earthquake: it strikes quickly and with great force, but no one knows how long it will take to form. The next day, Barsad visits the wine-shop. He masquerades as a sympathizer with the revolutionaries and comments on the horrible treatment of the peasants. Knowing that Defarge once worked as Doctor Manette's servant, he reports that Lucie Manette plans to marry, and that her husband is to be the Marquis's nephew, Darnay. After Barsad leaves, Madame Defarge adds Darnay's name to her registry, unsettling Defarge, the once loyal servant of Manette.

Summary: Chapter 17: One Night

It is the eve of Lucie's marriage to Darnay. Lucie and her father have enjoyed long days of happiness together. Doctor Manette finally has begun to put his imprisonment behind him. For the first time since his release, Manette speaks of his days in the Bastille. In prison, he passed much time imagining what sort of person Lucie would grow up to be. He is very happy now, thanks to Lucie, who has brought him "consolation and restoration." Later that night, Lucie sneaks down to her father's room and finds him sleeping soundly.

Analysis: Chapters 14–17

Of the many shadows throughout the novel, that of death looms most largely. Given the novel's concern with resurrection, death acquires an inevitable presence. Although young Jerry Cruncher's aborted trip to the cemetery at the heels of his grave-robbing father serves little dramatic purpose, it functions as an important tableau. As the boy runs home with visions in his head of Roger Cly's coffin chasing behind him, Dickens creates a suggestive symbol of the death that overshadows and pursues everyone.

As critic G. Robert Stange has noted, "the tableau technique" plays an important role in the novel. "Dickens tends throughout to make important episodes into set-pieces which are more visual than strictly dramatic." Chapter 14 opens with such a tableau—that of Cly's funeral scene. In the scene's emphasis on bizarre and freakish imagery, we see a clear example of Dickens's characteristic sense of the grotesque. The scene's importance also lies in its depiction of the throng attending Cly's funeral. Here, Dickens continues his criticism of mob mentality. Although Dickens intends the scene as largely comic, he also prepares the reader for his later, darker scenes of mindless frenzy and group violence in Paris. For example, as Cruncher participates in the burial of a man he does not know, his spirited condemnation of the deceased testifies to the contagious nature of the crowd's anger and excitement. Indeed, once the body is interred, the mob's energy remains unexhausted. Thus the group sets off to harass casual passers-by. Dickens later taps into the same frightening group psychology in the tableaux that portray the French revolutionaries as they gather around the grindstone and dance the Carmagnole.

The comedic atmosphere effected by Cruncher quickly lapses into a tone of ominous danger as the story comes to focus on Madame Defarge. For this woman possesses a vengeance and hatred that exceed all bounds. Indeed, the preceding scene presages her vindictive nature: the funeral-goers' boisterous accusations of espionage against innocent passers-by, which they voice for the sake of "vengeance," foreshadow the sweeping tide of hatred that consumes the revolutionaries, and Madame Defarge in particular. Two of the chapters in this section centre around her knitting, her symbolic hatred of the aristocracy. When one of the Jacques inquires as to whether Madame Defarge will always be able to decipher this register, his query presages a time in which the woman will seek death even for those objectively innocent of any oppressive behaviours, a time in which her monomaniacal bloodlust will drive her to murder without heed of her scrupulous register.

Dickens derived his knitting motif from historical record: many scholars have recorded that women of the period would often knit as they stood and watched the daily executions. In the hands of Madame Defarge, however, the pastime takes on symbolic significance. In Greek mythology, the Fates were three sisters who controlled human life: one sister spun the web of life, one measured it, and the last cut it. Dickens employs a similar metaphor. As Madame Defarge weaves the names of the condemned into shrouds, her knitting becomes a symbol of her victims' fate, their death at the hands of a vengeful peasantry.

As critic G. Robert Stange has noted, "the tableau technique" plays an important role in the novel. "Dickens tends throughout to make important episodes into set-pieces which are more visual than strictly dramatic." Chapter 14 opens with such a tableau—that of Cly's funeral scene. In the scene's emphasis on bizarre and freakish imagery, we see a clear example of Dickens's characteristic sense of the grotesque. The scene's importance also lies in its depiction of the throng attending Cly's funeral. Here, Dickens continues his criticism of mob mentality. Although Dickens intends the scene as largely comic, he also prepares the reader for his later, darker scenes of mindless frenzy and group violence in Paris. For example, as Cruncher participates in the burial of a man he does not know, his spirited condemnation of the deceased testifies to the contagious nature of the crowd's anger and excitement. Indeed, once the body is interred, the mob's energy remains unexhausted. Thus the group sets off to harass casual passers-by. Dickens later taps into the same frightening group psychology in the tableaux that portray the French revolutionaries as they gather around the grindstone and dance the Carmagnole.

The comedic atmosphere effected by Cruncher quickly lapses into a tone of ominous danger as the story comes to focus on Madame Defarge. For this woman possesses a vengeance and hatred that exceed all bounds. Indeed, the preceding scene presages her vindictive nature: the funeral-goers' boisterous accusations of espionage against innocent passers-by, which they voice for the sake of "vengeance," foreshadow the sweeping tide of hatred that consumes the revolutionaries, and Madame Defarge in particular. Two of the chapters in this section centre around her knitting, her symbolic hatred of the aristocracy. When one of the Jacques inquires as to whether Madame Defarge will always be able to decipher this register, his query presages a time in which the woman will seek death even for those objectively innocent of any oppressive behaviours, a time in which her monomaniacal bloodlust will drive her to murder without heed of her scrupulous register.

Dickens derived his knitting motif from historical record: many scholars have recorded that women of the period would often knit as they stood and watched the daily executions. In the hands of Madame Defarge, however, the pastime takes on symbolic significance. In Greek mythology, the Fates were three sisters who controlled human life: one sister spun the web of life, one measured it, and the last cut it. Dickens employs a similar metaphor. As Madame Defarge weaves the names of the condemned into shrouds, her knitting becomes a symbol of her victims' fate, their death at the hands of a vengeful peasantry.

On the tenth morning, Lorry wakes to find the shoemaker's bench put away and the Doctor reading a book. Lorry cautiously asks Manette what might have caused the now-ended relapse, relating Manette's strange case as though it had happened to someone else. Manette suggests that he himself anticipated the reversion. He goes on to say that some stimulus must have triggered a memory strong enough to cause it. Manette reassures Miss Pross and Lorry that such a relapse is not likely to recur because the circumstances that caused it are unlikely to surface again. Still speaking as though the afflicted party were someone other than Manette, Lorry creates a scenario about a blacksmith. He asks whether, if the smith's forge were associated with a trauma, the smith's tools should be taken from him in order to spare him painful memories. Manette answers that the man used those tools to comfort his tortured mind and should be allowed to keep them. Eventually, however, Manette agrees, for Lucie's sake, to let Lorry dispose of his tools while he is away. A few days later, Manette leaves to join Lucie and Darnay. In his absence, Lorry and Miss Pross hack the shoemaker's bench to pieces, burn it, and bury the tools.

Summary: Chapter 20: A Plea

When Lucie and Darnay return home from their honeymoon, Sydney Carton is their first visitor. He apologizes for his drunkenness on the night of the trial and delivers a self-effacing speech in which he asks for Darnay's friendship: "If you could endure to have such a worthless fellow... coming and going at odd times, I should ask that I might be permitted to come and go as a privileged person [in the household]...." Carton leaves. Afterward, Darnay comments that Carton tends to be careless and reckless. Lucie deems this judgment too harsh and insists that Carton possesses a good, though wounded, heart. Lucie's compassion touches Darnay, and he promises to regard Carton's faults with sympathy.

Summary: Chapter 21: Echoing Footsteps

Years go by, and Lucie and her family enjoy a tranquil life. She gives birth to a daughter, little Lucie, and a son, who dies young. Lucie still maintains her habit of sitting in a corner of the parlor, listening to the echoing footsteps on the street below. By 1789, the echoes reverberate "from a distance" and make a sound "as of a great storm in France with a dreadful sea rising." One day in July, Lorry visits the Darnays and reports that an alarming number of French citizens are sending their money and property to England.

The scene then shifts to the storming of the Bastille in Paris. Defarge and Madame Defarge serve as leaders among the mob. Once inside the Bastille, Defarge grabs a guard and demands to be taken to 105 North Tower. Defarge searches the cell. When he is finished, he rejoins the mob as it murders and mutilates the governor who had defended the fortress. Madame Defarge cuts off the man's head.

Analysis: Chapters 18–21

Nearly every character in the novel battles against some form of imprisonment. In the case of Doctor Manette and Charles Darnay, this imprisonment is quite literal. But subtler, psychological confines torture other characters as much as any stone cell. Sydney Carton, for instance, cannot seem to escape his listlessness. Darnay struggles to free himself from the legacy of his family history. Lorry tries to unshackle his heart from its enslavement to Tellson's Bank. Finally, although Manette long ago escaped the Bastille, in this section he battles the tormenting memories of his years there. Prompted by the discovery of Darnay's true identity, Manette reverts to pounding out shoes in order to calm his troubled mind. This episode brings the notion of the fight for freedom from the level of political revolution to the level of personal struggles, suggesting that men and women toil to free themselves from the forces that oppress them as surely as nations do.

Dickens further elaborates the parallel between personal and public struggles in Chapter 21, which begins with Lucie in her parlor listening to the echo of footsteps on the street, and then shifts to the storming of the Bastille in Paris. The footsteps sweep the reader along, from the intimate struggles of private life to a revolution that will shape the future of an entire country and continent. Dickens's description of the battle contains exceptional power.

Consider the following passage from Chapter 21:

Flashing weapons, blazing torches, smoking waggon-loads of wet straw, hard work at neighbouring barricades in all directions, shrieks, volleys, execrations, bravery without stint, boom, smash and rattle, and the furious sounding of the living sea; but, still the deep ditch, and the single drawbridge, and the massive stone walls, and the eight great towers, and still Defarge of the wine-shop at his gun, grown doubly hot by the service of Four fierce hours.

Here Dickens captures the frantic and dangerous energy of the conflict. This passage's effect owes much to Dickens's language, which employs both alliteration and onomatopoeia to evoke the mood of battle. Alliteration, or the repetition of consonants, fills the passage with harsh sounds. The effect, in the last line for instance, mimics the regular bursts of gunfire: "at his *gun, grown* doubly hot by the service of *Four fierce* hours" (emphasis added). The passage's onomatopoeia, or use of words that imitate the sound to which they refer—such as "boom," "smash," and "rattle"—contributes to the overall impression of chaos as the sounds of the battle take over. Both methods cause an abstract description to give way to an eruption of noise, as the harsh and relentless pounding and battering of the siege becomes a palpable presence in the text.

As the battle rages on, Dickens introduces a symbol that plays a major role in the novel's theme of resurrection: blood, which begins to flow in the streets of Saint Antoine. Dickens links the image of blood to that of wine: after a day of butchery, the revolutionaries' clothes and hands bear stains of red, recalling the day on which the wine-cask breaks in front of Defarge's shop (Book the First, Chapter 5). With these allegorical images of blood and wine, the theme of resurrection takes on a decidedly Christian undertone. In the Catholic ritual of communion, the priest consecrates a cup of wine and it becomes the blood of Christ, whose entombment and miraculous ascent to Heaven on Easter Day have rendered him a symbol of resurrection in Christian tradition. In later chapters, Dickens will continue to draw upon this Christian association of blood, wine, and resurrection. Just as Christ shed his wine-red blood upon the Cross prior to being entombed and resurrected, so must the blood of the aristocracy flow before the commoners can take up their new lives.

BOOK THE SECOND: THE GOLDEN THREAD CHAPTERS 22–24

Summary: Chapter 22: The Sea Still Rises

One week later in Saint Antoine, Defarge arrives bearing news of the capture of Foulon, a wealthy man who once declared that if people were starving they should eat grass. Foulon had faked his own death to avoid the peasants' fury but was later discovered hiding in the country. The revolutionaries set out to meet Foulon, led by Madame Defarge and a woman known only as The Vengeance. The mob strings Foulon up, but the rope breaks and he does not die until his third hanging. The peasants put his head on a pike and fill his mouth with grass. When they have finished, the peasants eat their "scanty and insufficient suppers," parents play with their children, and lovers love.

Summary: Chapter 23: Fire Rises

The French countryside lies ruined and desolate. An unidentified man, weary from travel, meets the mender of roads. They address each other as "Jacques" to indicate their status as revolutionaries. The mender of roads directs the man to the chateau of the murdered Marquis. Later that night, the man sets the castle on fire. A rider from the chateau urges the village soldiers to help put out the fire and salvage the valuables there, but they refuse, and the villagers go inside their homes and put "candles in every dull little pane of glass." The peasants nearly kill Gabelle, the local tax collector, but he escapes to the roof of his house, where he watches the chateau burn. The narrator reports that scenes such as this are occurring all over France.

Chapter 24: Drawn to the Loadstone Rock

Three years pass. Political turmoil continues in France, causing England to become a refuge for persecuted aristocrats. Tellson's Bank in London becomes a "great gathering-place of Monseigneur." Tellson's has decided to dispatch Mr. Lorry to its Paris branch, in hopes that he can protect their valuable ledgers, papers, and records from destruction. Darnay arrives to persuade Lorry not to go, but Lorry insists, saying that he will bring Jerry Cruncher as his bodyguard.

Lorry receives an urgent letter, addressed to the Marquis St. Evrémonde, along with instructions for its delivery. Lorry laments the extreme difficulty of locating the Marquis, who has abandoned the estate willed to him by his murdered uncle. Darnay, careful to let no one suspect that he is in fact the missing Marquis, says that the Marquis is an acquaintance of his. He takes the letter, assuring Lorry that he will see it safely delivered. Darnay reads the letter, which contains a plea from Gabelle, whom the revolutionaries have imprisoned for his upkeep of the Marquis's property. Gabelle begs the new Marquis to return to France and save him. Darnay resolves to go to Paris, with a "glorious vision of doing good." After writing a farewell letter to Lucie and Doctor Manette, he departs.

Analysis

Before writing A *Tale of Two Cities*, Dickens had made one other attempt at historical fiction, entitled *Barnaby Rudge*

(1841). Dissatisfied with the outcome of that venture, Dickens set out to craft a novel that combined the panorama of history with his typical cast of exaggerated characters. Critical opinion differs on whether he achieved a successful balance. Most critics agree that *A Tale of Two Cities* somewhat sacrifices its characters to its historical scope. They claim that the story lacks the memorable types of characters that vitalize Dickens's most popular novels, such as *The Old Curiosity Shop* and *David Copperfield*. However, debate continues as to whether Dickens's use of history ultimately warranted this sacrifice. Some consider the author's treatment of the Revolution to be a triumphant success, while others believe that Dickens's indomitably fantastical imagination only waters down his history. Without doubt, Dickens relied heavily upon Thomas Carlyle's history of the French Revolution, a work that impressed Dickens greatly. Many of his details come directly from Carlyle's work, such as the description of the death of Foulon, which *A Tale of Two Cities* portrays as follows:

Once, he went aloft, and the rope broke, and they caught him shrieking... then, the rope was merciful, and held him, and his head was soon upon a pike, with grass enough in the mouth for all Saint Antoine to dance at the sight of.

The similarity to Carlyle's portrayal of the same incident in *The French Revolution* is obvious:

Only with the third rope (for two ropes broke, and the quavering voice still pleaded) can he be so much as got hanged! His Body is dragged through the streets; his Head goes aloft on a pike, the mouth filled with grass: amid sounds as of Tophet, from a grass-eating people.

Dickens acknowledges his debt to Carlyle in *A Tale of Two Cities'* preface, in which he states that he "hopes to add something to the popular and picturesque means of understanding [the French Revolution], though no one can hope to add anything to the philosophy of Mr Carlyle's wonderful book." Dickens's debt to Carlyle, however, runs deeper than the level of historical detail, extending to the book's philosophical outlook as well. Dickens believed, as

Carlyle did, that history is an evolutionary phenomenon. In other words, one era must be destroyed before a new one can develop and thrive, or, as Carlyle noted, "each new age [is] born like the phoenix out of the ashes of the past."

Yet although Dickens promotes this view of history in which the destruction of the old makes way for the new, he remains ambivalent about the violence accompanying the cycles of eradication. While he acknowledges the evils and oppression that motivated the peasant uprising—he does this most notably in the chapters chronicling the events that lead up to the death of the Marquis—he never goes so far as to romanticize the revolutionaries' struggles or idealize their cause. Indeed, it is with great horror that he recounts the fall of the Bastille and the ensuing chaos in the streets.

BOOK THE THIRD: THE TRACK OF A STORM CHAPTERS 1–5

Summary: Chapter 1: In Secret

Travel through France proves difficult for Darnay. Hostile revolutionaries frequently stop him and question him. Upon his arrival in Paris, the revolutionaries confine him to a prison called La Force. Darnay protests and reminds his jailers of his rights. However, the guard responds that, as an emigrant, Darnay—whom he refers to as Evrémonde—has no rights. The guard hands Darnay over to Defarge with the instructions, "In secret." As he is being led away, Darnay converses with the wine merchant. Defarge wonders aloud why Darnay would choose to return to France in the age of "that sharp female newly-born... called La Guillotine." Darnay asks Defarge for help, but Defarge refuses. At La Force, Darnay feels he has entered the world of the dead. A fellow prisoner welcomes him to the prison and says that he hopes that Darnay will not be kept "in secret"—the Anglicized form of en secret, meaning solitary confinement. But Darnay has indeed been sentenced to total isolation, and he soon finds himself in a cell measuring "five paces by four and a half."

Summary: Chapter 2: The Grindstone

Lucie and Doctor Manette storm into the Paris branch of Tellson's Bank to find Mr. Lorry. They inform him that Darnay sits imprisoned in La Force. Manette remains confident that he can use his standing as a one-time prisoner of the Bastille to help rescue his son-in-law. Lorry sends Lucie into the back room of the bank so that he can speak to Manette in private. He and Manette look out into the courtyard, where throngs of people sharpen their weapons on a grindstone. Lorry explains that the mob is preparing to kill the prisoners. Manette rushes into the crowd, and soon a cry arises: "Help for the Bastille prisoner's kindred in La Force!"

Summary: Chapter 3: The Shadow

Fearing that Lucie and Manette's presence might compromise the bank's business, Lorry ushers Lucie, her daughter, and Miss Pross to a nearby lodging. He leaves Jerry Cruncher to guard them. Back at Tellson's, Defarge approaches Lorry with a message from Manette. Following Manette's instructions, Lorry leads Defarge to Lucie. Defarge claims that Madame Defarge must accompany them, as she will familiarize herself with the faces of Lucie, her daughter, and Miss Pross, in order to better protect them in the future. The woman known as The Vengeance also comes. Upon arriving at the lodging, Defarge gives Lucie a note from the imprisoned Darnay. It urges her to take courage. Turning to Madame Defarge, Lucie begs her to show Darnay some mercy, but Madame Defarge coldly responds that the revolution will not stop for the sake of Lucie or her family.

Summary: Chapter 4: Calm in Storm

Four days later, Manette returns from La Force. Lorry notes a change in the once-fragile Manette, who now seems full of strength and power. Manette tells him that he has persuaded the Tribunal, a self-appointed body that tries and sentences the revolution's prisoners, to keep Darnay alive. Moreover, he has secured a job as the inspecting physician of three prisons, one of which is La Force. These duties will enable him to ensure Darnay's safety. Time passes, and France rages as though in a fever. The revolutionaries behead the king and queen, and the guillotine becomes a fixture in the Paris streets. Darnay remains in prison for a year and three months.

Summary; Chapter 5: The Wood-sawyer

While the family waits for Darnay's trial, Manette tells Lucie of a window in the prison from which Darnay might see her in the street. For two hours every day, Lucie stands in the area visible from this window. A wood-sawyer who works nearby talks with Lucie while she waits, pretending that his saw is a guillotine (it bears the inscription "Little Sainte Guillotine") and that each piece of wood that he cuts is the head of a prisoner. One day, a throng of people comes down the street, dancing a horrible and violent dance known as the Carmagnole. The dancers depart, and the distressed Lucie now sees her father standing before her. As he comforts Lucie, Madame Defarge happens by. She and Manette exchange salutes. Manette then tells Lucie that Darnay will stand trial on the following day and assures her that her husband will fare well in it.

Analysis: Chapters 1–5

The scene at the grindstone powerfully evokes the frantic and mindlessly violent mob of the revolution. A master of imagery, Dickens often connects one scene to another in such a manner that the images flow throughout the entire novel rather than stand in isolation. The reader feels this continuity as the crowd gathers around the grindstone to sharpen their weapons. The description of the people in blood-stained rags, "[not one] creature in the group free from the smear of blood," immediately recalls the breaking of the wine-cask outside Defarge's shop in Chapter 5; there, too, the people's rags are stained and "those who had been greedy with the staves of the cask, had acquired a tigerish smear about the mouth." These parallel scenes do more than testify to Dickens's artistry. They serve to place disparate motifs into symbolic relation. In repeating the motif of the red-stained peasants' rags, Dickens links wine with blood, invoking the Christian association between communion wine and the blood of Christ. However, Dickens complicates the symbol in his text. While the blood of Christ traditionally signifies salvation—Christians believe that Christ sacrificed his life for human deliverance from sin—Dickens's grisly depictions of the vicious, vengeful, and often sadistic revolutionaries express a deep skepticism in the redemptive power of political bloodshed.

Shadows constitute another symbol that permeates the entire novel, here providing the subheading for Chapter 3. Dickens uses light and dark much as a painter might, infusing his composition with a wide range of tone and depth. The reader can observe Dickens's use of light and shadow at various instances in the novel. Notably, the chilling opening of the novel, in which the mail coach weaves its way through the darkness and fog, sets a tone of ominous mystery for the story; conversely, the sweet sunrise that opens Book the Second, Chapter 18, lends Lucie's wedding day an air of promise and happiness. In the current section, Madame Defarge casts a menacing shadow:

> The shadow attendant on Madame Defarge and her party seemed to fall so threatening and dark on the child, that her mother instinctively kneeled on the ground beside her, and held her to her breast. The shadow attendant on Madame Defarge and her party seemed then to fall, threatening and dark, on both the mother and the child.

The narrator's focus on the looming presence of Madame Defarge and on Lucie's inability to escape this woman's shadow establishes a tension between the gentle and nurturing Lucie—the "golden-haired doll"—and the dark and cold Madame Defarge, an unrelenting instrument of the revolution. Indeed, the narrator implicitly likens Madame Defarge's shadow, which "fall[s]... threatening and dark," to the guillotine blade that she is so eager to see making its fatal descent.

The wood-sawyer who talks with Lucie in Chapter 5 possesses a grotesque zeal for decapitation, as evidenced by the religious nature of the moniker that he gives to his saw. He labels his imagined guillotine "Sainte"—that is, holy—illustrating his belief that the guillotine, in lopping off the heads of the aristocracy, is carrying out divine will. Similarly devoted but of opposite sympathy, Lucie waits steadfastly outside of her husband's prison, merely on the off-chance that Darnay might catch a glimpse of her. Whereas the violent and rambunctious Carmagnole dance, in which the wood-sawyer participates, symbolizes the ruthlessness of the revolution, the white snow that falls "quietly and... soft" in the very same chapter symbolizes Lucie's gentle soul and pure love for Darnay. When Madame Defarge passes by "like a shadow over the white road," the reader again senses the threat she poses to Lucie's happiness.

BOOK THE THIRD: THE TRACK OF A STORM CHAPTERS 1–5

Summary: Chapter 1: In Secret

Travel through France proves difficult for Darnay. Hostile revolutionaries frequently stop him and question him. Upon his arrival in Paris, the revolutionaries confine him to a prison called La Force. Darnay protests and reminds his jailers of his rights. However, the guard responds that, as an emigrant, Darnay—whom he refers to as Evrémonde—has no rights. The guard hands Darnay over to Defarge with the instructions, "In secret." As he is being led away, Darnay converses with the wine merchant. Defarge wonders aloud why Darnay would choose to return to France in the age of "that sharp female newly-born... called La Guillotine." Darnay asks Defarge for help, but Defarge refuses. At La Force, Darnay feels he has entered the world of the dead. A fellow prisoner welcomes him to the prison and says that he hopes that Darnay will not be kept "in secret"—the Anglicized form of en secret, meaning solitary confinement. But Darnay has indeed been sentenced to total isolation, and he soon finds himself in a cell measuring "five paces by four and a half."

Summary: Chapter 2: The Grindstone

Lucie and Doctor Manette storm into the Paris branch of Tellson's Bank to find Mr. Lorry. They inform him that Darnay sits imprisoned in La Force. Manette remains confident that he can use his standing as a one-time prisoner of the Bastille to help rescue his son-in-law. Lorry sends Lucie into the back room of the bank so that he can speak to Manette in private. He and Manette look out into the courtyard, where throngs of people sharpen their weapons on a grindstone. Lorry explains that the mob is preparing to kill the prisoners. Manette rushes into the crowd, and soon a cry arises: "Help for the Bastille prisoner's kindred in La Force!"

Summary: Chapter 3: The Shadow

Fearing that Lucie and Manette's presence might compromise the bank's business, Lorry ushers Lucie, her daughter, and Miss Pross to a nearby lodging. He leaves Jerry Cruncher to guard them. Back at Tellson's, Defarge approaches Lorry with a message from Manette. Following Manette's instructions, Lorry leads Defarge to Lucie. Defarge claims that Madame Defarge must accompany them, as she will familiarize herself with the faces of Lucie, her daughter, and Miss Pross, in order to better protect them in the future. The woman known as The Vengeance also comes. Upon arriving at the lodging, Defarge gives Lucie a note from the imprisoned Darnay. It urges her to take courage. Turning to Madame Defarge, Lucie begs her to show Darnay some mercy, but Madame Defarge coldly responds that the revolution will not stop for the sake of Lucie or her family.

Summary: Chapter 4: Calm in Storm

Four days later, Manette returns from La Force. Lorry notes a change in the once-fragile Manette, who now seems full of strength and power. Manette tells him that he has persuaded the Tribunal, a self-appointed body that tries and sentences the revolution's prisoners, to keep Darnay alive. Moreover, he has secured a job as the inspecting physician of three prisons, one of which is La Force. These duties will enable him to ensure Darnay's safety. Time passes, and France rages as though in a fever. The revolutionaries behead the king and queen, and the guillotine becomes a fixture in the Paris streets. Darnay remains in prison for a year and three months.

Summary; Chapter 5: The Wood-sawyer

While the family waits for Darnay's trial, Manette tells Lucie of a window in the prison from which Darnay might see her in the street. For two hours every day, Lucie stands in the area visible from this window. A wood-sawyer who works nearby talks with Lucie while she waits, pretending that his saw is a guillotine (it bears the inscription "Little Sainte Guillotine") and that each piece of wood that he cuts is the head of a prisoner. One day, a throng of people comes down the street, dancing a horrible and violent dance known as the Carmagnole. The dancers depart, and the distressed Lucie now sees her father standing before her. As he comforts Lucie, Madame Defarge happens by. She and Manette exchange salutes. Manette then tells Lucie that Darnay will stand trial on the following day and assures her that her husband will fare well in it.

Analysis: Chapters 1–5

The scene at the grindstone powerfully evokes the frantic and mindlessly violent mob of the revolution. A master of imagery, Dickens often connects one scene to another in such a manner that the images flow throughout the entire novel rather than stand in isolation. The reader feels this continuity as the crowd gathers around the grindstone to sharpen their weapons. The description of the people in blood-stained rags, "[not one] creature in the group free from the smear of blood," immediately recalls the breaking of the wine-cask outside Defarge's shop in Chapter 5; there, too, the people's rags are stained and "those who had been greedy with the staves of the cask, had acquired a tigerish smear about the mouth." These parallel scenes do more than testify to Dickens's artistry. They serve to place disparate motifs into symbolic relation. In repeating the motif of the red-stained peasants' rags, Dickens links wine with blood, invoking the Christian association between communion wine and the blood of Christ. However, Dickens complicates the symbol in his text. While the blood of Christ traditionally signifies salvation—Christians believe that Christ sacrificed his life for human deliverance from sin—Dickens's grisly depictions of the vicious, vengeful, and often sadistic revolutionaries express a deep skepticism in the redemptive power of political bloodshed.

Shadows constitute another symbol that permeates the entire novel, here providing the subheading for Chapter 3. Dickens uses light and dark much as a painter might, infusing his composition with a wide range of tone and depth. The reader can observe Dickens's use of light and shadow at various instances in the novel. Notably, the chilling opening of the novel, in which the mail coach weaves its way through the darkness and fog, sets a tone of ominous mystery for the story; conversely, the sweet sunrise that opens Book the Second, Chapter 18, lends Lucie's wedding day an air of promise and happiness. In the current section, Madame Defarge casts a menacing shadow:

> The shadow attendant on Madame Defarge and her party seemed to fall so threatening and dark on the child, that her mother instinctively kneeled on the ground beside her, and held her to her breast. The shadow attendant on Madame Defarge and her party seemed then to fall, threatening and dark, on both the mother and the child.

The narrator's focus on the looming presence of Madame Defarge and on Lucie's inability to escape this woman's shadow establishes a tension between the gentle and nurturing

Lucie—the "golden-haired doll"—and the dark and cold Madame Defarge, an unrelenting instrument of the revolution. Indeed, the narrator implicitly likens Madame Defarge's shadow, which "fall[s]... threatening and dark," to the guillotine blade that she is so eager to see making its fatal descent.

The wood-sawyer who talks with Lucie in Chapter 5 possesses a grotesque zeal for decapitation, as evidenced by the religious nature of the moniker that he gives to his saw. He labels his imagined guillotine "Sainte"—that is, holy—illustrating his belief that the guillotine, in lopping off the heads of the aristocracy, is carrying out divine will. Similarly devoted but of opposite sympathy, Lucie waits steadfastly outside of her husband's prison, merely on the off-chance that Darnay might catch a glimpse of her. Whereas the violent and rambunctious Carmagnole dance, in which the wood-sawyer participates, symbolizes the ruthlessness of the revolution, the white snow that falls "quietly and... soft" in the very same chapter symbolizes Lucie's gentle soul and pure love for Darnay. When Madame Defarge passes by "like a shadow over the white road," the reader again senses the threat she poses to Lucie's happiness.

BOOK THE THIRD: THE TRACK OF A STORM CHAPTERS 6–10

Summary: Chapter 6: Triumph

A motley and bloodthirsty crowd assembles at the trial of Charles Darnay. When Doctor Manette is announced as Darnay's father-in-law, a happy cry goes up among the audience. The court hears testimony from Darnay, Manette, and Gabelle, establishing that Darnay long ago had renounced his title out of disapproval of the aristocracy's treatment of peasants. These factors, in addition to Darnay's status as the son-in-law of the much-loved martyr Manette, persuade the jury to acquit him. The crowd carries Darnay home in a chair on their shoulders.

Summary: Chapter 7: A Knock at the Door

The next day, although Manette rejoices in having saved Darnay's life, Lucie remains terrified for her husband. Later that afternoon, she reports hearing footsteps on the stairs, and soon a knock comes at the door. Four soldiers enter and re-arrest Darnay. Manette protests, but one of the soldiers reminds him that if the Republic demands a sacrifice from him, he must make that sacrifice. Manette asks one of the soldiers to give the name of Darnay's accuser. Though it is against the law to divulge such information, the soldier replies that he is carrying out the arrest according to statements made by Defarge, Madame Defarge, and one other individual. When Manette asks for the identity of this third person, the soldier replies that Manette will receive his answer the next day.

Summary: Chapter 8: A Hand at Cards

Meanwhile, Jerry Cruncher and Miss Pross discover Miss Pross's long-lost brother, Solomon, in a wine-shop. Solomon scolds his sister for making a scene over their reunion. He cannot afford to be identified because he is working as a spy for the Republic. Meanwhile, Cruncher recognizes Solomon as the witness who accused Darnay of treason during his trial in England thirteen years earlier. He struggles to remember the man's name until Sydney Carton, who suddenly appears behind them, provides it: Barsad. Carton states that he has been in Paris for a day and has been lying low until he could be useful. He threatens to reveal Barsad's true identity to the revolutionaries unless the spy accompanies him to Tellson's.

Upon arriving at Tellson's, Carton informs Mr. Lorry and Jerry Cruncher that Darnay has been arrested again; he overheard Barsad discussing the news in a bar. Carton has a plan to help Darnay, should he be convicted, and he threatens to expose Barsad as an English spy should Barsad fail to cooperate. Carton reveals that he has seen Barsad conversing with Roger Cly, a known English spy. When Barsad counters that Cly is dead and presents the certificate of burial, Cruncher disproves the story by asserting that Cly's coffin contained only stones and dirt. Though Cruncher is unwilling to explain how he knows these details, Carton takes him at his word and again threatens to expose Barsad as an enemy of the Republic. Barsad finally gives in and agrees to help Carton with his secret plan.

Summary: Chapter 9: The Game Made

Lorry scolds Cruncher for leading a secret life (grave-robbing) outside his job at Tellson's. Cruncher hints that there may be many doctors involved in grave-robbing who bank at Tellson's. Cruncher then makes amends, saying that if Lorry will let young Jerry Cruncher inherit his own duties at the bank, he himself will become a gravedigger to make up for all the graves that he has "un-dug." After Barsad leaves, Carton tells Lorry and Cruncher that he has arranged a time to visit Darnay before his imminent execution. Carton reflects that a human being who has not secured the love of another has wasted his life, and Lorry agrees.

That night, as he wanders the streets of Paris, Carton thinks of Lucie. He enters a chemist's shop and buys a mysterious substance. The words spoken by the priest at his father's funeral echo through his mind: "I am the resurrection and the life, saith the Lord: he that believeth in me, though he were dead, yet shall he live: and whosoever liveth and believeth in me, shall never die." Carton helps a small girl across the muddy street, and she gives him a kiss. The priest's words echo again in his mind. He wanders until sunrise, then makes his way to the courthouse for Darnay's trial. The judge names Darnay's accusers: the Defarges and Doctor Manette. Manette reacts with shock and denies having ever denounced Darnay. Defarge then takes the stand and speaks of a letter that he found, hidden in 105 North Tower of the Bastille.

Summary: Chapter 10: The Substance of the Shadow

Defarge claims that Manette wrote the letter while imprisoned in the Bastille, and he reads it aloud. It tells the story of Manette's imprisonment. In 1757, a pair of brothers, one the Marquis Evrémonde (Darnay's father) and the other the next in line to be Marquis (Darnay's uncle, the man who ran over the child with his carriage in Book the Second, Chapter 7), ordered Doctor Manette to care for a young peasant woman, who was dying of a fever, and her brother, who was dying of a stab wound. The Marquis's brother had raped the young woman, killed her husband, and stabbed her brother, who died quickly. Although the woman was still alive, Manette failed to save her life. The next day a kind woman—the Marquis's wife and Darnay's mother—came to Manette's door. Having heard about the horrible things done to the peasant girl and her family, she offers to help the girl's sister, who was hidden away so the Marquis could not find her. Unfortunately, Manette does not know the sister's whereabouts. The next day, Manette was taken away and imprisoned in the Bastille on the orders of the Marquis Evrémonde. After hearing this story, the jury sentences Darnay to death, to pay for the sins of his father and uncle.

Analysis: Chapters 6–10

The echoing footsteps that Lucie hears in Chapter 21 of Book the Second now manifest themselves again, but this time they signify the immediate presence of pressing danger. No longer distant, dim, or scarcely audible, the footfalls in Chapter 7 announce the four soldiers come to take Darnay back to prison. Whereas the revolution only vaguely stirs Lucie when she sits in her comfortable parlor in England, it encroaches, physically and emotionally, upon her most intimate relationships now that she has come to Paris. This transformation of the revolution from an abstract notion into a direct presence in the lives of Lucie and Manette finds a parallel in the soldiers' words to them. In answering Manette's question as to the identity of Darnay's accusers, the soldiers first tell him that they are acting on the orders of Saint Antoine, the personified suburb of Paris at the heart of the revolution. However, Manette soon learns that Defarge and his wife have in fact occasioned the arrest. With the news of this betrayal by his former allies, the revolution reaches new heights of personal significance for Manette.

As the novel approaches its close, the reader encounters an ever-increasing number of coincidences, such as Miss Pross's discovery of her long-lost brother; Carton's timely arrival in the wine-shop to identify Barsad; and Defarge's discovery of Manette's letter denouncing the Evrémonde family. Moments such as these, endemic to Victorian fiction, constitute a device called *deus ex machina* (literally: "god out of the machine"), a term that refers to improbable contrivances used by the author to resolve the plot. Modern readers, more accustomed to realistic narratives, usually consider such unlikely developments to reflect a weakness in the plot's conception. Even in Dickens's time, certain readers objected to the contrived feeling created by these coincidences. Wilkie Collins, for instance—the author of *The Frozen Deep*, the play that inspired *A Tale of Two Cities*—found the discovery of Manette's letter in Dickens's work highly unlikely. But defenders of this style of writing believe that Dickens conceived a world in which everything is so interconnected to everything else that coincidence—no matter how unlikely—is inevitable. Dickens's biographer, John Forster, defended the author thus:

On the coincidences, resemblances, and surprises of life, Dickens liked especially to dwell, and few things moved his fancy so pleasantly. The world, he would say, was so much smaller than we thought it; we were all so connected by fate without knowing it; people supposed to be far apart were so constantly elbowing each other; and to-morrow bore so close a resemblance to nothing half so much as to yesterday.

The coincidences Dickens presents may seem excessive in number, but many critics have come to see these plot devices as yet another example of Dickens's talent for exaggeration. Just as his many caricatured figures serve to emphasize and comment on real human foibles, his coincidences and sudden surprising connections serve merely to exaggerate the frequency of what Dickens believed to be very real phenomena in our own world.

Regardless of how one feels about Carton's sudden appearance, one must acknowledge the transformation of his character as one of the novel's foremost achievements. Indeed, Carton proves the most psychologically complex and emotionally rich character that *A Tale of Two Cities* has to offer. By the time of his appearance in Paris, he has shed the skin of "the jackal." No longer insolent, lazy, and directionless, he emerges determined to save Darnay's life for the sake of the woman that he himself loves. He now has a purpose, and a purpose that he cherishes. In Chapter 9, the reader witnesses him preparing to make the ultimate sacrifice as he recites a passage from the Book of John. In the Christian tradition, worshippers speak these lines at the opening of the Burial Service in the Book of Common Prayer. Carton's utterance of these words has a dual significance. First, his words confirm that he has made a conscious decision to give of himself for Lucie's sake. (The reader might argue that Carton already has sacrificed himself to Lucie's benefit. However, although Carton has saved Darnay once before, in Book the Second, Chapter 3, this first occasion—his observation of the physical likeness that he and Darnay share—seemed more serendipitous than an act of valor performed deliberately to help Lucie.) Second, Carton's recitation of the biblical passage speaks beyond his personal psychology to the fates of the other characters in the novel, promising a final and satisfying resurrection.

BOOK THE THIRD: THE TRACK OF A STORM CHAPTERS 11–15

Summary: Chapter 11: Dusk

The courtroom crowd pours into the streets to celebrate Darnay's condemnation. John Barsad, charged with ushering Darnay back to his cell, lets Lucie embrace her husband one last time. Darnay insists that Doctor Manette not blame himself for the trial's outcome. Darnay is escorted back to his cell to await his execution the following morning, and Carton escorts the grieving Lucie to her apartment. Carton tells Manette to try his influence one last time with the prosecutors and then meet him at Tellson's, though Lorry feels certain that there is no hope for Darnay, and Carton echoes the sentiment.

Summary: Chapter 12: Darkness

Carton goes to Defarge's wine-shop. The Defarges marvel at how much he physically resembles the condemned Darnay. Carton overhears Madame Defarge's plan to accuse Lucie and Manette of spying, and to accuse Lucie's daughter as well. Defarge himself finds this course unnecessary, but his wife reminds him of her grievance against the family Evrémonde: she is the surviving sister of the woman and man killed by the Marquis and his brother. She demands the extermination of their heirs. Carton pays for his wine and returns to Tellson's.

At midnight, Manette arrives home completely out of his mind. He looks about madly for his shoemaking bench. After calming Manette, Carton takes from the doctor's coat the papers that will allow Lucie, the doctor, and the child to leave the city. He gives the documents to Lorry. Then, Carton gives Lorry his own papers, refusing to explain why. Afraid that the papers may soon be recalled because Madame Defarge intends to denounce the entire family, Carton insists to Lorry that time is of the essence: the family must leave tomorrow. Alone in the street that night, Carton utters a final good-bye and blessing to Lucie.

Summary: Chapter 13: Fifty-two

Fifty-two people have been condemned to die the next day. Darnay resolves to meet his death bravely. Carton appears at the door to Darnay's cell, and Darnay observes something new and bright in Carton's face. Carton tricks Darnay into switching clothes with him, dictates a letter of explanation, and then drugs him with the substance that he had purchased at the chemist's shop. He orders Barsad to carry the unconscious Darnay to the carriage waiting outside Tellson's. At two o'clock, guards take Carton from Darnay's cell, believing him to be Darnay. He stands in the long line of the condemned. A poor seamstress, also falsely sentenced to death, realises that Carton is not Darnay and asks, "Are you dying for him?" He replies, "And his wife and child." Meanwhile, Barsad delivers the real Darnay to Manette, Lorry, and Lucie, and sends the carriage on its way. Lorry presents the family's papers at the city gates as they leave. They flee through the countryside, fearing pursuit.

Summary: Chapter 14: The Knitting Done

Meanwhile, Madame Defarge heads toward Lucie's apartment to try to catch Lucie in the illegal act of mourning a prisoner. Evidence of such a crime, she believes, will strengthen her case against the family. At the apartment, Miss Pross and Jerry Cruncher are in the middle of making final arrangements to depart Paris. To avoid drawing the suspicion that leaving together might engender, Miss Pross tells Cruncher to wait for her with the carriage at the cathedral. When Cruncher leaves, Madame Defarge barges in and demands to know Lucie's whereabouts. The women fight, and Madame Defarge draws a gun. In the struggle, however, Miss Pross shoots her. She meets Cruncher as planned and reports that she has gone deaf from the gunshot.

Summary: Chapter 15: The Footsteps Die Out Forever

... Crush humanity out of shape once more... and it will twist itself into the same tortured forms. Sow the same seed of... oppression over again, and it will surely yield the same fruit according to its kind.

Carton and the young seamstress reach the guillotine. The Vengeance and the other revolutionary women worry that Madame Defarge will miss the beheading of Charles Darnay. The seamstress reflects that the new Republic may make life easier for poor people like herself and her surviving cousin. She kisses Carton and goes calmly to her death. Carton then goes to his.

The narrator recounts that those who saw Carton die witnessed a peaceful and even prophetic look on his face, and speculates confidently about Carton's final thoughts: Carton notes the fact that the oppressors in the crowd "have risen on the destruction of the old," but also realises that, someday, Paris will recover from these horrors and become beautiful.

Also in these imagined last moments, Carton sees Lucie and Darnay with a child named after himself. He sees Manette happy and healthy and sees Lorry living a long and peaceful life. He sees a future in which he holds a special place in their hearts and in the hearts of generations hence. He sees his own name "made illustrious," and the blots that he threw upon his life fade away. According to the narrator, Carton dies in the knowledge that "It is a far, far better thing that I do, than I have ever done; it is a far, far better rest that I go to than I have ever known."

"I see a beautiful city and a brilliant people rising from this abyss, and, in their struggles to be truly free,... I see the evil of this time... gradually making expiation for itself and wearing out."

Analysis: Chapters 11–15

Dickens uses the figure of Miss Pross to emphasize the power of love. As the devoted servant battles with Madame Defarge, he notes that "the vigourous tenacity of love [is] always so much stronger than hate." The showdown between the two women serves also as a commentary on social order and revolution. Revolution, as embodied by Madame Defarge, may prove fiercer and wilder, but the social order that Miss Pross represents emerges as stronger and steadier. Although Dickens denounces the cruelty and vengefulness of Madame Defarge, he acknowledges the unavoidable fact of such people's existence in the world:

And yet there is not in France, with its rich variety of soil and climate, a blade, a leaf, a root, a sprig, a peppercorn, which will grow to maturity under conditions more certain than those that have produced this horror. Crush humanity out of shape once more, under similar hammers, and it will twist itself into the same tortured forms. Sow the same seed of rapacious license and oppression over again, and it will surely yield the same fruit according to its kind.

Yet in noting the prevalence of evil, Dickens also shows an understanding of the processes by which evil arises. Madame Defarge certainly possesses a criminal bloodlust, but

Dickens suggests her own tragic past and suffering, rather than any innate ill-will toward humanity, have transformed her into the despicable creature that she has become. As such, Dickens is not so interested in criticizing Madame Defarge specifically as he is in using her as an example of the vices that society perpetrates. Although, at the end of the novel, the narrator, using Carton's voice, prophesies a restored and replenished France—true to Carlyle's theory of history in which one era emerges "like a phoenix" out of the ashes of another—*A Tale of Two Cities* ultimately extends a cautionary word toward its readers. In certain sublime instances—such as Carton's self-sacrifice—death may beget life, but oppression can beget nothing other than itself.

The novel ends with something of a Christian paradox: life is achieved through death. Carton's sacrifice of his life enables him to live in a way that he otherwise could not, for this sacrifice—the only means by which Darnay can be saved—assures Carton a place in the hearts of others and allows him to have undertaken one truly meaningful and valuable act before dying.

The final passage, in which the narrator imagines and records Carton's last thoughts, extends Carton's life beyond the moment of his death. He will live on in Lucie and Darnay, who will feel as deeply connected to him as they do to each other. He will live on in their child, who will bear his name and ambitiously follow a path that might have been Carton's own. Generations to come will honour his memory, endowing him with a glory that he could never have enjoyed had he continued living as Stryver's disaffected and drunken assistant. Carton's death emphasizes one of the novel's simpler philosophies—that love conquers all. Carton's love for Lucie allows him to overcome not only the purposelessness of his life but also his own death. Moreover, the event constitutes a Victorian ending, in that it provides the perfect resolution to various characters' problems. It ensures the continued happiness of Darnay and Lucie and it represents the redemption of the once spiritually aimless Carton.

The closing shift from third-person narration to the first-person supposed thoughts of Sydney Carton creates a powerful effect—it is as if Carton's beautiful act transcends even the narrator's control over the story. Indeed, the stunningly philosophical words that the narrator ascribes to Carton mirror Carton's quasi-religious ascension into the realm of the sublime. In his repetition of the phrase "I see" over the penultimate four paragraphs, Dickens uses anaphora, a rhetorical device in which a phrase recurs at the beginning of successive clauses. These paragraphs then culminate in the spiritually edifying and uplifting anaphora of "It is a far, far better thing" and "It is a far, far better rest." This device lends the closing passages a soothing, peaceful tone, and, in its repetition, evokes the language of prayer and reverence. The harmony between the style and content of these final paragraphs leaves the reader with a feeling of complete resolution.

Chapter 12

Important Quotations Explained

Quotation

It was the best of times, it was the worst of times, it was the age of wisdom, it was the age of foolishness, it was the epoch of belief, it was the epoch of incredulity, it was the season of Light, it was the season of Darkness, it was the spring of hope, it was the winter of despair, we had everything before us, we had nothing before us, we were all going direct to Heaven, we were all going direct the other way...

Explanation

These famous lines, which open *A Tale of Two Cities,* hint at the novel's central tension between love and family, on the one hand, and oppression and hatred, on the other. The passage makes marked use of anaphora, the repetition of a phrase at the beginning of consecutive clauses—for example, "it was the age... it was the age" and "it was the epoch... it was the epoch...." This technique, along with the passage's steady rhythm, suggests that good and evil, wisdom and folly, and light and darkness stand equally matched in their struggle. The opposing pairs in this passage also initiate one of the novel's most prominent motifs and structural figures—that of doubles, including London and Paris, Sydney Carton and Charles Darnay, Miss Pross and Madame Defarge, and Lucie and Madame Defarge.

Quotation

> *A wonderful fact to reflect upon, that every human creature is constituted to be that profound secret and mystery to every other. A solemn consideration, when I enter a great city by night, that every one of those darkly clustered houses encloses its own secret; that every room in every one of them encloses its own secret; that every beating heart in the hundreds of thousands of breasts there, is, in some of its imagin-ings, a secret to the heart nearest it! Something of the awfulness, even of Death itself, is referable to this.*

Explanation

The narrator makes this reflection at the beginning of Book the First, Chapter 3, after Jerry Cruncher delivers a cryptic message to Jarvis Lorry in the darkened mail coach. Lorry's mission—to recover the long-imprisoned Doctor Manette and "recall" him to life—establishes the essential dilemma that he and other characters face: namely, that human beings constitute perpetual mysteries to one another and always remain somewhat locked away, never fully reachable by outside minds. This fundamental inscrutability proves most evident in the case of Manette, whose private sufferings force him to relapse throughout the novel into bouts of cobbling, an occupation that he first took up in prison. Throughout the novel, Manette mentally returns to his prison, bound more by his own recollections than by any attempt of the other characters to "recall" him into the present. This passage's reference to death also evokes the deep secret revealed in Carton's self-sacrifice at the end of the novel. The exact profundity of his love and devotion for Lucie remains obscure until he commits to dying for her; the selflessness of his death leaves the reader to wonder at the ways in which he might have manifested this great love in life.

Quotation

> *The wine was red wine, and had stained the ground of the narrow street in the suburb of Saint Antoine, in Paris,*

where it was spilled. It had stained many hands, too, and many faces, and many naked feet, and many wooden shoes. The hands of the man who sawed the wood, left red marks on the billets; and the forehead of the woman who nursed her baby, was stained with the stain of the old rag she wound about her head again. Those who had been greedy with the staves of the cask, had acquired a tigerish smear about the mouth; and one tall joker so besmirched, his head more out of a long squalid bag of a night-cap than in it, scrawled upon a wall with his finger dipped in muddy wine-lees—blood.

Explanation

This passage, taken from Book the First, Chapter 5, describes the scramble after a wine cask breaks outside Defarge's wine-shop. This episode opens the novel's examination of Paris and acts as a potent depiction of the peasants' hunger. These oppressed individuals are not only physically starved—and thus willing to slurp wine from the city streets—but are also hungry for a new world order, for justice and freedom from misery. In this passage, Dickens foreshadows the lengths to which the peasants' desperation will take them. This scene is echoed later in the novel when the revolutionaries—now similarly smeared with red, but the red of blood—gather around the grindstone to sharpen their weapons. The emphasis here on the idea of staining, as well as the scrawling of the word "blood," furthers this connection, as does the appearance of the wood-sawyer, who later scares Lucie with his mock guillotine in Book the Third, Chapter 5. Additionally, the image of the wine lapping against naked feet anticipates the final showdown between Miss Pross and Madame Defarge in Book the Third, Chapter 14: "The basin fell to the ground broken, and the water flowed to the feet of Madame Defarge. By strange stern ways, and through much staining of blood, those feet had come to meet that water."

Quotation

Along the Paris streets, the death-carts rumble, hollow and harsh. Six tumbrels carry the day's wine to La Guillotine.

All the devouring and insatiate Monsters imagined since imagination could record itself, are fused in one realization, Guillotine. And yet there is not in France, with its rich variety of soil and climate, a blade, a leaf, a root, a sprig, a peppercorn, which will grow to maturity under conditions more certain than those that have produced this horror. Crush humanity out of shape once more, under similar hammers, and it will twist itself into the same tortured forms. Sow the same seed of rapacious license and oppression over again, and it will surely yield the same fruit according to its kind.

Explanation

In this concise and beautiful passage, which occurs in the final chapter of the novel, Dickens summarizes his ambivalent attitude toward the French Revolution. The author stops decidedly short of justifying the violence that the peasants use to overturn the social order, personifying "La Guillotine" as a sort of drunken lord who consumes human lives—"the day's wine." Nevertheless, Dickens shows a thorough understanding of how such violence and bloodlust can come about. The cruel aristocracy's oppression of the poor "sow[s] the same seed of rapacious license" in the poor and compels them to persecute the aristocracy and other enemies of the revolution with equal brutality. Dickens perceives these revolutionaries as "[c]rush[ed]... out of shape" and having been "hammer[ed]... into... tortured forms." These depictions evidence his belief that the lower classes' fundamental goodness has been perverted by the terrible conditions under which the aristocracy has forced them to live.

Quotation

I see a beautiful city and a brilliant people rising from this abyss, and, in their struggles to be truly free, in their triumphs and defeats, through long years to come, I see the evil of this time and of the previous time of which this is the natural birth, gradually making expiation for itself and wearing out....

I see that child who lay upon her bosom and who bore my name, a man winning his way up in that path of life which once was mine. I see him winning it so well, that my name is made illustrious there by the light of his....

It is a far, far better thing that I do, than I have ever done; it is a far, far better rest I go to than I have ever known.

Explanation

Though much debate has arisen regarding the value and meaning of Sydney Carton's sacrifice at the end of the novel, the surest key to interpretation rests in the thoughts contained in this passage, which the narrator attributes to Carton as he awaits his sacrificial death. This passage, which occurs in the final chapter, prophesies two resurrections: one personal, the other national. In a novel that seeks to examine the nature of revolution—the overturning of one way of life for another—the struggles of France and of Sydney Carton mirror each other. Here, Dickens articulates the outcome of those struggles: just as Paris will "ris[e] from [the] abyss" of the French Revolution's chaotic and bloody violence, so too will Carton be reborn into glory after a virtually wasted life. In the prophecy that Paris will become "a beautiful city" and that Carton's name will be "made illustrious," the reader sees evidence of Dickens's faith in the essential goodness of humankind. The very last thoughts attributed to Carton, in their poetic use of repetition, register this faith as a calm and soothing certainty.

QUOTES

1. The water of the fountain ran, the swift river ran, the day ran into evening, so much life in the city ran into death according to rule, time and tide waited for no man, the rats were sleeping close together in their dark holes again, the Fancy Ball was lighted up at supper, all things ran their course.
2. "You might, from your appearance, be the wife of Lucifer. Nevertheless, you shall not get the better of me. I am an Englishwoman."

3. "You anticipate what I would say, though you cannot know how earnestly I say it, how earnestly I feel it, without knowing my secret heart, and the hopes and fears and anxieties with which it has long been laden. Dear Doctor Manette, I love your daughter fondly, dearly, disinterestedly, devotedly. If ever there were love in the world, I love her...."

4. "... I wish you to know that you have been the last dream of my soul. In my degradation I have not been so degraded but that the sight of you with your father, and of this home made such a home by you, has stirred old shadows that I thought had died out of me. Since I knew you, I have been troubled by a remorse that I thought would never reproach me again, and have heard whispers from old voices impelling me upward, that I thought were silent for ever. I have had unformed ideas of striving afresh, beginning anew, shaking off sloth and sensuality, and fighting out the abandoned fight. A dream, all a dream, that ends in nothing, and leaves the sleeper where he lay down, but I wish you to know that you inspired it."

5. Sadly, sadly, the sun rose; it rose upon no sadder sight than the man of good abilities and good emotions, incapable of their directed exercise, incapable of his own help and his own happiness, sensible of the blight on him, and resigning him-self to let it eat him away.

6. Up the two terrace flights of steps the rain ran wildly, and beat at the great door, like a swift messenger rousing those within;...

7. "I go so far as to say, miss, morehover," proceeded Mr. Cruncher, with a most alarming tendency to hold forth as from a pulpit—"and let my words be took down and took to Mrs. Cruncher through yourself—that wot my opinions respectin' flopping has undergone a change, and that wot I only hope with

all my heart as Mrs. Cruncher may be a flopping at the present time."

8. Chateau and hut, stone face and dangling figure, the red stain on the stone floor, and the pure water in the village well—thousands of acres of land—a whole province of France—all France itself—lay under the night sky, concentrated into a faint hairbreadth line. So does a whole world, with all its greatnesses and littlenesses, lie in a twinkling star. And as mere human knowledge can split a ray of light and analyse the manner of its composition, so, sublimer intelligences may read in the feeble shining of this earth of ours, every thought and act, every vice and virtue, of every responsible creature on it.

9. Charles Darnay seemed to stand in a company of the dead. Ghosts all! The ghost of beauty, the ghost of stateliness, the ghost of elegance, the ghost of pride, the ghost of frivolity, the ghost of wit, the ghost of youth, the ghost of age, all waiting their dismissal from the desolate shore, all turning on him eyes that were changed by the death they had died in coming there.

10. "... tell Wind and Fire where to stop," returned madame; "but don't tell me."

11. "If you could say, with truth, to your own solitary heart, to-night, 'I have secured to myself the love and attachment, the gratitude or respect, of no human creature; I have won myself a tender place in no regard; I have done nothing good or serviceable to be remembered by!' your seventy-eight years would be seventy-eight heavy curses; would they not?"

12. The two stand in the fast-thinning throng of victims, but they speak as if they were alone. Eye to eye, voice to voice, hand to hand, heart to heart, these two children of the Universal Mother, else so wide apart and differing, have come together on the dark

highway, to repair home together, and to rest in her bosom.

13. Cramped in all kinds of dim cupboards and hutches at Tellson's, the oldest of men carried on the business gravely. When they took a young man into Tellson's London house, they hid him somewhere till he was old. They kept him in a dark place, like a cheese, until he had the full Tellson flavour and blue-mould upon him. Then only was he permitted to be seen, spectacularly poring over large books, and casting his breeches and gaiters into the general weight of the establishment.
14. It is a far, far better thing that I do, than I have ever done; it is a far, far better rest that I go to, than I have ever known.
15. She was truest to them in the season of trial, as all the quietly loyal and good will always be.
16. It was the best of times, it was the worst of times, it was the age of wisdom, it was the age of foolishness, it was the epoch of belief, it was the epoch of incredulity, it was the season of light, it was the season of darkness, it was the spring of hope, it was the winter of despair, we had everything before us, we had nothing before us, we were all going direct to heaven, we were all going direct the other way— in short, the period was so far like the present period, that some of its noisiest authorities insisted on its being received, for good or for evil, in the superlative degree of comparison only.
17. He lowered the window, and looked out at the rising sun. There was a ridge of ploughed land, with a plough upon it where it had been left last night when the horses were unyoked; beyond, a quiet coppice-wood, in which many leaves of burning red and golden yellow still remained upon the trees. Though the earth was cold and wet, the sky was clear, and the sun rose bright, placid, and beautiful.

18. The wind is rushing after us, and the clouds are flying after us, and the moon is plunging after us, and the whole wild night is in pursuit of us; but, so far we are pursued by nothing else.
19. "... judiciously show a cat milk, if you wish her to thirst for it. Judiciously show a dog his natural prey, if you wish him to bring it down one day."

Chapter 13

Major Themes and Issues

THEMES

"Recalled to Life"

The themes of death, committal and resurrection are general and recurrent throughout the novel. It may be said that they are in fact its most important themes, for Dickens intended originally to entitle the book *Recalled to Life*. (This instead became the heading for the first chapter.)

The aforementioned concepts draw obvious parallels with the Christian faith and its ideals of deliverance and eternal life. Employing a less all-embracing interpretation, "Book the First" can safely be said to deal with the rebirth of Dr. Manette from the living death that is his incarceration.

The theme of resurrection is first brought to the reader's attention by Mr Lorry, who thinks obsessively of the words "buried alive". He regards himself as the vehicle for Dr. Manette's revival when he passes on the message "Recalled to Life" to Jerry Cruncher. He sees the candles on the table in the inn as being buried "in deep graves of black mahogany". He believes that he will physically "dig" (a word repeated often to enforce its connotation) Dr. Manette from his grave.

Jerry is also drawn into the theme: he himself is involved in death and resurrection in way that the reader does not yet know. The first piece of foreshadowing comes in his remark to himself: "You'd be in a blazing bad way, if recalling to life was to come into fashion, Jerry!" The black humour becomes obvious only in hindsight, and Dickens keeps the mystery alive until it is finally solved. One stormy night, a number of years later in the novel, Mr Lorry reawakens the reader's interest by telling Jerry that it is "Almost night [...] to bring the dead out of their graves". Jerry responds firmly that he has never seen the night do that.

The author revels in parallels. The theme of resurrection is illustrated with figurative genius in the case of Charles Darnay, with his triumvirate of imprisonments and subsequent escapes.

It is interesting to note that the demolition of Dr. Manette's shoe-making workbench is described as "the burning of the body". This is one of the few cases where that sub-theme has a positive connotation, liberating the doctor from his emotional slavery and the torturous memory of his long imprisonment.

Death is a theme dealt with almost solely by the French Revolution, although there is a brief mention of the passing of Lucie's son. His death, together with that of Sydney Carton, denotes a peaceful transition to deliverance and resurrection, in particular when we compare it to all the other deaths, which are brutal, violent and graceless.

Dickens holds the French and English equally liable for the social and judicial injustices in their respective countries. In both, death sentences are handed out for the most insignificant crimes, and life has little value. "From this room," the Marquis informs Darnay, "many such dogs have been taken out to be hanged." One peasant, the Marquis recalls, was run through with a sword because he dared mention his master's daughter. The Marquis and his cohorts believe in and take their "right of life and earth over the surrounding vulgar", which takes its revenge to similarly extreme proportions. The tables are turned, the roles of lord and slave reversed, and bloody retribution wrought.

It turns out that Jerry Cruncher's involvement in the theme is that he "resurrects" dead bodies to sell to medical men. As often happens with such Dickensian characters, Jerry has a change of heart and changes his ways, becoming a grave-digger instead of a grave-robber.

The devastating impact on Dr. Manette of his imprisonment in the Bastille might capture Dickens' sense of being trapped in his marriage to a woman he no longer loved. Even once he is freed, only Lucie can rescue Manette from recurrent delusions that he is still in prison; their relationship of father and daughter may have reflected aspects of Dickens' feelings for Ternan (who was the same age as his own daughters).

Sydney Carton's self-sacrificing death atones for all his past wrongdoings. He even finds God during the last few days of his life, repeating Christ's soothing words "I am the resurrection and the life". Resurrection, therefore, becomes the predominant theme of the final part of the novel. Darnay is rescued at the last moment and recalled to life; Carton chooses death and resurrection to a life better than that which he has ever known: "it was the peacefullest man's face ever beheld there [...] he looked sublime and prophetic".

Dickens, in conclusion, foresees a new and improved social order, rising from the ashes of the destruction which preceded it.

Mob violence

Dickens roundly denounces mob violence, using Roger Cly's funeral to show that the British are no less susceptible than the French. This helps to maintain a balance between the two cities of the tale.

Love and Hate

Lucie Manette is the central figure around whom the theme of love revolves. There is first the love between father and daughter, jointly thoughtful and altruistic. Their feelings for one another are summed up in Chapter 17, Book the Second, where she promises him that nothing can come between them, not even Charles. He asks her in turn, "How could my happiness be perfect, while yours was incomplete?"

Miss Pross, on the other hand, loves Lucie with a passion that is both obsessive and over-protective but also noble. She is prepared to die at Madame Defarge's hands to rescue Lucie. Mr Lorry loves her with the committed affection of an uncle, becoming soppy at her wedding and being courageously primed to jump to her defence against Mr Stryver. He too, risks his own life to save those of Lucie and his good friend Doctor Manette, helping them to escape Paris.

Charles and Sydney both fall in love with Lucie, Charles offering chivalrous loyalty and Sydney obsessive passion and valiant selflessness. When Charles is ready to admit to his love for Lucie, he speaks to Dr. Manette first: "Heaven is my witness that I love her". Sydney, meanwhile, divulges the depths of his anguished persona to her: "You have been the last dream of my soul [....] You kindled me, heap of ashes that I am, into fire." This is not as over-the-top in Sydney as it could be in other men: his admission is the bare reality. He walks the streets at night to be near Lucie and finally gives his life for her, "to keep a life you love beside you!"

Selfless love, such as that offered by Dr. Manette in trying to save Charles for Lucie even though he knows him to be the nephew of the Marquis d'Evrémonde responsible for his eighteen-year custody, is the point which Dickens wants to make as the benchmark to aim at in life. Sydney Carton and Miss Pross exemplify this notion, too, as does Lucie.

Hatred is personified principally by Madame Defarge (backed up by the Vengeance and Jacques III) on the poor side, and the Marquis on the side of the rich. Madame Defarge has a very private (and general) reason for hating the Evrémondes: they cruelly abused her sister, brought about the deaths of her husband and little brother, and have repressed her family for hundreds of years. It is understandable if not condonable that Madame Defarge should become obsessed with annihilating all the Evrémondes, including Lucie and her daughter. As she explains to Lucie, "All our lives, we have seen our sister-women suffer, in themselves and in their children, poverty, nakedness, hunger, thirst, sickness, misery, oppression and neglect of all kinds Is it likely that the trouble of one wife and mother would be much to us now?"

By way of uncomplimentary comparison, the Marquis has no reason at all to hate the peasants. They are spurned only for their low social standing. He sees them as less than animals and has anxiety only for his horses when his coach runs over and kills a young child. He shows his disdain for them to their faces: "You dogs! I would ride over any of you very willingly, and exterminate you from the earth."

It is unsurprising that the French Revolution should be so blood-spattered for so long a time, and that even the guiltless were murdered with the guilty. Dickens believes that, ultimately, good will triumph over evil and that love is stronger than hate: the inexperienced Miss Pross, for example, gets the better of the toughened Madame Defarge. Likewise, Sydney's love seizes Charles from the clutches of the executioner and thwarts Madame Defarge's evil plans.

Darkness and Light

As is common practice in English literature, Dickens depicts good and evil as expressions of light and darkness. Danger and fright are associated with darkness, while pleasure and happiness are associated with light. Lucie Manette embodies the theme of light and Madame Defarge that of darkness. Book the Second, "The Golden Thread", is intended to demonstrate Lucie's entwining a thread of bliss around those who come into contact with her, thus bringing them into her life and entangling them in her destiny.

Lucie meets her father for the first time in the Defarges' attic: "His old white head mingled with her radiant hair which warmed and lighted it as though it were the light of freedom shining on him." Lucie's hair symbolises joy as she winds "the golden thread that bound them all together". She is adorned with "diamonds, very bright and sparkling", and symbolic of the happiness of the day of her marriage.

Dickens does, however, go deliberately against the grain on one occasion: he has light show peril and fear, and thus presents a good technical range. When the ill-fated nobles are brought every day into the light from the dark vaults of their abhorrent prisons, the light heralds their journey to death.'

Sydney shows both pain and joy when Mr Lorry mentions Lucie's grieving for her spouse: "A light, or a shade [...] passed from it [his face], as swiftly as a change will sweep over a hill-side on a wild, bright day."

It is on a wild, tempestuous night that the Manettes flee from Paris: "The night comes on dark [....] The wind is rushing after us."

In more a traditional sense, we see the rising sun illuminate the way to Sydney's deliverance: "the glorious sun seemed to strike those words [...] straight and warn to his heart."

Darkness represents uncertainty, fear and peril. It is dark when Mr Lorry rides to Dover; it is dark in the prisons; dark shadows follow Madame Defarge; dark, gloomy doldrums disturb Dr. Manette; his capture and captivity are shrouded in darkness; the Marquis's estate is burned in the dark of night; Jerry Cruncher raids graves in the darkness; Charles's second arrest also occurs at night. Both Lucie and Mr Lorry feel the dark threat that is Madame Defarge. "That dreadful woman seems to throw a shadow on me," remarks Lucie. Although Mr Lorry tries to comfort her, "the shadow of the manner of these Defarges was dark upon himself". Madame Defarge is "like a shadow over the white road", the snow symbolising purity and Madame Defarge's darkness corruption. Dickens also compares the dark colour of blood to the pure white snow: the blood takes on the shade of the crimes of its shedders.

Social Injustice

On the serios part lifelong champion of the deprived and exploited because of his personal experiences as a young boy. His sympathies however, lie only up to a point with the revolutionaries; he condemns the mob madness which sets in after the insurrection. When mad men and women massacre eleven-hundred detainees in one night and hustle back to sharpen their weapons on the grindstone, they have "eyes which any unbrutalised beholder would have given twenty years of life, to petrify with a well-directed gun".

The reader is given numerous examples of the ways in which the poor are tyrannised in France and England alike. Amidst the common anarchy, the executioner in England is "stringing up long rows of miscellaneous criminals; now hanging housebreaker [...] now burning people in the hand" or hanging a broke man for stealing sixpence. In France, a boy is sentenced to have his hands removed and is burned alive, because he did not kneel down in the rain before a parade of monks, passing some fifty metres away. The clergy are extremely dishonest. At the lavish chateau of Monseigneur, we find "brazen ecclesiastics of the worst world worldly, with sensual eyes, loose tongues, and looser lives [...] Military officers destitute of military knowledge [...] Doctors who made great fortunes [...] for imaginary disorders".

The Marquis recalls with pleasure the days when his family had the right of life and death over their slaves, "when many such dogs were taken out to be hanged". He won't even allow a widow to put up a board bearing her dead husband's name, to discern his resting place from all the others. He orders Madame Defarge's sick brother-in-law to heave a cart all day and allay frogs at night to exacerbate the young man's illness and hasten his death.

In England, even banks endorse unbalanced sentences: a man may be condemned to death for nicking a horse or opening a letter. Conditions in the prisons are dreadful. "Most kinds of debauchery and villainy were practised, and [...] dire diseases were bred", sometimes killing the judge before the accused.

So riled is Dickens at the brutality of the law that he depicts some English establishments in acerbically sarcastic words: "the whipping-post, another deal old institution, very humanising and softening to behold in action." He faults the law for accepting the appalling conditions without seeking reform. "Whatever is, is right" is the dictum of the Old Bailey. The gruesome portrayal of quartering highlights the insane atrocity of the penalty.

Dickens is understanding of the reasons behind Jerry's grave-digging, reminding the reader that Mr Lorry is prone to rebuke Jerry more for his humble social status than anything else. Jerry reminds him that doctors, men of the cloth, undertakers and watchmen are also conspirators in the crime.

Dickens believes that there is little or no difference between the peers of the realm and the underprivileged as regards their dealings with each other. In spite of his compassion for the poor, he assumes the philosophical stance that what happened in the revolution was a predictable upshot. "Crush humanity out of shape once more, under similar hammers, and it will twist itself into the same tortured forms. Sow the same seed of rapacious licence and oppression over again, and it will surely yield the same fruit [...]."

The Ever-Present Possibility of Resurrection

With *A Tale of Two Cities,* Dickens asserts his belief in the possibility of resurrection and transformation, both on a personal level and on a societal level. The narrative suggests that Sydney Carton's death secures a new, peaceful life for Lucie Manette, Charles Darnay, and even Carton himself. By delivering himself to the guillotine, Carton ascends to the plane of heroism, becoming a Christ-like figure whose death serves to save the lives of others. His own life thus gains meaning and value. Moreover, the final pages of the novel suggest that, like Christ, Carton will be resurrected—Carton is reborn in the hearts of those he has died to save. Similarly, the text implies that the death of the old regime in France prepares the way for the beautiful and renewed Paris that Carton supposedly envisions from the guillotine. Although Carton spends most of the novel in a life of indolence and apathy, the supreme selflessness of his final act speaks to a human capacity for change. Although the novel dedicates much time to describing the atrocities committed both by the aristocracy and by the outraged peasants, it ultimately expresses the belief that this violence will give way to a new and better society.

Dickens elaborates his theme with the character of Doctor Manette. Early on in the novel, Lorry holds an imaginary conversation with him in which he says that Manette has been "recalled to life." As this statement implies, the doctor's eighteen-year imprisonment has constituted a death of sorts. Lucie's love enables Manette's spiritual renewal, and her maternal cradling of him on her breast reinforces this notion of rebirth.

The Necessity of Sacrifice

Connected to the theme of the possibility of resurrection is the notion that sacrifice is necessary to achieve happiness. Dickens examines this second theme, again, on both a national and personal level. For example, the revolutionaries prove that a new, egalitarian French republic can come about only with a heavy and terrible cost—personal loves and loyalties must be sacrificed for the good of the nation. Also, when Darnay is arrested for the second time, in Book the Third, Chapter 7, the guard who seizes him reminds Manette of the primacy of state interests over personal loyalties. Moreover, Madame Defarge gives her husband a similar lesson when she chastises him for his devotion to Manette—an emotion that, in her opinion, only clouds his obligation to the revolutionary cause. Most important, Carton's transformation into a man of moral worth depends upon his sacrificing of his former self. In choosing to die for his friends, Carton not only enables their happiness but also ensures his spiritual rebirth.

The Tendency toward Violence and Oppression in Revolutionaries

Throughout the novel, Dickens approaches his historical subject with some ambivalence. While he supports the revolutionary cause, he often points to the evil of the revolutionaries themselves. Dickens deeply sympathizes with the plight of the French peasantry and emphasizes their need for liberation. The several chapters that deal with the Marquis Evrémonde successfully paint a picture of a vicious aristocracy that shamelessly exploits and oppresses the nation's poor. Although Dickens condemns this oppression, however, he also condemns the peasants' strategies in overcoming it. For in fighting cruelty with cruelty, the peasants effect no true revolution; rather, they only perpetuate the violence that they themselves have suffered. Dickens makes his stance clear in his suspicious and cautionary depictions of the mobs. The scenes in which the people sharpen their weapons at the grindstone and dance the grisly Carmagnole come across as deeply macabre. Dickens's most concise and relevant view of revolution comes in the final chapter, in which he notes the slippery slope down from the oppressed to the oppressor: "Sow the same seed of rapacious license and oppression over again, and it will surely yield the same fruit according to its kind." Though Dickens sees the French Revolution as a great symbol of transformation and resurrection, he emphasizes that its violent means were ultimately antithetical to its end.

MOTIFS

Doubles

The novel's opening words ("It was the best of times, it was the worst of times....") immediately establish the centrality of doubles to the narrative. The story's action divides itself between two locales, the two cities of the title. Dickens positions various characters as doubles as well, thus heightening the various themes within the novel. The two most important females in the text function as diametrically opposed doubles: Lucie is as loving and nurturing as Madame Defarge is hateful and bloodthirsty. Dickens then uses this opposition to make judgments and thematic assertions. Thus, for example, while Lucie's love initiates her father's spiritual transformation and renewal, proving the possibility of resurrection, Madame

Defarge's vengefulness only propagates an infinite cycle of oppression, showing violence to be self-perpetuating.

Dickens's doubling technique functions not only to draw oppositions, but to reveal hidden parallels. Carton, for example, initially seems a foil to Darnay; Darnay as a figure reminds him of what he could have been but has failed to become. By the end of the novel, however, Carton transforms himself from a good-for-nothing to a hero whose goodness equals or even surpasses that of the honourable Darnay. While the two men's physical resemblance initially serves only to underscore Carton's moral inferiority to Darnay, it ultimately enables Carton's supremely self-elevating deed, allowing him to disguise himself as the condemned Darnay and die in his place. As Carton goes to the guillotine in his double's stead, he raises himself up to, or above, Darnay's virtuous status.

Shadows and Darkness

Shadows dominate the novel, creating a mood of thick obscurity and grave foreboding. An aura of gloom and apprehension surrounds the first images of the actual story—the mail coach's journey in the dark and Jerry Cruncher's emergence from the mist. The introduction of Lucie Manette to Jarvis Lorry furthers this motif, as Lucie stands in a room so darkened and awash with shadows that the candlelight seems buried in the dark panels of the walls. This atmosphere contributes to the mystery surrounding Lorry's mission to Paris and Manette's imprisonment. It also creates a literal manifestation of Dickens's observations about the shadowy depths of the human heart. As illustrated in the chapter with the appropriate subheading "The Night Shadows," every living person carries profound secrets and mysteries that will never see the light of day. Shadows continue to fall across the entire novel. The vengeful Madame Defarge casts a shadow on Lucie and all of her hopes, as emphasized in Book the Third, Chapter 5. As Lucie stands in the pure, fresh snow, Madame Defarge passes by "like a shadow over the white road." In addition, the letter that Defarge uses to condemn Darnay to death throws a crippling shadow over the entire family;

fittingly, the chapter that reveals the letter's contents bears the subheading "The Substance of the Shadow."

Imprisonment

Almost all of the characters in *A Tale of Two Cities* fight against some form of imprisonment. For Darnay and Manette, this struggle is quite literal. Both serve significant sentences in French jails. Still, as the novel demonstrates, the memories of what one has experienced prove no less confining than the walls of prison. Manette, for example, finds himself trapped, at times, by the recollection of life in the Bastille and can do nothing but revert, trembling, to his pathetic shoemaking compulsion. Similarly, Carton spends much of the novel struggling against the confines of his own personality, dissatisfied with a life that he regards as worthless.

SYMBOLS

The Broken Wine Cask

With his depiction of a broken wine cask outside Defarge's wine-shop, and with his portrayal of the passing peasants' scrambles to lap up the spilling wine, Dickens creates a symbol for the desperate quality of the people's hunger. This hunger is both the literal hunger for food—the French peasants were starving in their poverty—and the metaphorical hunger for political freedoms. On the surface, the scene shows the peasants in their desperation to satiate the first of these hungers. But it also evokes the violent measures that the peasants take in striving to satisfy their more metaphorical cravings. For instance, the narrative directly associates the wine with blood, noting that some of the peasants have acquired "a tigerish smear about the mouth" and portraying a drunken figure scrawling the word "blood" on the wall with a wine-dipped finger. Indeed, the blood of aristocrats later spills at the hands of a mob in these same streets.

Throughout the novel, Dickens sharply criticizes this mob mentality, which he condemns for perpetrating the very cruelty and oppression from which the revolutionaries hope to free themselves. The scene surrounding the wine cask is the novel's first tableau of the mob in action. The mindless frenzy with which these peasants scoop up the fallen liquid prefigures the scene at the grindstone, where the revolutionaries sharpen their weapons, as well as the dancing of the macabre Carmagnole.

Madame Defarge's Knitting

Even on a literal level, Madame Defarge's knitting constitutes a whole network of symbols. Into her needlework she stitches a registry, or list of names, of all those condemned to die in the name of a new republic. But on a metaphoric level, the knitting constitutes a symbol in itself, representing the stealthy, cold-blooded vengefulness of the revolutionaries. As Madame Defarge sits quietly knitting, she appears harmless and quaint. In fact, however, she sentences her victims to death. Similarly, the French peasants may appear simple and humble figures, but they eventually rise up to massacre their oppressors.

Dickens's knitting imagery also emphasizes an association between vengefulness and fate, which, in Greek mythology, is traditionally linked to knitting or weaving. The Fates, three sisters who control human life, busy themselves with the tasks of weavers or seamstresses: one sister spins the web of life, another measures it, and the last cuts it. Madame Defarge's knitting thus becomes a symbol of her victims' fate—death at the hands of a wrathful peasantry.

The Marquis

The Marquis Evrémonde is less a believable character than an archetype of an evil and corrupt social order. He is not only overly self-indulgent, as evidenced by the train of attendants who help him to drink his chocolate; he is also completely indifferent to the lives of the peasants whom he exploits, as evidenced by his lack of sympathy for the father of the child whom his carriage tramples to death. As such, the Marquis stands as a symbol of the ruthless aristocratic cruelty that the French Revolution seeks to overcome.

DESIRE AND THE IDEOLOGY OF VIOLENCE: AMERICA IN CHARLES DICKENS'S 'MARTIN CHUZZLEWIT'

by Robert E. Lougy

You preachers of equality, the tyrannomania of impotence clamors out of you for equality: your most secret ambitions to be tyrants thus shroud themselves in words of virtue. Aggrieved conceit, repressed envy—perhaps the conceit and envy of your fathers—erupt from you as a flame and as the frenzy of revenge.

Friedrich Nietzsche, Thus Spake Zarathrustra

Jacques Lacan has described with some eloquence how our lives are surrounded or "enveloped," even before we are born, by symbolic structures that precede our entrance into this world:

Symbols in fact envelop the life of man in a network so total that they join together, before he comes into the world, those who are going to engender him "by flesh and blood"; so total that they bring to his birth, along with the gift of the stars, if not with the gift of the fairies, the shape of his destiny; so total that they give the words that will make him faithful or renegade, the laws of the acts that will follow him right to the place where he is not yet and even beyond his death.

Dickens too was fascinated with the various configurations that destinies can assume and with how we are born into a network of signifiers that govern not only our birth into the social order, but also our exit from it. Intrigued by the ways in which we are the unconscious heirs of codes and laws that constitute human culture, Dickens realises that the shape of our destiny, if not bestowed by the stars or fairies, is the gift of equally ambiguous or mysterious forces. This fascination is evident in Dickens's earliest writings—for example, the "Madman's Manuscript" in The Pickwick

Papers—but it seems particularly true of Martin Chuzzlewit. Although the original title and epigraph for the novel were deleted by Dickens before it was published in its three-volume format in 1844, their presence within the genealogy of the text, like those buried archeological artifacts that Freud compared to the unconscious, enables us to trace the evolution of the text's form and to see how sharply it focused from its very beginning, in fact, on questions of genealogy, kinship, and family structure. The original title charted out for its readers those family dynamics that would be explored in the rest of the novel, making it clear that if they wanted to understand the House of Chuzzlewit, they had to read all of the history in front of them, for it alone provided "a Complete Key to the House of Chuzzlewit": "The Life and Adventures of Martin Chuzzlewit / His Relatives, Friends, and Enemies. / Comprising All His Wills and Ways: / With an Historical Record of What He Did, and What He Didn't: / Showing, Moreover, Who Inherited the Family Plate, Who Came in for the Silver Spoons, / The Whole Forming a Complete Key to the House of Chuzzlewit."

And while the title of Martin Chuzzlewit announced to its readers those questions of kinship and family that the rest of the novel would continue to explore, the epigraph that Dickens had intended to use—"Scene: your own house. Characters: yourselves"—apprised them of the fact that even as they read the history in front of them, they too were implicated in its narrative, since it told of matters concerning not only the House of the Chuzzlewits, but their own houses and themselves as well. The first chapter develops these questions yet still further, tracing the relationship between the Chuzzlewits and what Dickens refers to as "the antiquity of the race," as it follows the lineage of the Chuzzlewit family back to Adam and Eve. Martin Chuzzlewit is in fact haunted by the ways in which violent and unconscious aggressive traits are passed on from one generation to the next.

Tracing through the Chuzzlewits as Ur-family how particular characteristics of the human race, the "hereditary tastes" of each generation, are passed on "through the lives of their unconscious inheritors" (, emphasis mine), the narrator reminds us of how such characteristics or "tastes" are phylogenetically and ontogenetically encoded in our history. He reflects, for example, on how the roots of human "violence and vagabondism" can be traced back to Cain and Abel and to other subsequent "divers slaughterous conspiracies and bloody frays". Guy Fawkes's otherwise total inexplicable place in the Chuzzlewit family tree makes sense as an ancestral presence whose regicidal history anticipates other narratives of Oedipal desire and conflict (especially the story of attempted parricide involving Jonas and Anthony Chuzzlewit) woven into the English sections of the novel. As such, he is a mysterious ancestor not only in the Chuzzlewit family tree, but in all family trees and thus is also present in the American sections as well. For by the time young Martin and Mark Tapley arrive in America, Guy Fawkes is already there, his history anticipating those transgressions against authority and patriarchy that have been written into America's myths of its origin and destiny.

The unconscious, Freud reminds us, is eternal and timeless, and both the English and American sections of Martin Chuzzlewit chart the return of ancient and powerful stories plotted along what Ellie Ragland-Sullivan has referred to as the "path of repetition in the here and now." However, in the American episodes of the novel, these timeless stories assume their own particular paths and narrative patterns. The stormy and complex history of Dickens's relationship with America resembles that of a painful love affair, for it is a tale of love and hate, dreams nurtured and then betrayed. The editors of the third volume of the Pilgrim Edition of Dickens's letters, by far the single most important source for anyone interested in the full history of that relationship, suggest that Dickens's response to America moved from "delighted gratification at his welcome to disenchantment and even repulsion." As they also point out, "English travellers naturally read each others' books" (L, viii), and Dickens too, prior to his first American visit, read the writings of those who had preceded him to America, including Harriet Martineau's three-volume work,

Society in America (1837) and Retrospect of Western Travel (1838) and Marryat's A Diary in America (1839). After he returned from America, he also spoke warmly of Mrs. Trollope's Domestic Manners of the Americans (1832).

But however many earlier travellers Dickens might have read, the representation of America that we find in Martin Chuzzlewit is distinctly its own, differing not only from those that come before it, but also from Dickens's earlier American Notes as well. In writing to Forster of his American experiences, Dickens speaks of "the sublimated essence of comicality that I could distill, from the materials I have" (L, xv, emphasis Dickens's), and given the often abrasive as well as subversive nature of Dickens's comic vision, it should not surprise us that Dickens's America is a more disturbing and compelling landscape than that charted by his predecessors. For in Martin Chuzzlewit, we find a particular tale of national identity and repressed desire.

Questions of kinship and genealogy are at the heart of both the English and American sections of Martin Chuzzlewit, but the latter focus more on the question of human nature itself—in other words, on the relationship between human and nature, and specifically the ways in which we as human subjects cannot remain within nature, but rather must enter into those various symbolic structures that constitute culture. Introduced into the novel as early as the first chapter with its references to the eighteenth-century theories of Blumenbach and Monboddo, both concerned with the origin and nature of human nature, as they respectively trace our beginnings back to the swine or the orang-outang, this particular line of inquiry also suggests the degree to which, as is often the case, Dickens's concerns reflect those central philosophical questions of his age. Rousseau's and Marx's formulations, for example, concerning the relationship between the human and the natural are in this particular case especially helpful in amplifying those issues explored by Martin Chuzzlewit.

Readers such as Magnet and Meckier have spoken of Dickens's disillusionment with America—not only of his disenchantment with the American experiment itself, but also of his loss of faith in Rousseau's vision of nature and the possibilities of human fulfillment or happiness within it. However, one could argue that it is not so much a matter of Dickens having abandoned Rousseau's visions as of his having come closer to some of the more troubling or ambiguous aspects of that vision. Like Dickens, Rousseau found the relationship between the natural and the human to be problematic, arguing that sublimation and repression, the price we must pay to enter human culture, take their toll in fire, war, and other manifestations of violence and aggression. In the ninth chapter of his On the Origin of Languages, for example, Rousseau ponders the question of what could have prompted human beings to exchange a life of nature for a life of language and culture: "the earth nourishes men," he writes, "but when their initial needs have dispersed them, other needs arise, and it is only then that they speak, and that they have any incentive to speak".But why, he asks, would they ever give up a life of nature, especially when the "life of language and culture" inevitably leads to misery and crime: how could they "ever be induced to give up their primitive liberty" and create a society that "leads to property, government, and laws, and gradually to the misery and crime that are inseparable from the knowledge of good and evil".In his commentary on this chapter, Derrida suggests that "there is something catastrophic in the movement that brings about the emergence from the state of nature and in the awakening of the imagination", observing that such a movement for Rousseau is inextricably associated with the interdiction of incest, the need to prevent, as Rousseau expresses it, a man and woman from becoming "husband and wife without ceasing to be brother and sister". Only after the festival, Rousseau's image of human community and ritual, did incest become a transgressive act. Before that time, Rousseau suggests, "instinct held the place of passion, habit held the place of preference".

In his Economic and Philosophic Manuscripts of 1844, Marx does not raise the question of incest, but he similarly argues that human history is the story of our origins or beginnings in nature and also of our alienation from it. Marx points out, for example, that when we observe that "man's physical and spiritual life is linked to nature," we are really only saying that "nature is linked to itself, for man is a part of nature."Yet, Marx also stresses the fact that human history involves our estrangement from nature: "the nature which comes to bear in human history," he writes, "the genesis of human society—is man's real nature; hence nature as it comes to be through industry, even though in an estranged form, is true anthropological nature" (emphasis Marx's). We can come into full realization of consciousness, Marx argues, only within a social community that enables us to realise our "natural" or human capabilities. Transcendence of alienation is brought about not through an attempt to escape or flee from the human, but rather by embracing its possibilities within a society forged through history as shaped by the activity of men and women: thus Marx defines "communism" as the "complete return of man to himself as a social (i.e., human) being—a return become conscious, and accomplished within the entire wealth of previous development." It is, he suggests, "the genuine resolution of the conflict between man and nature and man and man", a state in which humanism and naturalism are no longer at odds, but rather are the equal of one another.

Dickens, as one might expect, approaches these questions from different angles than either Rousseau or Marx, but the questions themselves are strikingly similar. Magnet points out, for example, that Martin Chuzzlewit focuses "on how radically far from being a pure production of nature the truly human being is". In the America of Martin Chuzzlewit, however, Rousseau's festival becomes the psychic inversion of itself, an abnormal or grotesque celebration of a vision of community that even as it attempts to reject the human has its origins in Oedipal violence and transgressive incestuous desires. Similarly there is in Martin Chuzzlewit no resolution, genuine or otherwise, of that conflict between man and nature that Marx speaks of, even though the Americans speak ad nauseam of their reintegration back into a natural realm or kingdom.

Anticipating various modern and postmodern novels that have explored the ways in which psychoanalytic dynamics are textualized within the body politic of a nation, Martin Chuzzlewit suggests if we wish to understand the ways in which the repressed is inscribed as narrative within America's history, we must regard its language, myths, and legends as symptomatic gestures that disclose a desire whose presence remains repressed. "The powerful fiction," suggests Peter Brooks, "is that which is able to restage the complex and buried past history of desire as it covertly reconstitutes itself in the present language."Martin Chuzzlewit, I will argue, exemplifies such "powerful fiction" as it too restages this past history of desire. In so far as I will be examining those psychoanalytic dynamics of repression as they are inscribed in Dickens's fiction, I am pursuing paths of inquiry travelled earlier by others, going back at least as far as Edmund Wilson's groundbreaking "The Two Scrooges" and including a number of more recent studies. The distinctions between the directions of their inquiries and my own will, I trust, be evident. Jacques Lacan taught his students that "you must start from the text, start by treating it, as Freud does and as he recommends, as Holy Writ.

> The author, the scribe, is only a pen pusher, and he comes second.... please give more attention to the text than the psychology of the author—the entire orientation of my teaching is that." Following Lacan's advice, I too would argue that the text always knows more than the author does. I am interested in exploring the particular nature of the repressed desire that we find in Martin Chuzzlewit and the ways in which it drives the plot of the American sections of the novel. For although this history constitutes the repressed or "censored chapter" of the novel, it is neverthless a story that makes itself known.

Chapter 14

Critics on Dickens Work

by John L. Colle

At one of our many meetings held this past year where curriculum was developed, we learned that the one freshman literature book available however, that studying *A Tale of Two Cities* as the anthology presents it, is a less than satisfying experience for both me and for my students. As a teacher interested in having my students get as much possible from reading such a classic, I chose my topic in order to enhance the novel's teachability and its rewards. I also chose this particular novel because I love the book and have wanted for a number of years to increase my knowledge of it and of its background.

Many questions about *A Tale of Two Cities* have surfaced in my teaching the novel questions which I think need answering. What, for example, did historians or philosophers during the latter part of the eighteenth century think of the French Revolution? What did Dickens, himself a Victorian, think of it sixty years after it had occurred? And finally, what are the best ways to teach such a novel to students who may be reluctant to read any extended prose work?

Edmund Burke (1729-97), the Irish philosopher and public figure, is a man worth looking at because of his extensive treatment of the uprising in *Reflections on the Revolution in France* (1790). According to Samuel Johnson, Burke devoted his life to five causes: "the preservation of the English

Constitution, the emancipation of Ireland, the emancipation of the American Colonies, the protection of the people of India from the misgovernment of the East India Company, and opposition to the ravages of the French Revolution."[1] Burke, however, was not only opposed to the "ravages of the French Revolution," he was opposed to the Revolution *per se*. His *Reflections*, which began as a correspondence between Burke and a Parisian gentleman, was later expanded into a treatise but retained the letter form he had begun with his French friend. Burke plainly saw the French Revolution as unnecessary.

Were all these dreadful things necessary? Were they the inevitable results of the desperate struggle of determined patriots, compelled to wade through blood and tumult, to the quiet shore of a tranquil and prosperous liberty? No! nothing like it. The fresh ruins of France, which shock our feelings wherever we can turn our eyes, are not the devastation of civil war; they are the sad but instructive monuments of rash and ignorant counsel in time of profound peace. They are the display of inconsiderate and presumptuous, because unresisted and irresistible authority. The persons who have thus squandered away the precious treasure of their crimes, the persons who have made this prodigal and wild waste of public evils (the last stake reserved for the ultimate ransom of the state) have met in their progress with little, or rather with no opposition at all.

Their whole march was more like a triumphal procession than the progress of a war. Their pioneers have gone before them, and demolished and laid every thing level at their feet. Not one drop of *their* blood have they shed in the cause of the country they have ruined. They have made no sacrifices to their projects of greater consequence than their shoe-buckles, whilst they were imprisoning their king, murdering their fellow citizens, and bathing in tears, and plunging in poverty and distress, thousands of worthy men and worthy families. Their cruelty has not even been the base result of fear. It has been the effect of their sense of perfect safety, in authorizing treasons, robberies, rapes, assassinations, slaughters, and burnings throughout their harassed land.

Burke argued that the form of government instituted after the revolution was not a democracy, as Frenchmen were fond of calling it, but a "mischievous and ignoble oligarchy." He agreed with the ancients that an absolute democracy, like an absolute monarchy, is a legitimate form of government. But he cautioned that in a democracy, "the majority of the citizens is capable of exercising the most cruel oppressions upon the minority, whenever strong divisions prevail in that kind of polity, as they often must; and that oppression of the minority will extend to far greater numbers, and will be carried on with much greater fury, than can almost ever by apprehended from the dominion of a single scepter." Even under a cruel leader, he contended, the poor have other poor people to help assuage their wounds; in a democracy, they are deserted by others because they have become "overpowered by a conspiracy of their whole species." Burke agreed that the French government had needed reform, but he questioned why the 'Whole fabric should be at once pulled down, and the area cleared for the erection of a theoretic experiment edifice in its place."

Furthermore, the monarchy only *appeared* bad. As to the "all-atoning name" of liberty, Burke saw precious little of it when traveling in France. Instead, he saw an "oppressive degrading servitude. Forming a new government was, in Burke's view, a rather easy undertaking, as was giving freedom; but forming a free government was a task no one in France could achieve.

But had the Revolution achieved any good? Burke agreed that "among an infinite number of acts of violence and folly, some good may have been done. They who destroy every thing certainly will remove some grievance."The king, he argued, could have accomplished, or was intending to accomplish, the same things.

Edmund Burke, then, surely objected to the ravages of the revolution, but he condemned equally those who incited the revolt against the French monarchy. To him, the revolution was an attack on the settled institutions of society which he considered to be the only basis and guarantee of human liberty.

I do not expect all of my students to read Burke—he is perhaps a little too heavy for them. I do want them to see, however, that there is more than one side to any historical event. I may read a passage or two to my students, or, better yet, I may send a few of the more interested students to do a little research on their own. If they are captivated by Burke's prose, I may steer them to Paul Fussell:s *The Rhetorical* World of Augustan *Humanism*, an excellent book analyzing Burke's use of imagery and his rhetoric. Fussell says, for example, that in Burke's *Reflections*, certain passages are "so gorgeous, the effect so commandingly contrived, the issues so central to the conduct of human life" that they "deserved to be excerpted, bound in limp black leather, and appointed to be read in churches on Sundays."

Thomas Paine (1737-1809), the author of *Common Sense*, who did much to inspire the American Revolution, summarily answered Burke's condemnation of the French Revolution. In a treatise entitled *The Rights of Man*, which was sent to President George Washington, Paine complained that Burke's treatise was filled with "flagrant misrepresentations," and "that while it is an outrageous abuse on the French Revolution, and the principles of Liberty, it is an imposition on the rest of the world." Implying that Burke was fearful that England and France would cease to be enemies, Paine maintained that Burke had written his treatise because "there are men in all countries who get their living by war" and who "make it their study to sow discord, and cultivate prejudices between nations."

Paine condemned Burke's treatise of nearly four hundred pages as being filled with almost every abusive epithet found in the English language. However, his own railing at Burke is also forcefully worded. For example:

Hitherto Mr. Burke has been mistaken and disappointed in the opinions he had formed of the affairs of France; but such is the ingenuity of his hope, or the malignancy of his despair, that it furnished him with new pretenses to go on. There was a time when it was impossible to make Mr. Burke believe there would be any revolution in France. His opinion then was, that the French had neither spirit to undertake it, nor fortitude to support it; and now that there is one, he seeks an escape by condemning it.

Burke, according to Paine, made no distinction between *men* and *principles*. Because of this, Burke was unable to see that the revolt took place against the despotism of principles rather than the despotism of the king. Even though Louis XVI was a moderate, according to Paine, he nevertheless did nothing to change the tyrannies of the former reigns; it was this and other despotisms—the monarchy, parliament, church, ministerial policies in general, and feudalism itself—that precipitated the revolt. Finally, when the Bastille was taken, says Paine, its downfall "included the idea of the downfall to despotism; and this compounded image was become as figuratively united as Bunyan's Doubting Castle and Giant Despair."

Paine is a joy to read. His prose is clear, and his invective cuts like a double-edged sword. He is *fun* to real, too; I may even read my class this excerpt, which I am sure students will enjoy:

Mr. Burke, who does not call himself a madman, whatever other people may do, has libeled, in the most unprovoked manner, and in the grossest style of the most vulgar abuse, the whole representative authority of France; and yet Mr. Burke takes his seat in the British House of Commons!

From his violence and his grief, his silence on some points, and his excess on others, it is difficult not to believe that Mr. Burke is sorry, extremely sorry, that arbitrary power, the power of the Pope, and the Bastille, are pulled down.

Not one glance of compassion, not one commiserating reflection, that I can find throughout his book, has he bestowed on those who lingered out the most wretched of lives, a life without hope, in the most miserable of prisons.

It is painful to behold a man employing his talents to corrupt himself. Nature has been kinder to Mr. Burke than he is to her. He is not affected by the reality of distress touching his heart, but by the showy resemblage of it striking his imagination. He pities the plumage, but forgets the dying bird.

Accustomed to kiss the aristocratical hand that hath purloined him from himself, he degenerates into a composition of art, and the genuine soul of nature forsakes him. His hero or his heroine must be a tragedyvictim expiring in show, and not the real prisoner of mystery, sinking into death in the silence of a dungeon.

The students may ask at this point, "With whom—Burke or Paine—does Charles Dickens himself agree?" They will be able to answer this question after delving into the novel and reading closely Chapter VII, "Monseigneur in Town," of the *Tale*. In this chapter the Monseigneur, here used to personify the French aristocracy, is about to drink his chocolate. Dickens writes:

Monseigneur could swallow a great many things with ease, and was by some few sullen minds supposed to be rapidly swallowing France; but his morning:s chocolate could not so much as get into the throat of Monseigneur, without the aid of four strong men besides the Cook.

Yes. It took four men, all four ablaze with gorgeous decoration, and the Chief of them unable to exist with fewer than two gold watches in his pocket, emulative of the noble and chaste fashion set by Monseigneur, to conduct the happy chocolate to Monseigneur's lips. One lackey carried the chocolate pot into the sacred presence; a second milled and frothed the chocolate with the little instrument he bore for that function; a third presented the favoured napkin; a fourth—he of the two gold watches—poured the chocolate out. It was impossible for Monseigneur to dispense with one of these attendants... he must have died of two.

In the same chapter Monsieur the Marquis, who also personifies the pampered aristocracy who is one of the truly despicable characters in the novel, heartlessly runs down a child and considers the accident a mere inconvenience to him and a hazard to his horses. Students are quick to understand the Marquis's total lack of compassion when Dickens has the aristocrat say:

"It is extraordinary to me," said he, "that you people cannot take care of yourselves and your children. One or the other of you is forever in the way. How do I know what injury you have done my horses? See! Give him that."

The Marquis thinks that magnanimously tossing a gold coin to the grieving father more than compensates for his dead child. Even the more unsophisticated student will grasp this heartless gesture of the Marquis and the unfeeling attitude of the aristocracy toward the downtrodden masses. From there, it is a short step to their understanding that Dickens's attitudes towards the Revolution are closer to Paine's than they are to Burke's.

At this point students should be introduced to Thomas Carlyle. That Carlyle was a friend and admirer of Dickens is shown in this short anecdote: When Dickens asked Carlyle for some material on the French Revolution, Carlyle actually sent two cartloads from the London Library! In fact, Dickens thanked Carlyle in t he preface of his novel; the novelist supposedly used many details from Carlyle's history, *The French Revolution*. The better students in the class might be directed to a few chapters or so of Carlyle's history. For example, the storming of the Bastille is particularly interesting. Carlyle writes,

And so it lashes and it roars. Cholat the wine-merchant has become an impromptu cannoneer.... Let conflagration rage; of whatsoever is combustible! Guard-rooms are burnt, Invalides mess-rooms.... Straw is burnt; three cartloads of it, hauled thither, go up in white smoke: almost to the choking of Patriotism itself.... How the great Bastille clock ticks (inaudible) in its Inner Court there, at its ease, hour after hour; as if nothing special, for it or the world, were passing! It tolled One when the firing began; and is now pointing towards Five, and still the firing slakes not.—Far down, in their vaults, the seven Prisoners hear muffled din as of earthquakes; their Turnkeys answer vaguely.... For four hours now has the World-Bedlam roared: call it the World-Chimaera, blowing fire!... the Bastille is fallen! *Victoire! La Bastille est*

The students should then compare Dickens's account of the storming.

He writes:

Deep ditches, double drawbridge, massive stone walls, eight great towers, cannon, muskets, fire, and smoke. Through the fire and through the smoke—in the fire and in the smoke, for the sea cast him up against a cannon, and on the instant he became a cannoneer—Defarge of the wine shop worked like a manful soldier, two fierce hours... grown doubly hot by the service of four fierce hours. A white flag from within the fortress, and a parley—suddenly the sea rose and swept Defarge of the wine shop over the lowered drawbridge, past the massive stone outer walls, in among the eight great towers surrendered!

Then, too, students might see the similarities between the Manettes' flight from Paris and Carlyle's account of Louis XVI and Marie Antoinette's near-escape from the revolutionaries. Carlyle writes:

The eyes of the Villagers look enlightened, as such eyes do when a coach-transit, which is an event, occurs for them. Strolling Dragoons respectfully, so fine are the yellow liveries, bring hand to helmet; and a Lady in gypsy-hat responds with a grace peculiar to her.

That Lady in slouched gypsy-hat, though sitting back in carriage, does she not resemble some one we have seen, some time;—at the Feast of Pikes, or elsewhere? And this *Grosse-Tete* in round hat and peruke, which, looking rearward, pokes itself out from time to time, methinks there are features in it? Quick, Sieur Guillaume, Clerk of the *Directoire,* bring me a new Assignat! Drouet scans the new Assignat; compares the Paper-money Picture with the Gross Head in round hat there: by Day and Night! you might say the one was an attempted Engraving of the other. And this march of Toops; this sauntering and whispering,—I see it!

If students read Carlyle closely, they will quickly see that Dickens not only borrowed a few cartloads of materials from Carlyle, but he adopted much of his social philosophy, tone, and subject matter as well.

As mentioned earlier, for years now I have wondered how critics viewed *A Tale of Two Cities;* and in doing some research on the critics of Dickens, I found as many who condemned the novel as praised it. For example, when *Tale* was published in 1859, it was scarcely noticed by the reviewers, according to Professor Michael Wolff, "but, where noticed, almost universally scorned." And James Fitzjames Stephens (?), in an unsigned review in *The Uncommercial Traveller, Saturday* called the novel "melodramatic, pretentious, and above all, deadly dull." G. K. Chesterton thought that Dickens entirely missed the intellectual side of the French Revolution. Finally, Louis Cazamian had some scathing comments on Dickens the writer, and many of these apply to Dickens' *Tale*. He wrote:

His faults in taste and in style, the failings of his intuitive verve, are obvious; his literary individuality lacks polish. He sacrifices balance for the sake of intense effects; his expression obeys monotonous habits; he repeats himself to excess. His pathos is cheap or exaggerated; his imagination in its continual effort to emphasize the character of things tends rather to distort them; his vision, fond of agitated outlines, is apt to lose the very sense of repose.... At every turn in his stories, we come upon the favourable or unfavourable opinions of the author—a kind of sentimental commentary on his own work; and these instances of bias, intensified by polemical preferences and arguments, too often bore or annoy the reader.

Yet even Chesterton added that in terms of dignity and eloquence, Two Cities "almost stands alone among the books by Dickens." And notwithstanding Dickens's faults, Cazamian feels that Dickens is "the most national, the most typical, and the greatest [author] of them all." Wilkie Collins, whose play

The Frozen Deep is alluded to in Dickens s preface to the novel, called *Two Cities* Dickens's "most perfect work of constructive art," and Dickens himself wrote: "I hope it is the best story I have written." However, it is the book itself which is the main concern here—not its sources, not what others thought about it, and not even what Dickens himself thought of it. The real question remains: Can the book succeed with inner-city students who may be reluctant to read such a classic?

I firmly believe it can, depending on the approach. I recently came across, quite by accident, a New Haven curriculum guide published in the summer of 1970. Although the guides approach to the novel is somewhat general, it nevertheless has some good points for teaching a book like *A Tale of Two Cities*. It is a low-keyed approach, one purporting to develop confidence in students who dislike or mistrust novels as a genre. I have included the approach in the following pages, and I suggest strongly that each teacher modify or expand it as he/she sees fit. (The third part of the approach, "Narration," is given as an example below.)

In this approach, the teacher is encouraged to become a "book pimp," using any device that might attract a reluctant reader. In this case, perhaps a vivid description of the guillotine might be a good attention-getter or pimping device for the students. In *Outlooks* we find a fairly comprehensive description of the guillotine, but it comes too late in the book to interest the students much. Before beginning the book, then, students might read or be read the following:

Dr. Joseph I. Guillotin, a surgeon and a member of the Revolutionary Assembly, proposed in 1789 that persons condemned to death be executed swiftly and mercifully by a beheading machine, which thereafter came to bear his name. Before the revolution only French nobles had the privilege of being decapitated for capital crimes; common people were hanged, broken on the wheel, burned at the stake, or tortured to death on the rack. Guillotin sought a quick, painless, uniform method of execution to be used democratically for all condemned persons, regardless of rank.... The victim was strapped to a board and then laid horizontally on a table, which extended at right angles from the base of the upright posts. His neck was confined in a round opening between two planks, the upper one of which could be raised and then lowered. Since the falling blade would cover the round opening, the head would be severed from the body. In front of the opening was an oblong trough or basket to receive the head, and on the right of the table was a large wicker-work basket to receive the body.... Between August 10, 1792 and July 31, 1794, approximately 20,000 persons were executed. Though no longer used for political terrorism, the guillotine remains today the legal *method of execution in France.*

The approach mentioned above gives five "handles"—terms used, I imagine, for devices whereby students may gain a feeling of control and of mastery of the text in question. The first handle is entitled "Data," and the teacher should encourage students to write in their notebooks, after having read the first chapter, their answers to the following:

1. When?
2. Where?
3. What time?
4. Who?
5. Who speaks?
6. Who listens?
7. Who does what?
8. Why?

One good feature about the Outlooks edition is that the first chapter, "The Period," is left almost intact. This is the famous chapter beginning, "It was the best of times, it was the worst of times." Several other school editions of the novel have omitted it entire! At any rate, the questions above are so basic that any one will able to answer them and feel he has mastered much of the material, even if he actually has not.

At this point, perhaps, some general background information about the revolution can be given the students. I think the approach may vary, for we know that lecturing might be fine for some students, but doing research in the library might be better for others. I firmly believe, though, that students should have the information before they get very far in the novel.

For the interested teacher, an excellent background introduction to the novel can be found in the abridged version of *Two Cities* edited by Youngham. The introduction is complete—covering biographical sketches of Louis XVI and Marie Antoinette, court life during the Old Regime, the extravagance of the King:s house, the King s *levée*, Versailles, the dress of the period, the people of France, the three estates, taxes, the Bastille, Louis's attempt at reform, the guillotine, and the Reign of Terror. A sample which would interest students follows:

Can you imagine yourself as a fashionable young man or woman living at the time of Louis XVI and Marie Antoinette? As a gentleman of those days, you would have worn a triangular cocked hat on your powdered hair, which would be tied back with a black ribbon. Your coat, of satin, possibly striped in light blue and pink, would be open to disclose an elaborate waistcoat and knee-length breeches of pale yellow, trimmed with pink bindings and blue buttons. Your long white silk stockings, embroidered with blue clocks and fastened by blue garters, would show to advantage your well-shaped leg, for you would make a sorry figure in the minuet if your legs did not measure up to the current idea of manly good looks. In addition, as a well-dressed gentleman of fashion, you would wear silver buckles on your black shoes, a ring on your finger, and you would carry a handsome jewelled or enameled snuffbox which would be used with exaggeratedly graceful gestures as you flirted back your long, ruffled lace cuffs.

As a lady of the late eighteenth century, your dress would be elaborate and heavy in contrast to the delicacy of the gentleman's costume. The material of stiff brocade would be fashioned into a long whale-boned waist, beneath which would billow a skirt with panniers or heavy folds looped over the hips. Down the front would show a petticoat trimmed with lace, velvet bows, and artificial flowers. Most characteristic of the period, however, would be the mountainous headdress which you, as a lady in keeping with the times, would wear. Coiffures varied from one to three feet in height, and were so intricate in design that they could not often be taken down or combed.

Students also would enjoy seeing paintings and drawings showing the strange costumes of the period, Several excellent books are given in the bibliography section of this paper. Showing the costumes on the opaque projector would really interest the students. Perhaps, too, bringing to class a plastic back-scratcher might be a good idea, for the original back-scratcher was used, not for the back, but for the perukes which sometimes reached a height of six feet and which would become verminous between trips to the hairdresser!

The second handle in the approach is entitled "Character," a crucial part in teaching Dickens. Indeed, as one critic writes, "To think of Dickens is first of all to remember the great characters." I have found that students have no trouble remembering Madam Defarge—in fact, many think she is the novel's protagonist—or Sydney Carton. To be sure, these characters are drawn so that we do remember them, and it plea se s me and the students when, at the end of the school year, they still remember the names covered back in September or October. I have found that one way to insure that everyone will have a good chance to remember the characters is to make the students write in their notebooks the names of any new characters as they appear in the novel. It might be useful, also, to include the scenes in which there appears to be any kind of character change, for change is important if we later want to teach the difference between the static and dynamic characters. As a device to aid students' understanding of character, the teacher might indicate the following points for students to remember when working with character:

1. What the character says about others.
2. What the character says about himself.
3. What other people say about him.

4. What he has done before.
5. What he thinks.
6. What he does.
7. How he does it.

While it is true that in English literature, Dickens probably is second only to Shakespeare in the number of memorable characters created, students do have trouble remembering some others from *Tale*.[25] There are undoubtedly good reasons for this. Jerry Cruncher, for example, is not very memorable, although students find his secondary occupation an interesting one. But before we think Dickens did a shoddy piece of writing with this humourous character, we must remember that with *Tale*, Dickens was experimenting a bit. He actually tried to subdue his typical comic extravagances and even his dialogue. In a letter to his friend, John Forster, Dickens wrote that his new novel was a "picturesque story, rising in every chapter with characters true to nature, but whom t should express, more than they should express themselves, by dialogue."[26] Plot, then, at least as far as this novel is concerned, is primary. In spite of this, however, I hope that students will be able to see for themselves how insipid Lucie and Charles Darnay are.

The third handle in the above approach is "Narration," intended also to clear a student's perspective on how the story is told. Here the student should be told to look for the following:

1. The story just happening.
2. A character telling the story.
3. A hero-character telling the story.
4. A combination of any of the above.

Earlier in the paper I mentioned that teachers should modify or expand these "handles." My modification might look like this:

1. **Read the first paragraph in Book I, Chapter III, "The Night Shadows" (pp. 454-6), and answer the following questions:**

a. Who is the "I" in this paragraph? Is it Dickens or the narrator?

b. What does the "I" mean when he says, "A wonderful fact to reflect upon, that every human creature is constituted to be that profound secret and mystery to every other"?

c. Why does Dickens begin his chapter in the first person and then switch to the third person in the second paragraph?

2. Read the third paragraph, column B, of Chapter IV, "The Preparation" (p. 461), and answer the following:

a. Why is this paragraph in parentheses?

b. Why does Dickens say that Mr. Lorry's reflection was "breathless"?

c. Why would a narrator want us, the readers, to know what is in Mr. Lorry's mind at this point?

d. Is the paragraph in question really necessary? What would be lost without it?

3. Read the last two sentences of Chapter XVIII, "Echoing Footsteps" p. 533), and answer the following:

a. Who is hoping that the footsteps of Saint Antoine never enter Lucie Darnay's life?

b. What does the above tell us about the narrator?

c. What does the above tell us about Dickens?

As teachers we should be able to elicit correct responses concerning the sometimes fine line between the narrator and the author. Students will probably argue that the line is always a fine one, but we must remember that their reading has been scanty at best. Moreover, many read for plot alone. They have not yet learned to appreciate the finer points. For a more in-depth coverage of the narrator in literature, see Booth's *The Rhetoric of Fiction*.

The fourth handle, "Plot," comes only after students have read into the book and feel comfortable with the facts. The teacher could ask them to do the following:

1. Strip plot to essential details.
2. Indicate what they have eliminated from the novel.
3. Indicate what elements they would add first if they were reconstructing the novel.
4. When, if at any time, did they have a tip-off that something was going to happen? (See below for the element of foreshadowing.)
5. How logical" was the chain of events?
6. What seemed real to them?
7. How do they test for reality in a book?

After that, one might go on to describe different kinds of plots and to talk about sequence and chronology. Students should have a good time with this, since there is a flashback near the end of the novel, taking the students back to 1767, eighteen years prior to the beginning of the novel! At this point in the approach the students should be ready to embellish the action with details, and the teacher should ask them for alternative actions and alternative details.

The most interesting handle, at least for some students, might be the fifth handle, "Setting." I can already see them doing well, especially with the second chapter, "The Mail," where Jerry Cruncher meets Mr. Lorry on the Dover road. The following series of questions should be placed on the board:

1. Where?
2. What does it look like?
3. What does it smell like?
4. What would you touch there?
5. When did it last rain?
6. How hot or cold is it?
7. Are the characters sweating or shivering?
8. How does it sound at night?
9. What would you see if you walked around the place?
10. If you were a detective, what would you notice?
11. Would you like to visit or live there?

From there, the students may move on to talk of atmosphere, very often controlled by setting. These questions might prove helpful:

1. What makes atmosphere?
2. How does one describe it?
3. What do you know? *versus* What do you feel?
4. What kinds of details are important to know?
5. What is physical? *versus* What is psychological?

With the above "handles," I feel that almost everyone placed in the average or above-average tracks in the high schools could grasp the riches being offered by Dickens. Certainly, the slower and reluctant reader would approach the novel with less loathing and intrepidation at such bulk. Moreover, we know that *Two Cities* was written in installments and since the chapters are very often short and suspenseful, many students will want to continue to read.

There are a few techniques or activities which might enhance student appreciation of the novel. One good exercise might be having the students guess where each installment ended as Dickens wrote it. Any standard edition will tell where the original installment ended. Another activity is an occasional oral reading of a particular chapter or scene. Students can always increase their oral reading skills this way, and most of them enjoy it. Also, because Dickens was such an avid theatre buff, a few of his chapters can be read play-fashion. Chapter Six, "The Shoemaker," is one that particularly lends itself to dramatic reading. This past year, for example, playing the part of Dr. Manette, I pulled out from around my neck a small locket made from string and paper, in which were several strands of blond hair. Gimmicks such as these are "scorny," as students are fond of pointing out, but I believe they are appreciated at the same time. Furthermore, I will sometimes read an entire chapter to students. They love it as a change from the worksheet and discussion blues. Also, students might wish to adapt a scene they have read into a dramatic presentation.

Something I would like to try next year is to have students make a list of all the foreshadowing elements found in the novel, but they may need a little help at first. Foreshadowing is a technique that every student should master when studying *Tale,* for Dickens uses the technique to perfection. The teacher knows that these clues relate to coming events and will recognize them before the students. For this reason, the students will have to be guided as they read the novel. In Chapter VII of Book I, for example, Gaspard's child is killed by the Marquis's carriage; and in Chapter VIII, Dickens says that the carriage "might have been lighter." After reading the eighth chapter, the teacher should have the students explain the significance of the line.

And in Chapter IX, as the Marquis is awaiting Charles' arrival, he thinks he hears someone outside his window. The reader is not told anything other than that the servant finds no one there lurking about. Finally, when the Marquis is murdered in Chapter X, the students will understand all the clues given earlier. The puzzle finally fits, and no one should have trouble with the plausibility of the actions. The students will enjoy finding examples of foreshadowing after they have been given a little help, and many of them will want to race ahead to see what will happen. The students will want to explain, later in the novel, the significance of the rainstorm in Soho, Darnay's mention of the English prisoner in the London Tower, Miss Pross's strength when she first appears in the novel, Jerry's penchant for funerals, and so on. All of these incidents relate to coming events; the teacher would do well to remind the students about the importance of the incidents as they are first encountered.

Next year, too, I plan to impose upon the good graces of the Yale Film Library to lend us *Two Cities.* Because I like students to make lists of things, we will undoubtedly list the differences between the book and the movie, or we may list the differences between what we pictured from the book and what we actually saw in the movie. These lists, of course, provide good outlines for future compositions, too.

I am rather satisfied with the edition of *Two Cities* in *Outlooks* for the majority of my students, but this year I had a class that could have handled, with possibly a few exceptions, an unbridged version. I might add that an excellent unabridged school edition is published by Macmillan Company. It includes a fair introduction, vocabulary definitions at the bottom of pages, and questions of fact and writer's craft at the back of the book. Another reason I would like to use an unabridged edition for some classes is that in Outlooks some important information is left out.

For example, an entire chapter is omitted where Stryver, an important foil to Carton, foolishly believes that Lucie would enthusiastically accept his proposal of marriage. Humourous incidents such as these are already too few in *Two Cities* to have them omitted willy-nilly! In addition, Lucie's first-born son, who dies from a childhood disease, is omitted in Outlooks. But the best argument by far for reading the unabridged classic is that very often an editor will omit valuable description. I heartily agree with one critic who wrote:

Description, with Dickens, is more than a means; very often it is an end in itself. It contributes to the general effect, but with such varied and powerful resources at its command that it subordinates the other elements of the narrative to itself.

I will be ordering a set of the unabridged version of *Tale* for those teachers who feel that their classes might be able to handle them. These books will be made available at the Hall of Graduate Studies.

Chapter 15

Study Questions

Q1. Critically Analyse Dickens Tale of Two Cities.

Or

Q. How does Dickens combines humour, sentiment, autobiography, spirituality, and both Gothic and realistic elements in his novels?

(Full name Charles John Huffam Dickens; also wrote under the pseudonym of Boz) English novelist, short story writer, dramatist, and essayist.

Although Dickens is perhaps best known for his novels, he wrote short fiction throughout his career, from the early *Sketches by Boz* to the acclaimed Christmas stories and the journalistic *Uncommercial Traveller*. Dickens's short stories, like his longer works, mix humour with macabre imagery to create vivid illustrations of the lives of ordinary people. Designed to uncover social injustices and promote reform in his own time, the endearing characterizations and moving situations presented in Dickens's shorter pieces have appealed to audiences up to the present day; indeed, his short story *A Christmas Carol* is one of his most enduring works.

For much of the Englishspeaking world, this tale has played an important role in defining the Yule spirit; according to May Lamberton Becker, "every year at Christmas time, thousands of families wherever the English language is known would scarcely think Christmas really Christmas without listening to this story read aloud."

Dickens was the son of John Dickens, a minor government official who, because he continually lived beyond his means, was briefly imprisoned for debt. During his father's confinement, the twelve-year-old Dickens was forced to leave home and work in dreadful conditions in a blacking (shoe polish) warehouse. This experience left an indelible impression on Dickens, who portrayed the difficulties of the poor in most of his writings. Late in his teens, Dickens learned shorthand and worked as a reporter. In 1833 he began contributing sketches and short stories to various periodicals. These were eventually compiled into two volumes under the title *Sketches by Boz*. He continued to use serial publication for all of his works, including his novels, for he cherished the constant contact with his readers the method provided. Throughout his career, Dickens gave numerous public readings from his works in both England and America, an activity that left him exhausted. Many believe that increasing physical and mental strain led to the stroke Dickens suffered while working on the novel *The Mystery of Edwin Drood*, which he left unfinished at his death.

In his short fiction, Dickens variously combines humour, sentiment, autobiography, spirituality, and both Gothic and realistic elements. *Sketches by Boz*, provides comic and closely observed characterizations drawn from Victorian London's lower and middle classes. Celebrated stories from this compilation include: "A Visit to Newgate," which details a criminal's final hours before his execution; "The Black Veil," a tale about a woman whose life is evaluated according to the worth of her husband; and "Mr. Minns and His Cousin," which shows that adherence to social conventions can cause misery. Continuing to focus on the lives of ordinary people, Dickens began writing Christmas stories, which include *A Christmas Carol, The Chimes, The Cricket on the Hearth,* and *The Haunted Man and the Ghost's Bargain*. His intention for these tales was, he wrote, "a whimsical kind of masque which the good humour of the season justified, to waken some loving and forbearing thoughts, never out of season in a Christian land." Generally, these books feature fallen protagonists who, through a chain of remarkable, even otherworldly, events, realise the mistakes they have made in life. For example, *A Christmas Carol* chronicles the transformation of Ebenezer Scrooge (Dickens's most famous character) from a miser to a generous being after he receives startling visits from the Ghosts of Christmas Past, Present, and Future.

In *The Chimes* Toby Veck represents members of the lower class who have acceded to society's opinion that the poor are inferior; his conversion involves restoring faith in himself and his class. *The Haunted Man and the Ghost's Bargain*—the most sophisticated version of the common theme in the estimation of many critics—portrays Mr. Redlaw's realization that his new-found ability to erase memories is harmful to others. After writing these holiday tales, Dickens, using material from his own life, penned the more journalistic *The Uncommercial Traveller*. One story in this collection, "Dullborough Town," describes the setting of Dickens's childhood, and another, "City of London Churches," recounts a love affair similar to the writer's first relationship.

Hailed for his comic and journalistic abilities, powerful and provoking depictions of the poor, unforgettable characters, and the moral-filled Christmas stories, Dickens was one of the most successful writers of his time. Enormously popular in England, he was, before he turned thirty, honourably received in America as well. Dickens wrote of the reception: "There never was a king or emperor upon the earth so cheered and followed by crowds, and entertained in public at splendid halls and dinners, and waited on by public bodies and deputations of all kinds." Although some critics have asserted that *Sketches by Boz* focuses too heavily on the lower class and that the author's stories are at times too sentimental and laden with exaggeration, many have extolled them for their expressions of a fundamental faith in humanity and their unflagging censure of social injustice. A. Edward Newton perhaps best summarized the high esteem in which countless readers hold Dickens when he declared that "in the resplendent firmament of English literature there is only one name I would rank above his for sheer genius: Shakespeare."

Q2. Discuss at least one way in which Dickens parallels the personal and the political in A Tale of Two Cities.

In his dual focus on the French Revolution and the individual lives of his characters, Dickens draws many comparisons between the historical developments taking place and the characters' triumphs and travails. Perhaps the most direct example of this parallel comes in the final chapter of the novel, in which Dickens matches Sydney Carton's death with the French Revolution's most frenzied violence, linking the two through the concept of resurrection.

Throughout the novel, Carton struggles to free himself from a life of apathy and meaninglessness while the French lower classes fight for political emancipation. Each of these struggles involves death—Carton decides to give his life so that Charles Darnay may escape, and the revolutionaries make a spectator-sport out of the execution of aristocrats. Still, each struggle holds the promise of renewed life. Nowhere is this promise more evident than in the prophecy that the narrator ascribes to Carton at the novel's end. Here, Carton envisions a new city rising up from the ashes of the ruined Paris as clearly as he sees Lucie, Darnay, and their son celebrating and extending his life as a man of worth and honour. Dickens thus closes his novel with a note of triumphant hope both political and personal.

Q3. One of the novel's most important motifs is the figure of the double. What is the effect of Dickens's doubling technique? Does he use doubles to draw contrasts, comparisons, or both?

From early on in the novel, various characters seemed paired as opposites. Darnay, for instance, appears capable and accomplished, while Carton seems lazy and lacks ambition. Similarly, Miss Pross represents respectable English order while Madame Defarge embodies its opposite: hot-blooded revolution. As the novel progresses, however, these doubled characters come to relate more as twins than as opposites. Both Carton and Darnay share a common love for Lucie, and Lucie exerts a power over Carton that enables him to shed his skin as a "jackal" and adopt a life that actually may exceed Darnay's in terms of devotion and heroism. A common ground exists even between Miss Pross and Madame Defarge. The two women share a sense of uncompromising duty, as becomes manifest in their confrontation in Lucie's apartment. Miss Pross proves as fiercely devoted to Lucie's life and safety as Madame Defarge is to the idea of a new French Republic purged of all aristocrats. Each is willing to give up her life for her beliefs. In revealing these resemblances, Dickens suggests that even seeming opposites can possess underlying similarities. This gesture, along with Dickens's inclusion of multiple coincidences in his plot, contributes to the author's larger message that human beings inhabit a world of multiple hidden patterns and connections.

Q4. Discuss Dickens's use of foreshadowing in A Tale of Two Cities.

Dickens makes frequent use of foreshadowing, as it allows him to build suspense throughout his narrative and imbue it with a haunting atmosphere. He fills the novel with details that anticipate future events. For example, the wine cask breaking in the street and the echoing footsteps that can be heard in the Manettes' apartment hint to the reader about the imminence of the great and violent mob that eventually overtakes Paris. In this way, the reader becomes more aware of the situation than Dickens's characters and feels ever more emotionally and psychologically involved in the narrative. Given that Dickens published *A Tale of Two Cities* in short, weekly installments, this technique was a particularly effective means of sustaining the reader's interest in the novel. The reader was teased by hints of terrific events on the horizon and satisfied only by reading (and first buying) further installments.

Q5. The theme of resurrection is predominant throughout this novel. Elaborate.

The theme of resurrection ("rebirth," saving or redeeming in one's soul, renewed interest in and zest for life, salvation from death, harm, or "nothingness," etc.) is predominant throughout this novel. Identify two characters whose lives were resurrected; explain their previous lifestyle, their previous emotional state, and who/what inspired them to become resurrected. Additionally, discuss one other character whose life was improved or also resurrected due to this change in one of the first characters.

Essay

In A Tale of Two Cities, by Charles Dickens, many characters are given second chances as their lives are resurrected. The central heroine woman, Lucy Manette, is responsible for the resurrections of Sydney Carton and Dr. Alexander Manette's lives. She gives them inspiration and love to help them recover from their seemingly hopeless states. In turn, Carton gives up his own life in order to save a friend. The lives of Sydney Carton, Dr. Manette, and Charles Darnay are all resurrected at times when hope is lost.

Lucie Manette is a compassionate and benevolent character that aids in the resurrection of Sydney Carton and Dr. Manette. At the beginning of the book Lucie is only 17, but maturity beyond her age is reflected in her character. She is the ideal Victorian lady, perfect in every way. Lucie is gorgeous, with long, beautiful golden hair. She is very positive and unselfish, always willing to help others. Her wonderfully kind and sympathetic nature causes the men to fall in love with her. She doesn't look down upon anyone and sees the best in who some may see the worst. These qualities in Lucy are what make possible the resurrections of Sydney Carton and Dr. Manette's lives.

Dr. Alexander Manette's life is resurrected by his daughter, Lucie, after he is rescued from prison. Dr. Manette was imprisoned in the Bastille for 18 years, driving him to insanity. He was jailed because he knew information that the Marquis St. Evremonde did not want to get out. He is saved when the Defarges get him out of the Bastille and bring him to their wine shop, where he is then picked up by his daughter and family friend, Mr. Lorry. At the time they bring Dr. Manette back to his house, he is insane. He refers to himself as "One Hundred and Five, North Tower," his prison cell number. He knows of nothing other than his prison life and frequently reverts to busily making shoes, a hobby he picked up while jailed. He is completely incapable of functioning in the outside world, having entirely forgotten what life outside of prison is like. Lucie loves him unconditionally and helps him regain his sanity. Dr. Manette recovers gradually with the help of family and friends. It is a long process, but Lucie is dedicated to her father and assists in recovering from his crazed state. As time passes, Dr. Manette becomes more mentally stable and his regressions to shoe-making become less often. By the end of the book, Dr. Manette is nearly back to normal; he is once again a fully functional person. Lucie's love and determination nurse Dr. Manette back to normality.

Sydney Carton's life is made meaningful by the hope that he receives from Lucy Manette. At the beginning of the story, Sydney Carton's life has no significance. He is a drunkard with a seemingly worthless life. Sydney is working as a clerk for the lawyer C.J. Stryver, and though Sydney is the real brains behind the ideas, the attorney receives all the credit. Carton has had an unfavourable life and has no inspiration, nothing to live for. Sydney really wants for his life to have served some purpose, for him to have made a difference. He changes his life around after a conversation with Miss Manette in which Carton professes his love to her. Carton describes himself as a "self-flung away, wasted, drunken, poor creature of misuse" and states that there is no hope for bettering his life. However, Lucy explains that she believes in him and that he is "capable of better things." As Carton leaves he tells her, "For you, and for any dear to you, I would to anything," a promise he winds up keeping. Carton feels much better about himself knowing that Lucie, the woman he idolizes, believes in him. He strives to be a better person and tries to change his life around. He stops getting drunk and begins to lead a respectable life. Because Lucie sees potential for Carton, he is inspired to better his life.

Sydney Carton twice saves Charles Darnay, first from prison and then from death. Charles Darnay is a wealthy aristocrat, but he chooses to live a more modest life. He marries Lucy Manette, Sydney Carton's love. In the beginning of the book, Darnay is put on trial for treason, though he really has not done anything wrong. Sydney Carton is the clerk for Darnay's attorney. Things do not look hopeful for Charles, but then the court notices a remarkable resemblance of Darnay to Carton. Darnay is luckily set free because of this similarity. Had Carton not been present, Charles would have almost surely been found guilty. Darnay is later imprisoned and sentenced to death in France because of something his uncle and father did many years before. All hope is lost after every attempt to set Darnay free ends up in failure. The day of the execution, Carton has a plan of his own that is completely unexpected. He goes to the prison and trades places with Charles Darnay. Darnay safely leaves the prison while Carton stays in his place, awaiting his own death. Sydney does this because of his promise to Lucy earlier, that he would do anything for her or for anyone dear to her. Carton sees that Darnay has a family to go home to, while he does not. This serves as the perfect opportunity for Sydney to make his life meaningful, allowing a person with purpose to live on. There is no hope for Sydney after the change is made, he goes to the guillotine later that day. But Sydney dies with dignity, knowing his life did not go to waste. Because Sydney Carton bravely sacrifices his own life for Charles Darnay, Darnay is given an extra chance.

The characters in A Tale of Two Cities all play significant roles in each other's lives. None of the characters would be the same if it wasn't for the influence and impact of someone else. Resurrection is a predominant theme throughout the book, and three of the characters are resurrected. Dr. Manette is resurrected by his daughter and he is returned to sanity. Sydney Carton's life is changed from despair to honour. Because of the great change in Carton, Darnay's life is spared. The power of love and determination is clearly exemplified by the resurrection of Dr. Alexander Manette, Sydney Carton, and Charles Darnay.

Q6. The Bluest Aesthetic Is An Ethos Of Bluest People. Justify

Or

Discussthe Narrative Techniques in Bluest Eye.

The bluest aesthetic is an ethos of bluest people that manifests itself in everything done, not just in the music. (Salaam) Readers of Toni Morrison's first novel, The Bluest Eye, are often so overwhelmed by the narrative's emotional content—the child Pecola's incestuous rape, ensuing pregnancy, and subsequent abandonment by her community and descent into madness—that they miss the music in this lyrically "songified" narrative. Morrison has stated that her narrative "effort is to be like something that has probably only been fully expressed perhaps in music... " ("Interview"). The Bluest Eye is the genesis of her effort "to do what the music did for blacks, what we used to be able to do with each other in private and in that civilization that existed underneath the white civilization" (Morrison, "Language"). The catharsis and the transmission of cultural knowledge and values that have always been central to the blues form the thematic and rhetorical underpinnings of The Bluest Eye. The narrative's structure follows a pattern common to traditional blues lyrics: a movement from an initial emphasis on loss to a concluding suggestion of resolution of grief through motion. In between its initial statement of loss and its final emphasis on moving' on, The Bluest Eye contains an abundance of cultural wisdom. The blues lyrics that punctuate the narrative at critical points suggest a system of folk knowledge and values that is crucial to a young black woman's survival in the 1930s and '40s and which supports Claudia's cathartic role as storyteller. The lyrics also illustrate the folk knowledge and values that are not transmitted to Pecola—information without which she cannot survive as a whole and healthy human being.

In traditional blues songs, the singer is the subject, the I who tells her (or his) own story. In The Bluest Eye, however, Claudia tells Pecola's story. Except for a few fragmented lines of dialogue, Pecola remains silent within Claudia's narrative.

Much of the critical discourse on the novel has focused on the relationship between voice and empowerment, and on the problematics of a narrative that silences its dispossessed protagonist while seeking to empower the dispossessed and to critique power relations. This essay addresses the apparent contradiction between The Bluest Eye's silenced protagonist and its traditionally African American equation of voice with empowerment by situating Claudia's narrative voice within African American oral traditions and a blues aesthetic. I posit Claudia as the narrative's blues subject, its bluest "I" and representative blues figure, and Pecola as the abject tabula rasa on which the community's blues are inscribed. I assert that, rather than singing Pecola's blues, Claudia "sings" the community's blues. Claudia bears witness, through the oral tradition of testifying, to the community's lack of self-love and its transference of this lack onto the abject body of Pecola.

In the first section below, I address the initial reference to a specific blues song in the novel by discussing the lyrics and structure of "The St. Louis Blues" as representative of traditional blues. I then lay the foundation for a discussion of The Bluest Eye as a blues narrative. In the ensuing section, I build upon this foundation to discern a female blues subjectivity in The Bluest Eye, a subjectivity constructed through African American oral traditions and embodied in the three whores' speech, song, and laughter, and in Claudia's narrative voice. Finally, I position Claudia's subjectivity within a blues aesthetic and her voice within the oral tradition of testifying.

The earliest reference to a specific blues in The Bluest Eye follows the scene in which Mrs. MacTeer harangues the girls after Pecola consumes what Mrs. MacTeer deems more than her share of the milk in the refrigerator, and it precedes the narrative of Pecola's first menstruation. This reference to the blues, then, forms a bridge between childhood (the milk consumption represents Pecola's effort to consume—and become—Shirley Temple) and womanhood. The blues to which Claudia refers exemplify the cultural knowledge and values transmitted orally to Claudia that ease and assist her transition into womanhood—folk wisdom that is not conveyed to Pecola. The blues are first represented in the text in Claudia's reminiscence about the Saturdays when her "mother was in a singing mood." Claudia recalls snatches of lyrics from "hard times" songs her mother frequently sings, including the phrase "hate to see that evening sun go down," a reference to one of the earliest recorded and most popular blues songs, "St. Louis B lues,"

by W. C. Handy.

Q7. Discuss the Lyrical Language in A Tale of Two Cities.

Musicians from the early twentieth century to the present have revised, improvised, and recorded Handy's classic, whose lyrics convey a wealth of folk knowledge and cultural values. Hearing her mother sing the blues, Claudia finds herself longing for those hard times, yearning to be grown without "a thin di-ime to my name." I looked forward to the delicious time when "my man" would leave me, when I would "hate to see that evening sun go down..."' cause then I would know "my man has left this town." Misery coloured by the greens and blues in my mother's voice took all the grief out of the words and left me with a conviction that pain was not only endurable, it was sweet.The lyrical language in which Claudia describes her mother's singing is suggestive of the sweet and cathartic tone of traditional blues. The tone and the positive spectrum of emotion she describes as the colours of her mother's voice are more powerfully affecting than the pain signified by the words. Morrison tells us that music was one of "the most prominent elements" in her own early life ("Interview"). Her mother was a singer, and her home was filled with the seductive blues yearning that Claudia describes, a yearning at the emotional centre of the "St. Louis Blues" and The Bluest Eye.

In referring to the "St. Louis Blues," Morrison has chosen a blues that registers all of the central concerns of The Bluest Eye. Both the song and the novel exhibit a lyrical progression from an initial statement of loss to a concluding statement of resolve to move on, literally and figuratively. The song opens on the traditional blues note of loss or lack: The speaker's man has left her with an empty bed, and consequently she hates to see the lonely nighttime come. The song then proceeds immediately, in the second verse, to the suggestion of resolution through the motion nearly always implied in the blues:

"Feelin' tomorrow lak I feel today

I'll pack mah trunk, an' make mah getaway."

Houston Baker writes that the notion of resolution of earthly problems through motion is implied in the sound of the blues:

The dominant blues syntagm in America is an instrumental imitation of train-wheels-over-track-junctures. The sound is the "sign," as it were, of the blues, and it combines an intriguing melange of phonics: rattling gondolas, clattering flatbeds, quilling whistles, clanging bells, rumbling boxcars, and other railroad sounds.... If desire and absence are driving conditions of blues performance, the amelioration of such conditions is implied by the onomatopoeic training of blues voice and instrument.

Baker add that, "even as [the blues] speak of paralyzing absence and ineradicable desire, their instrumental rhythms suggest change, movement, action...". This observation certainly applies to the "St. Louis Blues," a traditional twelve-bar blues augmented with an eight-bar bridge and an additional twelve-bar blues. Its rhymed couplets, most of them obeying strict iambic pentameter, develop a complex iteration of cultural values and direct a black audience to sources of support and sustenance in times of trouble.

Like many other blues, the "St. Louis Blues" suggests a literal as well as a tropological resolution through motion: The speaker announces her intent to board a train and seek her lover who has left for St. Louis, invoking cultural wisdom that may be interpreted in literal as well as figurative terms. She suggests that looking up a friend employed by the railroad lines is the first step toward a way out of troubled times (verse seven). This is excellent practical advice in a time period when the railroads employed large numbers of black men in some of the better-paying, service-oriented positions in the urban North. For black people negotiating the route of the Great Migration, from the Jim Crow South to the urban North, friends on the railroad line were indispensable. A friend on the railroad could be a poor person's only ticket to ride. In figurative terms this verse suggests that there is a way out of troubled times and that this way out involves forming and relying on a close-knit community and making on e's needs known. It also suggests that the two-timing man may not be the speaker's only love interest ("mah ol' frien', Jeff / Gwine to pin mahself close to his side / If I flag his train, I sho can ride"), and that women can give as well as they get in the field of intimate intrigues. Figuratively, in referring to the train, the song suggests to the listener's imagination the sound of the train, echoed in the sound of the blues, and at this juncture of sound and reference to sound, the promise of motion and change is magnified and enhanced.

James McPherson, in Railroad: Trains and Train People in American Culture, notes that to nineteenth-century backwoodsmen, Africans, and recent immigrants—the people who comprised the vernacular segment of society... the [steam engine locomotive] might have been loud and frightening, but its whistle and its wheels promised movement. And since a commitment to both freedom and movement was the basic premise of democracy, it was probable that such people would view the locomotive as a challenge to the integrative powers of their imaginations.

Claudia tells the reader twice that Mrs. MacTeer is "all the time singing about trains and Arkansas". Claudia, with her keen sense of justice, hears freedom and democracy in what Houston Baker would call the "trained" sound of her mother's singing voice. The Saturdays on which her mother does not sing are "lonesome, fussy, soapy days. Second in misery only to those tight, starchy, cough-drop Sundays, so full of 'don'ts' and 'set' cha self downs'". The singing Saturdays are full of possibility; her mother's "voice so sweet and her singing-eyes so melty" stir her imagination and yearning, and leave her with a sense of "conviction" that sustains her in times of trouble.

The singing subject of the "St. Louis Blues" is a female,and in verse seven she yearns for the sense of dominion, motion, and freedom represented by the masculine railroad line ("If I flag his train, I sho can ride"). The tone and tenor of Claudia's narrative express a similar longing. In employing the "St. Louis Blues" to provoke and represent Claudia's yearning, Morrison inverts traditional notions of the masculine and the feminine and claims for Claudia some of the "masculinity" that she will later claim for Sula. The notion that there is always somewhere else to go when hard times hit, and a way to get there, sustains Claudia. The only somewhere else for Pecola to go is insane. The poverty of her imagination, an imagination which has not been nurtured by the blues or any other source of cultural sustenance, is reflected in the destitution of the Breedlove home.

Q8. The traditional progression from cathartic statement of loss to announcement of the intent to achieve resolution through motion is accomplished in the first two verses of the "St. Louis Blues." Elucidate.

The traditional progression from cathartic statement of loss to announcement of the intent to achieve resolution through motion is accomplished in the first two verses of the "St. Louis Blues." The remaining eight verses that Claudia would have become familiar with through her mother's repeated performances affirm cultural values essential to her growth and development—and the growth and development of any young, black, working-class person. The third verse of the song iterates a theme that is central to this novel and that runs throughout the body of Morrison's work: The glitz of beauty industry consumer products that reify light skin and straight hair—the make-up and fashion apparel ruined in the rain on Hagar's fatal shopping spree in Song of Solomon, for example—can be both powerful and powerfully misleading. Verse three argues that it is not the St. Louis woman who has stolen the speaker's man, it is "diamon' rings... / powder an'... store-bought hair." The St. Louis woman is not present in this ver se; rather, her presence is suggested solely by the reified products with which she adorns herself. Verse four of the "St. Louis Blues" recapitulates the song's initial sense of loss. It echoes the soulless emptiness that the speaker asserts (in the third verse) lies beneath the St. Louis Woman's patina of beauty and success. In The Bluest Eye, Maureen Peal is more a conglomeration of signifying products—"patent-leather shoes with buckles... sweaters the colour of lemon drops... a brown velvet coat trimmed in white rabbit fur, and a matching muff"—than a presence. Her surname may be read as Morrison's signifying on the word peel to emphasize 'skin,' 'rind,' 'patina,' or 'husk.'

The last two verses of the "St. Louis Blues" relate cultural values absolutely crucial to Claudia's survival and Pecola's downfall, and speak to the sensitive issue at the emotional centre of The Bluest Eye: caste prejudice, or intraracism based upon skin tone. Verse nine describes the sought-after man as "stovepipe brown" and links his desirability to his dark-toned skin; and verse ten inverts the caste hierarchy that has filtered down from the dominant white culture into Lorain's black community, a caste hierarchy that privileges light skin, blue eyes, and European features and that is embodied in Maureen Peal. The speaking subject of the "St. Louis Blues" constructs a striking visual image of the desired man as "Blacker than midnight, teeth lak flags of truce / Blackest man in de whole St. Louis." She then employs this image in a direct inversion of the dominant caste hierarchy, closing the verse with a popular aphorism, passed down through generations of African Americans, that assigns the highest aesthe tic value to the darkest skin: "Blacker de berry, sweeter is de juice...." While Claudia is regularly serenaded—on Saturdays, when her mother was in a singing mood—with this concise, confident, and lyrical deconstruction of the Shirley Temple aesthetic, Pecola is rejected by Pauline, who embraces the "corn-yellow"-haired child of her white employers. One of the novel's more chilling scenes, rivaled in emotional content only by the rape scene, is the one in which Pauline slaps Pecola for accidentally overturning the blueberry cobbler, throws her out of the house, and then tenderly embraces the white Fisher child, who calls her by her first name (Pecola must call her mother "Mrs. Breedlove"). Clearly, Pauline has internalized the notion that black is not beautiful. Pecola and the dark berries in the bubbling cobbler with which she is associated are objects to be swept out of the way as Pauline rushes to embrace the rich white child.

Claudia's defiance of and Pecola's internalization of the Shirley Temple aesthetic are illustrated in the Maureen Peal "six-finger-dog-tooth-meringue-pie" episode. In rejecting Maureen and "calling her out of her name," Claudia rejects the intraracism implicit in the privileging of Maureen's "high yellow dream" complexion and her "two lynch ropes" of long brown hair. Pecola desires what Claudia rejects: light skin, straight hair, blue eyes, and the social status they represent. Claudia's defiance is a learned and nurtured defiance, encouraged by a severe but loving mother who sings to her on Saturdays. Pecola internalizes the caste aesthetic that the "St. Louis Blues" mediates against, an aesthetic that Morrison argues has insidiously infiltrated not only families like the Breedloves but whole communities.

Claudia tells us that she comes to embrace this aesthetic tentatively, reluctantly, and consciously. As IngerAnne Softing notes, "Claudia is the only character in this novel who consciously makes an attempt at deconstructing the ideology of the dominant society. This is seen in her dismembering of the dolls". Describing her gradual awareness that her violent dismembering of white baby dolls was unacceptable, Claudia speaks of a conversion "from pristine sadism to fabricated hatred to fraudulent love.... I learned much later to worship [Shirley Temple], just as I learned to delight in cleanliness, knowing, even as I learned, that the change was adjustment without improvement". This awareness of her reluctant capitulation to intraracism seems remarkable in a child. It is almost certainly the observation of the adult Claudia, who is engaged in the act of remembering and interpreting her childhood. Still, it is noteworthy that the child Claudia seems to stand alone in her critique of a "master" aesthet ic that is internalized by nearly everyone in her community, from the adults who give the gift of white baby dolls and Shirley Temple cups, to Geraldine, to the bully boys who taunt Pecola and whose words Maureen Peal repeats: "'Black and ugly black e mos'".

Morrison has stated that her purpose in writing the novel was to "peck away at the gaze that condemns" Pecola's blackness as ugly ("Afterword"); Morrison critiques the "racial self-loathing" implicit in the community's valorization of Maureen Peal and the peel/skin colour/caste hierarchy that she represents. Whereas Maureen Peal and Shirley Temple serve as icons of the destructive reification of caste and whiteness, respectively, the "St. Louis Blues" singing subject recognizes the vapidity beneath the husk of powder, rings, and store-bought hair. Claudia, too, even as a child, recognizes the self-loathing inherent in the condemning gaze, and the blues wisdom that fills the house on Claudia's mother's singing Saturdays has fostered this recognition.

Thus, Morrison implies that the MacTeers have retained a connection to ancestral knowledge essential to survival in their current situation, a connection lost to the Breedloves.

The Breedloves follow a trajectory away from the values of the black, poor, rural South and toward values that serve the interests of a privileged, white upper-middle class and of capitalism itself. This trajectory serves to instill in the Breedloves' own family a sense of worthlessness and lack. Morrison makes it clear that Cholly and Pauline Breedlove, and particularly Pauline, were once connected to a community that embodied the cultural values expressed in the blues. In Pauline's italicized narrative fragments concerning her girlhood in the rural South, she recalls a delicious yearning and pleasure associated not with consumer products but with community and with the associated fruits of the earth:

When I first seed Cholly I want you to know it was like all the bits of colour from that time down home when us children went berry picking after a funeral and I put some in the pocket of my Sunday dress, and they mashed up and stained my hips. My whole dress was messed with purple, and it never did wash out. Not the dress nor me. I could feel that purple deep inside me. And that lemonade Mama used to make when Pap came in out the fields. It be cool and yellowish.... And that streak of green the june bugs made on the trees the night we left from down home. All of them colours was in me.

Pauline's use of the word colours to name an abstract emotional yearning recalls the blues yearning instilled in Claudia by the sound of her mother's voice. The above passage is, in essence, Pauline's blues, and it expresses a longing for home and community and a choice to move on, to "go down to the crossroads," as Robert Johnson put it in his historic blues, and head north. In lyrically expressing a longing for the rural Southern community that revolved around church ("Sunday dress") and ritual ("berry picking," "funeral"). Pauline accomplishes what the blues singer accomplishes: She recreates that which is lost and for which she longs, transforming lack into poetry. Unfortunately, the transformation is temporary and exists only in her memory. Pauline's narrative traces her movement toward the white bourgeois values represented by the Hollywood films that seduce her, and by the flawless home of the Fishers. The lure of the material supplants her memories of community, even though she can never hope to posses s what she longs for.

Pauline seeks acceptance and success in terms defined by a white power structure that excludes her, whereas Claudia possesses an altogether different understanding of social structures. She seems intuitively to understand a central tenet of blues wisdom embodied in the "St. Louis Blues": Seek alternative forms of knowledge and understanding within the community, not in the white power structure. These forms are represented by the song's reference to the "gypsy," a figure who has a long history in African American literature and oral culture.

The "gypsy" fortune teller or root doctor figure is negatively personified in The Bluest Eye by Soaphead Church. Claudia understands that Soaphead Church may reside within the community, but he is not of the community. She seems instinctively to understand that Church despises blackness and lives in thrall to a value system that excludes him. Because Claudia is part of the community, she is privy to information circulated orally about Church's "nasty" habit of molesting young girls. But Pecola, because she is treated as an outcast, is not privy to this knowledge. She sees in Church an outcast like herself, living on the fringes of the community, and in her first visit to him she is made to understand that he despises blackness just as she despises her own blackness. Pecola visits Church hoping for some magic, but Morrison twists the root doctor/fortune teller figure into a self-loathing, obsessive-compulsive child molester in order to underscore the dangerous nature of the only alternative sources of knowled ge and succor available to children like Pecola, whose families and communities are not looking out for their well-being.

The cultural values and knowledge embodied in the blues and transmitted orally to Claudia enable her to develop what would much later come to be called a black aesthetic. Claudia does not, however, passively absorb this body of cultural knowledge and draw strength from it. She not only hears the blues, but she listens to and, more importantly, "sings" the blues. Indeed, the blues define her storytelling voice and style. Claudia is a blues subject engaged in what Kalamu ya Salaam calls the act of "reclaiming the black blues self."

As a singing subject, Claudia has some talented and versatile models in The Bluest Eye. Mrs. MacTeer and Poland serenade the reader with only a few lines, but these lines constitute a rich variety of blues expression that reflects the range of techniques Claudia employs as a blues narrator. Like Mrs. MacTeer singing the "St. Louis Blues" and Pauline reconstructing the rural South in blues prose, Poland transforms lack into poetry:

I got blues in my mealbarrel
Blues up on the shelf
I got blues in my mealbarrel
Blues up on the shelf
Blues in my bedroom
'Cause I'm sleeping by myself.

The transformation of lack, loss, and grief into poetic catharsis is the constitutive task of the blues singer, and it is the labour that Claudia accomplishes in narrating The Bluest Eye. Central to the transmogrification of lack into poetry in Poland's "Mealbarrel Blues" is an assertion of subjectivity: In singing to affirm not having (blues, not meal, fill the mealbarrel), Poland establishes a desiring self. In desiring, she exists, and in naming her desire, she acts to fulfill it.

In the act of naming the blues (which Poland does five times in the verse above, in every line but the last), she calls down the power of Nommo, defined by Angela Y. Davis as a "West African philosophical concept... 'the magic power of the word'... the very basis of music". In naming the blues, Poland activates the catharsis that holds the promise of ameliorating the blues. Davis goes on to assert that, in keeping with the tradition of Nommo, black women blues artists historically have shaped and interpreted a female blues subject who yearns for freedom. She emphasizes that the yearned-for freedom is not to be confused with Western notions of symbolic freedom; rather, given the material conditions of blues production, freedom must be understood first as literal—ownership of one's body—and, later (in history), as material—control over the means of production, and freedom from poverty, discrimination, debt, and disenfranchisement. Davis asserts that the sexual desire expressed in African American wome n's blues lyrics is a "camouflaged dream of a new social order". It is also an assertion of women's control over their bodies.

When a woman is living in desperate material conditions, with nothing but the blues in her pantry, her body is all that she owns and controls; thus, assertion of ownership and control is a courageous political statement. Women blues singers from Ma Rainey to Koko Taylor have boldly and boastfully asserted their sexuality. When Mr. Henry molests Frieda and Frieda explains to Claudia the nature of his transgression, Claudia attempts to insert her voice into this tradition, and Morrison emphasizes the humour and naivete in the guileless child's attempt. Claudia enthusiastically asks, "'Really? How did it feel?'". She then asks if it didn't feel good, and displays an innocent jealousy at Mr. Henry's choosing Frieda instead of her, aligning herself with the blues singer who complains of an empty bed.

The three whores embody the blues singer's assertion of sexuality, desirability, and ownership of their bodies. Nowhere in the novel is this clearer than in the paragraph describing their laughter:

All three of the women laughed. Marie threw back her head. From deep inside, her laughter came like the sound of many rivers.... China giggled spastically. Each gasp seemed to be yanked out of her by an unseen hand jerking an unseen string. Poland, who seldom spoke unless she was drunk, laughed without sound. When she was sobre, she hummed mostly or chanted blues songs, of which she knew many.

Inger-Anne Softing writes that Poland, in addition to carrying "on the old tradition of blending the sweet and the sad," introduces into the text "true carnival laughter... nonauthoritarian and nonhierarchical". Softing points out that all three of the whores in The Bluest Eye laugh with their whole bodies, from the depths of being, constituting "true carnivalesque" in "a novel which, on the whole, is not filled with the liberating force of laughter". The whores' laughter is the quintessential blues utterance: It wells up from within, with the force and rhythm of a freight train, and it erupts into pure catharsis. It is a public communication of emotions that are both private and shared.

Although the blues typically feature a first-person singular subject, and exhibit a concern "with the problems and/or experiences of the individual" (Southern), Davis observes in women's blues a "public communication of private troubles" that "allows for the development of a collective social consciousness within the black population". Houston A. Baker, Jr., describes the blues as "an anonymous (nameless) voice issuing from the black whole". Poland's "Blues in my bedroom / 'Cause I'm sleeping by myself" may be read as a sensual and a political expression of collective need. Her "Mealbarrel Blues" conflates the language of sexual desire and the desire for freedom from poverty.

The conflation of material lack and sexual desire is humourously developed, in storytelling rather than singing form, in exchanges between Marie and China as China attempts to insert herself into the legend of John Dillinger. Marie and China enact a tradition that blends call-and-response, an erotic blues sensuality, and tongue-in-cheek humour—signifying. Miss Marie responds to Pecola's earnest "'How come they [men] all love you?' " with, " 'What else they gone do? They know I'm rich and good lookin'.' " Marie proceeds to tell a tall tale of how she came to be rich, the story in which she claims to be the mysterious Lady in Red who turned John Dillinger in to the " 'F. B. and I.' " China responds with guffaws and interrupts Marie's story, first with questions mimicking Pecola's earnestness (" 'Yeah.... Where you get it from?' "), then with affirmations (" 'We know that' "), and finally with goading insults, to which Marie responds playfully and aggressively:

"I was little and cute then. No more than ninety pounds, soaking wet."

"You ain't never been soaking wet," China said.

"Well you ain't never been dry. Shut up...."

China hoots, " 'She makin' like she's the Lady in Red that told on John Dillinger. Dillinger wouldn't have come near you lessen he was going hunting in Africa and shoot you for a hippo' ".

China and Marie engage in the black vernacular tradition of signifying, which Geneva Smitherman defines as "the verbal art of insult in which a speaker humourously puts down, talks about, needles—that is, signifies on—the listener". Signifying has been enacted in musical forms from blues to rap; it is a component of some of the earliest recorded blues, and it has remained a staple in the blues repertoire. Pecola hears Poland singing, and she listens to China signifying on Marie's story, but she lacks the cultural knowledge necessary to understanding. She is exiled from the collective consciousness; it is as though she doesn't speak the language of the blues, although she most certainly lives the blues. Although she is close in age to Claudia and Frieda, she lacks Claudia's sense of irony and humour and both sisters' mastery of language.

Throughout the novel, Claudia's observations are guided by a sharp-edged humour. Her narrative is characterized by the adaptive laughing-to-keep-from-crying perspective that is central to the blues and that Bernard Bell, in his study of the African American novel, terms "double vision." Some of the most humourous moments in The Bluest Eye occur in the scenes following Frieda's molestation by Mr. Henry. Claudia and Frieda's unwitting play on the meaning of ruined and their misinterpretation of vague and confusing adult speech leads them to believe that the only cure for the ruination that has been wrought on Frieda by Mr. Henry is for Frieda to become an alcoholic. Their youthful logic and the examples of China and Poland lead them to conclude that drinking whisky will prevent Frieda from getting fat, the ruinous result, they believe, of molestation. When Claudia and Frieda signify on Maureen Peal and play a child's version of the dozens when Maureen goads them, Pecola "fold[s] into herself, like a broken wing, " because she is ashamed and lacks the double vision necessary to participation in this ritual.Listening to China and Marie signifying, Pecola misses the humour and the innuendo; she responds with guileless earnestness: "'You rich, Miss Marie?'"; "'But what about the money?'". Her responses to the whores' language play foreground her focus on the lack and need (" rich...?...money?'") that always marks the first verse(s) of a blues song—in this case it is material, a material desire, later reified in her desire for blue eyes. But Pecola's development as a blues subject stops at the first verse: She is entirely defined and consumed by lack. It is as though she is entrapped in the opening lines of a blues song; her character is never developed, as blues subjectivity is always developed, to the point of agency.

In Maxine Hong Kingston's The Woman Warrior, the narrator's mother explains "'the difference between mad people and sane people'": "'Sane people have variety when they talk-story. Mad people have only one story that they talk over and over'". By the closing pages of The Bluest Eye, Pecola has only one story, the story of her beautiful blue eyes. Her identity is hopelessly fragmented; and, as Madonne Miner notes, "tragically, even when combined, [Pecola and her 'imaginary friend'] do not compose one whole being....she no longer exists as a reasonable human being". Claudia's voice gathers strength as Pecola fragments. Guided by a blues aesthetic, Claudia constructs a wealth of stories and a variety of perspectives from which to interpret her childhood experiences and Pecola's story. Even as a child, Claudia subverts the consumer culture and the outside gaze that seek to impose impossible standards of beauty on her community; she subsumes the master narrative into a blues narrative.

Central to Claudia's narrative style is the oral tradition of testifying. Geneva Smitherman defines this oral tradition that came out of the traditional black church as "a ritualized form of black communication in which the speaker gives verbal witness to the efficacy, truth and power of some experience in which all blacks have shared". She adds that "to testify is to tell the truth through story"; testifying is not "plain and simple commentary but a dramatic narration and a communal reenactment of one's feelings and experiences" Testifying is a tradition which, like call-and-response, is rooted in African American religious practice and can be traced to West African sons and speech. The testifying utterance is a chronicle initiated by an individual—a registering of emotion, rather than an outpouring of emotion in response to a call. In Song of Solomon, when Pilate stalks into the church at Hagar's funeral and calls out "'Mercy'" and Reba sings out "'I hear you,'" and they continue in this vein, singing back and forth," In the nighttime. / Mercy/ In the darkness. / Mercy...," they are performing call-and-response. Moments later, in the same scene, when Pilate repeats, "'My baby girl,'" as she gazes into the coffin, and then speaks these three words to the audience, she is testifying. Yvonne Atkinson observes that the emotional impact of this scene is the result of the layering of call-and-response and testifying, and that the layering of these two and of other residually oral forms throughout Morrison's fiction is central to her artistry.

The accomplished blues singer blends these two oral forms, as does Claudia in The Bluest Eye. When she offers up Pecola's story, she is testifying to the community's failings and the community's unspoken desire, which Pecola vocalizes. Morrison places Claudia in a position similar to that of Pilate gazing into the coffin. Claudia is gazing, in the novel's final pages, at Pecola picking among the garbage, and she turns her gaze outward toward the reader and testifies that Pecola is the site of inscription of a communal shame. This act of testifying is a narrative act that is central to Morrison's work. Morrison asserts that her

... work bears witness and suggests who the outlaws were, who survived under what circumstances and why....All that is in the fabric of the story in order to do what the music used to do. The music kept us alive, but it's not enough any more. Whenever I feel uneasy about my writing, I think: what would be the response of people in the book if they read the book? That's my way of staying on track. Those are the people for whom I write. ("Language")

Inherent in testifying is the assumption of commonalties between the testifying subject and her audience (Atkinson). Claudia skillfully bridges the dramatic distance she has constructed as a blues narrator—just as Morrison bridges that distance as a blues writer—and she assumes crucial commonalties with the community she speaks from, to, and about, critiquing it firmly but lovingly and absolving its guilt and shame.

Throughout The Bluest Eye, Claudia sets herself up as an individual who questions the community's tastes and judgments and often finds them suspect; but she is not outside of or in opposition to the community—she critiques the community from within. Morrison places her in a call-and-response dialectic with a community chorus. The traditional blues singer did not speak for the community, but she did speak from the community. As Giles Oakley puts it,

> Many black people would have been... offended by the idea that the blues singer "spoke" for them, in much the same way that others would reject the spokesmanship of the preacher. Nevertheless, there did exist what almost amounted to a blues community. Its significance was in the process of communal creation and participation in a shared culture....the idea that the blues were an expression of deeply felt emotions made the music more than simply entertainment.

In addition to Claudia's voice, we hear Pauline's, an omniscient narrator's, and fragments of dialogue representing nearly every quarter of the community, from the three whores to Geraldine and Junior to Soaphead Church to unidentified gossips. Claudia develops an individual voice that taps into the community's repressed racial self-hatred and its deeply concealed guilt at displacing that self-hatred onto Pecola. Hers is not what Robert Cataliotti calls "a traditional country blues, which were most frequently performed by solo artists."

The country blues was thought of and enacted, for the most part, as a masculine tradition. Claudia's blues are what Cataliotti and others before him have termed a "Classic Blues... performed by a female singer with accompaniment provided by a pianist, possibly augmented by a small instrumental combo. Nonetheless, the singer certainly remained the dominant personality in the performance". Claudia's is the dominant voice in the novel, and Frieda frequently responds in the affirmative to Claudia's blues" call," as do Mrs. MacTeer's and Poland's blues and China's signifying. They are the blues chorus that mediates against the buzzing of voices that condemns Pecola.

The playwright August Wilson has said that the blues provide "a way of processing information about Black life, particularly information about the nobility... the beauty... and the resiliency of Black life." Claudia's embodiment of the blues aesthetic enables her to "process" precisely the "information" to which Wilson refers. The Bluest Eye does not appear to be a novel about beauty and nobility; it seems largely bereft of these elements. Even marigolds fail to grow in this fictional world.

"Beauty" is a deeply problematic concept in Morrison's work. In fact, the omniscient narrator of The Bluest Eye asserts that "physical beauty" and romantic love "are probably the most destructive ideas in the history of human thought". As Morrison interrogates a master narrative of beauty, her blues aesthetic lends structure, style, and form to the interrogation. The emphasis in Claudia's blues narrative is on resiliency, and the resiliency she develops as a blues subject allows her to appreciate the beauty and the nobility even in a community that fails its most destitute resident. At the novel's close, after blame has been assigned ("we were not strong, only aggressive; we were not free, merely licensed; we were not compassionate, we were polite; not good, but well behaved") and limited absolution granted ("I even think now that the soil of the entire country was hostile to marigolds that year"), Claudia is able to look "among the garbage.., of [her] town" and focus, in the novel's final line, on beauty: "sunflowers".

Morrison constructs Claudia as a blues subject: sensuous, brutally honest, poetic, ironically humourous, and adept at call-and-response, signifying, and testifying. She learns to sing from her mother, and her blues is The Bluest Eye. Her storytelling mode is a blues mode in its sensuality, honesty, lyricism, ironic distance, humour, dialectic with the community, and open-endedness. Blues narratives, like blues lyrics, never end on a closed note, and The Bluest Eye is no exception. At the end of a "typical" blues there is affirmation, as there is in "St. Louis Blues" (of the beauty in blackness), and there is movement, or a statement of intent to move, but there is no closure, no neatly wrapped-up ending.

The subjects of blues narratives achieve, by their narratives' close, an ironic distance—and often a physical distance—from the lack and loss expressed in the narratives' beginnings. Indeed, the construction of ironic distance and open-endedness is a primary function of the blues, which codify a means of resistance to oppression and a call to "move on" up and out. Claudia's blues narrative may be understood as a sustained signifying on the master aesthetic of physical beauty and the racial self-loathing that this master aesthetic produces. Hers is a complex and polyvocal signifying, involving a call-and-response dialectic with her community. Claudia could not carry on this dialectic, could not "sing" this blues without first living the blues. As Janie in Hurston's Their Eyes Were Watching God puts it," 'It's uh known fact.... you got tuh go there tuh know there'". Claudia's narrative traces a trajectory from the childhood experience and naming of lack—her community's lack of a sense of the intrinsi c beauty of blackness and hence its scapegoating of the Breedloves and of Pecola, in particular—to a sense of resolution through movement.

At the novel's close, Claudia claims membership in the community ("my town"), but she has achieved sufficient distance from her subject to enable her to reconstruct Pecola's story. She sees Pecola in her mind, or on the streets of her present-day community, "searching through the garbage—for what?" but she also sees across the dramatic distance between the blues subject and her narrative. Claudia does not see this traversing of distance as unequivocally positive, but she sees it as necessary. She has stood at a blues crossroads and resolved to assert her independence. She has distanced herself from Pecola and from her community in order to engage the community in a dialectic, but she looks back upon this move with a nostalgia for a time and place that no longer exist. Claudia can look back in time and see clearly because she has achieved a metaphoric distance, albeit at a price. The novel closes with a sense that Claudia has moved on while Pecola remains frozen in time—a child, trapped in the tragic first verse of her own blues, with her imagined blue eyes and the lack and self-loathing they signify, "frozen in the glare of the lover's inward eye". The loving eye is Claudia's, and The Bluest Eye is her testifying to Pecola's pain and the community's shame.

The "Eye" of the title may refer to Pecola's disastrous longing for blue eyes, but it also refers to the eye that takes Pecola as its subject, and to the J who narrates her story. The Bluest Eye is Claudia's blues for Pecola and her community. The novel's central paucity is the community's lack of self-love, a lack precipitated by the imposition of a master aesthetic that privileges the light skin and blue eyes inherent in the community's internalization of this master aesthetic. Claudia is the voice for the community's blues, and Pecola is the site of the inscription of the community's blues.

Further Study Questions

1. Which aspects of English life were being criticized by Dickens in *Hard Times*?
2. Which characters do you consider to be heroes in the story? Explain.
3. Which characters struck you as being the villains? Explain.
4. Does the story have a sad ending, or does it give you hope for better times?
5 Some critics charge that Dickens, in much of his work, failed to create meaningful characters because he exaggerated them to parodic extremes. Do you find this a fair assessment of his characterization in *A Tale of Two Cities*? Does the author's use of caricature detract from his novel's ability to speak to human nature?
6 Dickens relies heavily on coincidence to fuel the plot of *A Tale of Two Cities*: letters are found bearing crucial infor-mation, for example, and long-lost brothers are discovered in crowded public places. Do such incidents strengthen or weaken the plot and overall themes of the novel?

7 Discuss Dickens's attitude toward the French Revolution. Does he sympathize with the revolutionaries?

8 Based on Dickens's portrayals of the villainous characters in his novel (particularly Madame Defarge), what conclusions might the reader draw about the author's notions of human evil? Does he seem to think that people are born evil? If so, do they lack the ability to change? Or does he suggest that circumstances drive human beings to their acts of cruelty?

Chapter 16

Important Chapters from the Text

CHAPTER I

The Period

It was the best of times, it was the worst of times, it was the age of wisdom, it was the age of foolishness, it was the epoch of belief, it was the epoch of incredulity, it was the season of Light, it was the season of Darkness, it was the spring of hope, it was the winter of despair, we had everything before us, we had nothing before us, we were all going direct to Heaven, we were all going direct the other way—in short, the period was so far like the present period, that some of its noisiest authorities insisted on its being received, for good or for evil, in the superlative degree of comparison only.

There were a king with a large jaw and a queen with a plain face, on the throne of England; there were a king with a large jaw and a queen with a fair face, on the throne of France. In both countries it was clearer than crystal to the lords of the State preserves of loaves and fishes, that things in general were settled for ever.

It was the year of Our Lord one thousand seven hundred and seventy-five. Spiritual revelations were conceded to England at that favoured period, as at this. Mrs. Southcott had recently attained her five-and-twentieth blessed birthday, of whom a prophetic private in the Life Guards had heralded the sublime appearance by announcing that arrangements were made for the swallowing up of London and Westminster. Even the Cock-lane ghost had been laid only a round dozen of years, after rapping out its messages, as the spirits of this very year last past (supernaturally deficient in originality) rapped out theirs. Mere messages in the earthly order of events had lately come to the English Crown and People, from a congress of British subjects in America: which, strange to relate, have proved more important to the human race than any communications yet received through any of the chickens of the Cock-lane brood.

France, less favoured on the whole as to matters spiritual than her sister of the shield and trident, rolled with exceeding smoothness down hill, making paper money and spending it. Under the guidance of her Christian pastors, she entertained herself, besides, with such humane achievements as sentencing a youth to have his hands cut off, his tongue torn out with pincers, and his body burned alive, because he had not kneeled down in the rain to do honour to a dirty procession of monks which passed within his view, at a distance of some fifty or sixty yards. It is likely enough that, rooted in the woods of France and Norway, there were growing trees, when that sufferer was put to death, already marked by the Woodman, Fate, to come down and be sawn into boards, to make a certain movable framework with a sack and a knife in it, terrible in history. It is likely enough that in the rough outhouses of some tillers of the heavy lands adjacent to Paris, there were sheltered from the weather that very day, rude carts, bespattered with rustic mire, snuffed about by pigs, and roosted in by poultry, which the Farmer, Death, had already set apart to be his tumbrils of the Revolution. But that Woodman and that Farmer, though they work unceasingly, work silently, and no one heard them as they went about with muffled tread: the rather, forasmuch as to entertain any suspicion that they were awake, was to be atheistical and traitorous.

In England, there was scarcely an amount of order and protection to justify much national boasting. Daring burglaries by armed men, and highway robberies, took place in the capital itself every night; families were publicly cautioned not to go out of town without removing their furniture to upholsterers' warehouses for security; the highwayman in the dark was a City tradesman in the light, and, being recognised and challenged by his fellow- tradesman whom he stopped in his character of "the Captain," gallantly shot him through the head and rode away; the mall was waylaid by seven robbers, and the guard shot three dead, and then got shot dead himself by the other four, "in consequence of the failure of his ammunition:" after which the mall was robbed in peace; that magnificent potentate, the Lord Mayor of London, was made to stand and deliver on Turnham Green, by one highwayman, who despoiled the illustrious creature in sight of all his retinue; prisoners in London gaols fought battles with their turnkeys, and the majesty of the law fired blunderbusses in among them, loaded with rounds of shot and ball; thieves snipped off diamond crosses from the necks of noble lords at Court drawing-rooms; musketeers went into St. Giles's, to search for contraband goods, and the mob fired on the musketeers, and the musketeers fired on the mob, and nobody thought any of these occurrences much out of the common way. In the midst of them, the hangman, ever busy and ever worse than useless, was in constant requisition; now, stringing up long rows of miscellaneous criminals; now, hanging a housebreaker on Saturday who had been taken on Tuesday; now, burning people in the hand at Newgate by the dozen, and now burning pamphlets at the door of Westminster Hall; to-day, taking the life of an atrocious murderer, and to-morrow of a wretched pilferer who had robbed a farmer's boy of sixpence.

All these things, and a thousand like them, came to pass in and close upon the dear old year one thousand seven hundred and seventy-five. Environed by them, while the Woodman and the Farmer worked unheeded, those two of the large jaws, and those other two of the plain and the fair faces, trod with stir enough, and carried their divine rights with a high hand. Thus did the year one thousand seven hundred and seventy-five conduct their Greatnesses, and myriads of small creatures—the creatures of this chronicle among the rest—along the roads that lay before them.

CHAPTER IV

The Preparation

When the mail got successfully to Dover, in the course of the forenoon, the head drawer at the Royal George Hotel opened the coach-door as his custom was. He did it with some flourish of ceremony, for a mail journey from London in winter was an achievement to congratulate an adventurous traveller upon.

By that time, there was only one adventurous traveller left be congratulated: for the two others had been set down at their respective roadside destinations. The mildewy inside of the coach, with its damp and dirty straw, its disageeable smell, and its obscurity, was rather like a larger dog-kennel. Mr. Lorry, the passenger, shaking himself out of it in chains of straw, a tangle of shaggy wrapper, flapping hat, and muddy legs, was rather like a larger sort of dog.

"There will be a packet to Calais, tomorrow, drawer?"

"Yes, sir, if the weather holds and the wind sets tolerable fair. The tide will serve pretty nicely at about two in the afternoon, sir. Bed, sir?"

"I shall not go to bed till night; but I want a bedroom, and a barber."

"And then breakfast, sir? Yes, sir. That way, sir, if you please. Show Concord! Gentleman's valise and hot water to Concord. Pull off gentleman's boots in Concord. (You will find a fine sea-coal fire, sir.) Fetch barber to Concord. Stir about there, now, for Concord!"

The Concord bed-chamber being always assigned to a passenger by the mail, and passengers by the mail being always heavily wrapped up from bead to foot, the room had the odd interest for the establishment of the Royal George, that although but one kind of man was seen to go into it, all kinds and varieties of men came out of it. Consequently, another drawer, and two porters, and several maids and the landlady, were all loitering by accident at various points of the road between the Concord and the coffee-room, when a gentleman of sixty, formally dressed in a brown suit of clothes, pretty well worn, but very well kept, with large square cuffs and large flaps to the pockets, passed along on his way to his breakfast.

The coffee-room had no other occupant, that forenoon, than the gentleman in brown. His breakfast-table was drawn before the fire, and as he sat, with its light shining on him, waiting for the meal, he sat so still, that he might have been sitting for his portrait.

Very orderly and methodical he looked, with a hand on each knee, and a loud watch ticking a sonorous sermon under his flapped waist-coat, as though it pitted its gravity and longevity against the levity and evanescence of the brisk fire. He had a good leg, and was a little vain of it, for his brown stockings fitted sleek and close, and were of a fine texture; his shoes and buckles, too, though plain, were trim. He wore an odd little sleek crisp flaxen wig, setting very close to his head: which wig, it is to be presumed, was made of hair, but which looked far more as though it were spun from filaments of silk or glass. His linen, though not of a fineness in accordance with his stockings, was as white as the tops of the waves that broke upon the neighbouring beach, or the specks of sail that glinted in the sunlight far at sea. A face habitually suppressed and quieted, was still lighted up under the quaint wig by a pair of moist bright eyes that it must have cost their owner, in years gone by, some pains to drill to the composed and reserved expression of Tellson's Bank. He had a healthy colour in his cheeks, and his face, though lined, bore few traces of anxiety. But, perhaps the confidential bachelor clerks in Tellson's Bank were principally occupied with the cares of other people; and perhaps second-hand cares, like second-hand clothes, come easily off and on.

Completing his resemblance to a man who was sitting for his portrait, Mr. Lorry dropped off to sleep. The arrival of his breakfast roused him, and he said to the drawer, as he moved his chair to it:

"I wish accommodation prepared for a young lady who may come here at any time to-day. She may ask for Mr. Jarvis Lorry, or she may only ask for a gentleman from Tellson's Bank. Please to let me know."

"Yes, sir. Tellson's Bank in London, sir?"

"Yes."

"Yes, sir. We have oftentimes the honour to entertain your gentlemen in their travelling backwards and forwards betwixt London and Paris, sir. A vast deal of travelling, sir, in Tellson and Company's House."

"Yes. We are quite a French House, as well as an English one."

"Yes, sir. Not much in the habit of such travelling yourself, I think, sir?"

"Not of late years. It is fifteen years since we—since I—came last from France."

"Indeed, sir? That was before my time here, sir. Before our people's time here, sir. The George was in other hands at that time, sir."

"I believe so."

"But I would hold a pretty wager, sir, that a House like Tellson and Company was flourishing, a matter of fifty, not to speak of fifteen years ago?"

"You might treble that, and say a hundred and fifty, yet not be far from the truth."

"Indeed, sir!"

Rounding his mouth and both his eyes, as he stepped backward from the table, the waiter shifted his napkin from his right arm to his left, dropped into a comfortable attitude, and stood surveying the guest while he ate and drank, as from an observatory or watchtower. According to the immemorial usage of waiters in all ages.

When Mr. Lorry had finished his breakfast, he went out for a stroll on the beach. The little narrow, crooked town of Dover hid itself away from the beach, and ran its head into the chalk cliffs, like a marine ostrich. The beach was a desert of heaps of sea and stones tumbling wildly about, and the sea did what it liked, and what it liked was destruction. It thundered at the town, and thundered at the cliffs, and brought the coast down, madly. The air among the houses was of so strong a piscatory flavour that one might have supposed sick fish went up to be dipped in it, as sick people went down to be dipped in the sea. A little fishing was done in the port, and a quantity of strolling about by night, and looking seaward: particularly at those times when the tide made, and was near flood. Small tradesmen, who did no business whatever, sometimes unaccountably realised large fortunes, and it was remarkable that nobody in the neighbourhood could endure a lamplighter.

As the day declined into the afternoon, and the air, which had been at intervals clear enough to allow the French coast to be seen, became again charged with mist and vapour, Mr. Lorry's thoughts seemed to cloud too. When it was dark, and he sat before the coffee-room fire, awaiting his dinner as he had awaited his breakfast, his mind was busily digging, digging, digging, in the live red coals.

A bottle of good claret after dinner does a digger in the red coals no harm, otherwise than as it has a tendency to throw him out of work. Mr. Lorry had been idle a long time, and had just poured out his last glassful of wine with as complete an appearance of satisfaction as is ever to be found in an elderly gentleman of a fresh complexion who has got to the end of a bottle, when a rattling of wheels came up the narrow street, and rumbled into the inn-yard.

He set down his glass untouched. "This is Mam'selle!" said he.

In a very few minutes the waiter came in to announce that Miss Manette had arrived from London, and would be happy to see the gentleman from Tellson's.

"So soon?"

Miss Manette had taken some refreshment on the road, and required none then, and was extremely anxious to see the gentleman from Tellson's immediately, if it suited his pleasure and convenience.

The gentleman from Tellson's had nothing left for it but to empty his glass with an air of stolid desperation, settle his odd little flaxen wig at the ears, and follow the waiter to Miss Manette's apartment. It was a large, dark room, furnished in a funereal manner with black horsehair, and loaded with heavy dark tables. These had been oiled and oiled, until the two tall candles on the table in the middle of the room were gloomily reflected on every leaf; as if THEY were buried, in deep graves of black mahogany, and no light to speak of could be expected from them until they were dug out.

The obscurity was so difficult to penetrate that Mr. Lorry, picking his way over the well-worn Turkey carpet, supposed Miss Manette to be, for the moment, in some adjacent room, until, having got past the two tall candles, he saw standing to receive him by the table between them and the fire, a young lady of not more than seventeen, in a riding-cloak, and still holding her straw travelling- hat by its ribbon in her hand. As his eyes rested on a short, slight, pretty figure, a quantity of golden hair, a pair of blue eyes that met his own with an inquiring look, and a forehead with a singular capacity (remembering how young and smooth it was), of rifting and knitting itself into an expression that was not quite one of perplexity, or wonder, or alarm, or merely of a bright fixed attention, though it included all the four expressions-as his eyes rested on these things, a sudden vivid likeness passed before him, of a child whom he had held in his arms on the passage across that very Channel, one cold time, when the hail drifted heavily and the sea ran high. The likeness passed away, like a breath along the surface of the gaunt pier-glass behind her, on the frame of which, a hospital procession of negro cupids, several headless and all cripples, were offering black baskets of Dead Sea fruit to black divinities of the feminine gender-and he made his formal bow to Miss Manette.

"Pray take a seat, sir." In a very clear and pleasant young voice; a little foreign in its accent, but a very little indeed.

"I kiss your hand, miss," said Mr. Lorry, with the manners of an earlier date, as he made his formal bow again, and took his seat.

"I received a letter from the Bank, sir, yesterday, informing me that some intelligence—or discovery—"

"The word is not material, miss; either word will do."

"—respecting the small property of my poor father, whom I never saw—so long dead—"

Mr. Lorry moved in his chair, and cast a troubled look towards the hospital procession of negro cupids. As if they had any help for anybody in their absurd baskets!

"—rendered it necessary that I should go to Paris, there to communicate with a gentleman of the Bank, so good as to be despatched to Paris for the purpose."

"Myself."

"As I was prepared to hear, sir."

She curtseyed to him (young ladies made curtseys in those days), with a pretty desire to convey to him that she felt how much older and wiser he was than she. He made her another bow.

"I replied to the Bank, sir, that as it was considered necessary, by those who know, and who are so kind as to advise me, that I should go to France, and that as I am an orphan and have no friend who could go with me, I should esteem it highly if I might be permitted to place myself, during the journey, under that worthy gentleman's protection. The gentleman had left London, but I think a messenger was sent after him to beg the favour of his waiting for me here."

"I was happy," said Mr. Lorry, "to be entrusted with the charge. I shall be more happy to execute it."

"Sir, I thank you indeed. I thank you very gratefully. It was told me by the Bank that the gentleman would explain to me the details of the business, and that I must prepare myself to find them of a surprising nature. I have done my best to prepare myself, and I naturally have a strong and eager interest to know what they are."

"Naturally," said Mr. Lorry. "Yes—I—"

After a pause, he added, again settling the crisp flaxen wig at the ears, "It is very difficult to begin."

He did not begin, but, in his indecision, met her glance. The young forehead lifted itself into that singular expression—but it was pretty and characteristic, besides being singular—and she raised her hand, as if with an involuntary action she caught at, or stayed some passing shadow.

"Are you quite a stranger to me, sir?"

"Am I not?" Mr. Lorry opened his hands, and extended them outwards with an argumentative smile.

Between the eyebrows and just over the little feminine nose, the line of which was as delicate and fine as it was possible to be, the expression deepened itself as she took her seat thoughtfully in the chair by which she had hitherto remained standing. He watched her as she mused, and the moment she raised her eyes again, went on:

"In your adopted country, I presume, I cannot do better than address you as a young English lady, Miss Manette?"

"If you please, sir."

"Miss Manette, I am a man of business. I have a business charge to acquit myself of. In your reception of it, don't heed me any more than if I was a speaking machine-truly, I am not much else. I will, with your leave, relate to you, miss, the story of one of our customers."

"Story!"

He seemed wilfully to mistake the word she had repeated, when he added, in a hurry, "Yes, customers; in the banking business we usually call our connection our customers. He was a French gentleman; a scientific gentleman; a man of great acquirements— a Doctor."

"Not of Beauvais?"

"Why, yes, of Beauvais. Like Monsieur Manette, your father, the gentleman was of Beauvais. Like Monsieur Manette, your father, the gentleman was of repute in Paris. I had the honour of knowing him there. Our relations were business relations, but confidential. I was at that time in our French House, and had been—oh! twenty years."

"At that time—I may ask, at what time, sir?"

"I speak, miss, of twenty years ago. He married—an English lady—and I was one of the trustees. His affairs, like the affairs of many other French gentlemen and French families, were entirely in Tellson's hands. In a similar way I am, or I have been, trustee of one kind or other for scores of our customers. These are mere business relations, miss; there is no friendship in them, no particular interest, nothing like sentiment. I have passed from one to another, in the course of my business life, just as I pass from one of our customers to another in the course of my business day; in short, I have no feelings; I am a mere machine. To go on—"

"But this is my father's story, sir; and I begin to think" —the curiously roughened forehead was very intent upon him—"that when I was left an orphan through my mother's surviving my father only two years, it was you who brought me to England. I am almost sure it was you."

Mr. Lorry took the hesitating little hand that confidingly advanced to take his, and he put it with some ceremony to his lips. He then conducted the young lady straightway to her chair again, and, holding the chair-back with his left hand, and using his right by turns to rub his chin, pull his wig at the ears, or point what he said, stood looking down into her face while she sat looking up into his.

"Miss Manette, it was I. And you will see how truly I spoke of myself just now, in saying I had no feelings, and that all the relations I hold with my fellow-creatures are mere business relations, when you reflect that I have never seen you since. No; you have been the ward of Tellson's House since, and I have been busy with the other business of Tellson's House since. Feelings! I have no time for them, no chance of them. I pass my whole life, miss, in turning an immense pecuniary Mangle."

After this odd description of his daily routine of employment, Mr. Lorry flattened his flaxen wig upon his head with both hands (which was most unnecessary, for nothing could be flatter than its shining surface was before), and resumed his former attitude.

"So far, miss (as you have remarked), this is the story of your gretted father. Now comes the difference. If your father had not died when he did—Don't be frightened! How you start!"

She did, indeed, start. And she caught his wrist with both her hands.

"Pray," said Mr. Lorry, in a soothing tone, bringing his left hand from the back of the chair to lay it on the supplicatory fingers that clasped him in so violent a tremble: "pray control your agitation— a matter of business. As I was saying—"

Her look so discomposed him that he stopped, wandered, and began anew:

"As I was saying; if Monsieur Manette had not died; if he had suddenly and silently disappeared; if he had been spirited away; if it had not been difficult to guess to what dreadful place, though no art could trace him; if he had an enemy in some compatriot who could exercise a privilege that I in my own time have known the boldest people afraid to speak of in a whisper, across the water there; for instance, the privilege of filling up blank forms for the consignment of any one to the oblivion of a prison for any length of time; if his wife had implored the king, the queen, the court, the clergy, for any tidings of him, and all quite in vain;—then the history of your father would have been the history of this unfortunate gentleman, the Doctor of Beauvais."

"I entreat you to tell me more, sir."

"I will. I am going to. You can bear it?"

"I can bear anything but the uncertainty you leave me in at this moment."

"You speak collectedly, and you—ARE collected. That's good!" (Though his manner was less satisfied than his words.) "A matter of business. Regard it as a matter of business-business that must be done. Now if this doctor's wife, though a lady of great courage and spirit, had suffered so intensely from this cause before her little child was born—"

"The little child was a daughter, sir."

"A daughter. A-a-matter of business—don't be distressed. Miss, if the poor lady had suffered so intensely before her little child was born, that she came to the determination of sparing the poor child the inheritance of any part of the agony she had known the pains of, by rearing her in the belief that her father was dead— No, don't kneel! In Heaven's name why should you kneel to me!"

"For the truth. O dear, good, compassionate sir, for the truth!"

"A-a matter of business. You confuse me, and how can I transact business if I am confused? Let us be clear-headed. If you could kindly mention now, for instance, what nine times ninepence are, or how many shillings in twenty guineas, it would be so encouraging. I should be so much more at my ease about your state of mind."

Without directly answering to this appeal, she sat so still when he had very gently raised her, and the hands that had not ceased to clasp his wrists were so much more steady than they had been, that she communicated some reassurance to Mr. Jarvis Lorry.

"That's right, that's right. Courage! Business! You have business before you; useful business. Miss Manette, your mother took this course with you. And when she died—I believe broken-hearted— having never slackened her unavailing search for your father, she left you, at two years old, to grow to be blooming, beautiful, and happy, without the dark cloud upon you of living in uncertainty whether your father soon wore his heart out in prison, or wasted there through many lingering years."

As he said the words he looked down, with an admiring pity, on the flowing golden hair; as if he pictured to himself that it might have been already tinged with grey.

"You know that your parents had no great possession, and that what they had was secured to your mother and to you. There has been no new discovery, of money, or of any other property; but—"

He felt his wrist held closer, and he stopped. The expression in the forehead, which had so particularly attracted his notice, and which was now immovable, had deepened into one of pain and horror.

"But he has been-been found. He is alive. Greatly changed, it is too probable; almost a wreck, it is possible; though we will hope the best. Still, alive. Your father has been taken to the house of an old servant in Paris, and we are going there: I, to identify him if I can: you, to restore him to life, love, duty, rest, comfort."

A shiver ran through her frame, and from it through his. She said, in a low, distinct, awe-stricken voice, as if she were saying it in a dream,

"I am going to see his Ghost! It will be his Ghost—not him!"

Mr. Lorry quietly chafed the hands that held his arm. "There, there, there! See now, see now! The best and the worst are known to you, now. You are well on your way to the poor wronged gentleman, and, with a fair sea voyage, and a fair land journey, you will be soon at his dear side."

She repeated in the same tone, sunk to a whisper, "I have been free, I have been happy, yet his Ghost has never haunted me!"

"Only one thing more," said Mr. Lorry, laying stress upon it as a wholesome means of enforcing her attention: "he has been found under another name; his own, long forgotten or long concealed. It would be worse than useless now to inquire which; worse than useless to seek to know whether he has been for years overlooked, or always designedly held prisoner. It would be worse than useless now to make any inquiries, because it would be dangerous. Better not to mention the subject, anywhere or in any way, and to remove him—for a while at all events— out of France. Even I, safe as an Englishman, and even Tellson's, important as they are to French credit, avoid all naming of the matter. I carry about me, not a scrap of writing openly referring to it. This is a secret service altogether. My credentials, entries, and memoranda, are all comprehended in the one line, 'Recalled to Life;' which may mean anything. But what is the matter! She doesn't notice a word! Miss Manette!"

Perfectly still and silent, and not even fallen back in her chair, she sat under his hand, utterly insensible; with her eyes open and fixed upon him, and with that last expression looking as if it were carved or branded into her forehead. So close was her hold upon his arm, that he feared to detach himself lest he should hurt her; therefore he called out loudly for assistance without moving.

A wild-looking woman, whom even in his agitation, Mr. Lorry observed to be all of a red colour, and to have red hair, and to be dressed in some extraordinary tight-fitting fashion, and to have on her head a most wonderful bonnet like a Grenadier wooden measure, and good measure too, or a great Stilton cheese, came running into the room in advance of the inn servants, and soon settled the question of his detachment from the poor young lady, by laying a brawny hand upon his chest, and sending him flying back against the nearest wall.

("I really think this must be a man!" was Mr. Lorry's breathless reflection, simultaneously with his coming against the wall.)

"Why, look at you all!" bawled this figure, addressing the inn servants. "Why don't you go and fetch things, instead of standing there staring at me? I am not so much to look at, am I? Why don't you go and fetch things? I'll let you know, if you don't bring smelling-salts, cold water, and vinegar, quick, I will."

There was an immediate dispersal for these restoratives, and she softly laid the patient on a sofa, and tended her with great skill and gentleness: calling her "my precious!" and "my bird!" and spreading her golden hair aside over her shoulders with great pride and care.

"And you in brown!" she said, indignantly turning to Mr. Lorry; couldn't you tell her what you had to tell her, without frightening her to death? Look at her, with her pretty pale face and her cold hands. Do you call THAT being a Banker?"

Mr. Lorry was so exceedingly disconcerted by a question so hard to answer, that he could only look on, at a distance, with much feebler sympathy and humility, while the strong woman, having banished the inn servants under the mysterious penalty of "letting them know" something not mentioned if they stayed there, staring, recovered her charge by a regular series of gradations, and coaxed her to lay her drooping head upon her shoulder.

"I hope she will do well now," said Mr. Lorry.

"No thanks to you in brown, if she does. My darling pretty!"

"I hope," said Mr. Lorry, after another pause of feeble sympathy and humility, "that you accompany Miss Manette to France?"

"A likely thing, too!" replied the strong woman. "If it was ever intended that I should go across salt water, do you suppose Providence would have cast my lot in an island?"

This being another question hard to answer, Mr. Jarvis Lorry withdrew to consider it.

CHAPTER 8

A Sight

"You know the Old Bailey, well, no doubt?" said one of the oldest of clerks to Jerry the messenger.

"Ye-es, sir," returned Jerry, in something of a dogged manner. "I do know the Bailey."

"Just so. And you know Mr. Lorry."

"I know Mr. Lorry, sir, much better than I know the Bailey. Much better," said Jerry, not unlike a reluctant witness at the establishment in question, "than I, as a honest tradesman, wish to know the Bailey."

"Very well. Find the door where the witnesses go in, and show the door-keeper this note for Mr. Lorry. He will then let you in."

"Into the court, sir?"

"Into the court."

Mr. Cruncher's eyes seemed to get a little closer to one another, and to interchange the inquiry, "What do you think of this?"

"Am I to wait in the court, sir?" he asked, as the result of that conference.

"I am going to tell you. The door-keeper will pass the note to Mr. Lorry, and do you make any gesture that will attract Mr. Lorry's attention, and show him where you stand. Then what you have to do, is, to remain there until he wants you."

"Is that all, sir?"

"That's all. He wishes to have a messenger at hand. This is to tell him you are there."

As the ancient clerk deliberately folded and superscribed the note, Mr. Cruncher, after surveying him in silence until he came to the blotting-paper stage, remarked:

"I suppose they'll be trying Forgeries this morning?"

"Treason!"

"That's quartering," said Jerry. "Barbarous!"

"It is the law," remarked the ancient clerk, turning his surprised spectacles upon him. "It is the law."

"It's hard in the law to spile a man, I think. Ifs hard enough to kill him, but it's wery hard to spile him, sir."

"Not at all," retained the ancient clerk. "Speak well of the law. Take care of your chest and voice, my good friend, and leave the law to take care of itself. I give you that advice."

"It's the damp, sir, what settles on my chest and voice," said Jerry. "I leave you to judge what a damp way of earning a living mine is."

"WeB, well," said the old clerk; "we aa have our various ways of gaining a livelihood. Some of us have damp ways, and some of us have dry ways. Here is the letter. Go along."

Jerry took the letter, and, remarking to himself with less internal deference than he made an outward show of, "You are a lean old one, too," made his bow, informed his son, in passing, of his destination, and went his way.

They hanged at Tyburn, in those days, so the street outside Newgate had not obtained one infamous notoriety that has since attached to it. But, the gaol was a vile place, in which most kinds of debauchery and villainy were practised, and where dire diseases were bred, that came into court with the prisoners, and sometimes rushed straight from the dock at my Lord Chief Justice himself, and pulled him off the bench. It had more than once happened, that the Judge in the black cap pronounced his own doom as certainly as the prisoner's, and even died before him. For the rest, the Old Bailey was famous as a kind of deadly inn-yard, from which pale travellers set out continually, in carts and coaches, on a violent passage into the other world: traversing some two miles and a half of public street and road, and shaming few good citizens, if any. So powerful is use, and so desirable to be good use in the beginning. It was famous, too, for the pillory, a wise old institution, that inflicted a punishment of which no one could foresee the extent; also, for the whipping-post, another dear old institution, very humanising and softening to behold in action; also, for extensive transactions in blood-money, another fragment of ancestral wisdom, systematically leading to the most frightful mercenary crimes that could be committed under Heaven. Altogether, the Old Bailey, at that date, was a choice illustration of the precept, that "Whatever is is right;" an aphorism that would be as final as it is lazy, did it not include the troublesome consequence, that nothing that ever was, was wrong.

Making his way through the tainted crowd, dispersed up and down this hideous scene of action, with the skill of a man accustomed to make his way quietly, the messenger found out the door he sought, and handed in his letter through a trap in it. For, people then paid to see the play at the Old Bailey, just as they paid to see the play in Bedlam—only the former entertainment was much the dearer. Therefore, all the Old Bailey doors were well guarded—except, indeed, the social doors by which the criminals got there, and those were always left wide open.

After some delay and demur, the door grudgingly turned on its hinges a very little way, and allowed Mr. Jerry Cruncher to squeeze himself into court.

"What's on?" he asked, in a whisper, of the man he found himself next to.

"Nothing yet."

"What's coming on?"

"The Treason case."

"The quartering one, eh?"

"Ah!" returned the man, with a relish; "he'll be drawn on a hurdle to be half hanged, and then he'll be taken down and sliced before his own face, and then his inside will be taken out and burnt while he looks on, and then his head will be chopped off, and he'll be cut into quarters. That's the sentence."

"If he's found Guilty, you mean to say?" Jerry added, by way of proviso.

"Oh! they'll find him guilty," said the other. "Don't you be afraid of that."

Mr. Cruncher's attention was here diverted to the door-keeper, whom he saw making his way to Mr. Lorry, with the note in his hand. Mr. Lorry sat at a table, among the gentlemen in wigs: not far from a wigged gentleman, the prisoner's counsel, who had a great bundle of papers before him: and nearly opposite another wigged gentleman with his hands in his pockets, whose whole attention, when Mr. Cruncher looked at him then or afterwards, seemed to be concentrated on the ceiling of the court. After some gruff coughing and rubbing of his chin and signing with his hand, Jerry attracted the notice of Mr. Lorry, who had stood up to look for him, and who quietly nodded and sat down again.

"What's he got to do with the case?" asked the man he had spoken with.

"Blest if I know," said Jerry.

"What have YOU got to do with it, then, if a person may inquire?"

"Blest if I know that either," said Jerry.

The entrance of the Judge, and a consequent great stir and settling down in the court, stopped the dialogue. Presently, the dock became the central point of interest. Two gaolers, who had been standing there, wont out, and the prisoner was brought in, and put to the bar.

Everybody present, except the one wigged gentleman who looked at the ceiling, stared at him. All the human breath in the place, rolled at him, like a sea, or a wind, or a fire. Eager faces strained round pillars and corners, to get a sight of him; spectators in back rows stood up, not to miss a hair of him; people on the floor of the court, laid their hands on the shoulders of the people before them, to help themselves, at anybody's cost, to a view of him—stood a-tiptoe, got upon ledges, stood upon next to nothing, to see every inch of him. Conspicuous among these latter, like an animated bit of the spiked wall of Newgate, Jerry stood: aiming at the prisoner the beery breath of a whet he had taken as he came along, and discharging it to mingle with the waves of other beer, and gin, and tea, and coffee, and what not, that flowed at him, and already broke upon the great windows behind him in an impure mist and rain.

The object of all this staring and blaring, was a young man of about five-and-twenty, well-grown and well-looking, with a sunburnt cheek and a dark eye. His condition was that of a young gentleman. He was plainly dressed in black, or very dark grey, and his hair, which was long and dark, was gathered in a ribbon at the back of his neck; more to be out of his way than for ornament. As an emotion of the mind will express itself through any covering of the body, so the paleness which his situation engendered came through the brown upon his cheek, showing the soul to be stronger than the sun. He was otherwise quite self-possessed, bowed to the Judge, and stood quiet.

The sort of interest with which this man was stared and breathed at, was not a sort that elevated humanity. Had he stood in peril of a less horrible sentence—had there been a chance of any one of its savage details being spared—by just so much would he have lost in his fascination. The form that was to be doomed to be so shamefully mangled, was the sight; the immortal creature that was to be so butchered and torn asunder, yielded the sensation. Whatever gloss the various spectators put upon the interest, according to their several arts and powers of self-deceit, the interest was, at the root of it, Ogreish.

Silence in the court! Charles Darnay had yesterday pleaded Not Guilty to an indictment denouncing him (with infinite jingle and jangle) for that he was a false traitor to our serene, illustrious, excellent, and so forth, prince, our Lord the King, by reason of his having, on divers occasions, and by divers means and ways, assisted Lewis, the French King, in his wars against our said serene, illustrious, excellent, and so forth; that was to say, by coming and going, between the dominions of our said serene, illustrious, excellent, and so forth, and those of the said French Lewis, and wickedly, falsely, traitorously, and otherwise evil-adverbiously, revealing to the said French Lewis what forces our said serene, illustrious, excellent, and so forth, had in preparation to send to Canada and North America. This much, Jerry, with his head becoming more and more spiky as the law terms bristled it, made out with huge satisfaction, and so arrived circuitously at the understanding that the aforesaid, and over and over again aforesaid, Charles Darnay, stood there before him upon his trial; that the jury were swearing in; and that Mr. Attorney-General was making ready to speak.

The accused, who was (and who knew he was) being mentally hanged, beheaded, and quartered, by everybody there, neither flinched from the situation, nor assumed any theatrical air in it. He was quiet and attentive; watched the opening proceedings with a grave interest; and stood with his hands resting on the slab of wood before him, so composedly, that they had not displaced a leaf of the herbs with which it was strewn. The court was all bestrewn with herbs and sprinkled with vinegar, as a precaution against gaol air and gaol fever.

Over the prisoner's head there was a mirror, to throw the light down upon him. Crowds of the wicked and the wretched had been reflected in it, and had passed from its surface and this earth's together. Haunted in a most ghastly manner that abominable place would have been, if the glass could ever have rendered back its reflections, as the ocean is one day to give up its dead. Some passing thought of the infamy and disgrace for which it had been reserved, may have struck the prisoner's mind. Be that as it may, a change in his position making him conscious of a bar of light across his face, he looked up; and when he saw the glass his face flushed, and his right hand pushed the herbs away.

It happened, that the action turned his face to that side of the court which was on his left. About on a level with his eyes, there sat, in that corner of the Judge's bench, two persons upon whom his look immediately rested; so immediately, and so much to the changing of his aspect, that all the eyes that were tamed upon him, turned to them.

The spectators saw in the two figures, a young lady of little more than twenty, and a gentleman who was evidently her father; a man of a very remarkable appearance in respect of the absolute whiteness of his hair, and a certain indescribable intensity of face: not of an active kind, but pondering and self-communing. When this expression was upon him, he looked as if he were old; but when it was stirred and broken up—as it was now, in a moment, on his speaking to his daughter—he became a handsome man, not past the prime of life.

His daughter had one of her hands drawn through his arm, as she sat by him, and the other pressed upon it. She had drawn close to him, in her dread of the scene, and in her pity for the prisoner. Her forehead had been strikingly expressive of an engrossing terror and compassion that saw nothing but the peril of the accused. This had been so very noticeable, so very powerfully and naturally shown, that starers who had had no pity for him were touched by her; and the whisper went about, "Who are they?"

Jerry, the messenger, who had made his own observations, in his own manner, and who had been sucking the rust off his fingers in his absorption, stretched his neck to hear who they were. The crowd about him had pressed and passed the inquiry on to the nearest attendant, and from him it had been more slowly pressed and passed back; at last it got to Jerry:

"Witnesses."

"For which side?"

"Against."

"Against what side?"

"The prisoner's."

The Judge, whose eyes had gone in the general direction, recalled them, leaned back in his seat, and looked steadily at the man whose life was in his hand, as Mr. Attorney-General rose to spin the rope, grind the axe, and hammer the nails into the scaffold.

CHAPTER 19

The Fellow of No Delicacy

If Sydney Carton ever shone anywhere, he certainly never shone in the house of Doctor Manette. He had been there often, during a whole year, and had always been the same moody and morose lounger there. When he cared to talk, he talked well; but, the cloud of caring for nothing, which overshadowed him with such a fatal darkness, was very rarely pierced by the light within him.

And yet he did care something for the streets that environed that house, and for the senseless stones that made their pavements. Many a night he vaguely and unhappily wandered there, when wine had brought no transitory gladness to him; many a dreary daybreak revealed his solitary figure lingering there, and still lingering there when the first beams of the sun brought into strong relief, removed beauties of architecture in spires of churches and lofty buildings, as perhaps the quiet time brought some sense of better things, else forgotten and unattainable, into his mind. Of late, the neglected bed in the Temple Court had known him more scantily than ever; and often when he had thrown himself upon it no longer than a few minutes, he had got up again, and haunted that neighbourhood.

On a day in August, when Mr. Stryver (after notifying to his jackal that "he had thought better of that marrying matter") had carried his delicacy into Devonshire, and when the sight and scent of flowers in the City streets had some waifs of goodness in them for the worst, of health for the sickliest, and of youth for the oldest, Sydney's feet still trod those stones. From being irresolute and purposeless, his feet became animated by an intention, and, in the working out of that intention, they took him to the Doctor's door.

He was shown up-stairs, and found Lucie at her work, alone. She had never been quite at her ease with him, and received him with some little embarrassment as he seated himself near her table. But, looking up at his face in the interchange of the first few common-places, she observed a change in it.

"I fear you are not well, Mr. Carton!"

"No. But the life I lead, Miss Manette, is not conducive to health. What is to be expected of, or by, such profligates?"

"Is it not—forgive me; I have begun the question on my lips—a pity to live no better life?"

"God knows it is a shame!"

"Then why not change it?"

Looking gently at him again, she was surprised and saddened to see that there were tears in his eyes. There were tears in his voice too, as he answered:

"It is too late for that. I shall never be better than I am. I shall sink lower, and be worse."

He leaned an elbow on her table, and covered his eyes with his hand. The table trembled in the silence that followed.

She had never seen him softened, and was much distressed. He knew her to be so, without looking at her, and said:

"Pray forgive me, Miss Manette. I break down before the knowledge of what I want to say to you. Will you hear me?"

"If it will do you any good, Mr. Carton, if it would make you happier, it would make me very glad!"

"God bless you for your sweet compassion!"

He unshaded his face after a little while, and spoke steadily.

"Don't be afraid to hear me. Don't shrink from anything I say. I am like one who died young. All my life might have been."

"No, Mr. Carton. I am sure that the best part of it might still be; I am sure that you might be much, much worthier of yourself."

"Say of you, Miss Manette, and although I know better—although in the mystery of my own wretched heart I know better—I shall never forget it!"

She was pale and trembling. He came to her relief with a fixed despair of himself which made the interview unlike any other that could have been holden.

"If it had been possible, Miss Manette, that you could have returned the love of the man you see before yourself—flung away, wasted, drunken, poor creature of misuse as you know him to be—he would have been conscious this day and hour, in spite of his happiness, that he would bring you to misery, bring you to sorrow and repentance, blight you, disgrace you, pull you down with him. I know very well that you can have no tenderness for me; I ask for none; I am even thankful that it cannot be."

"Without it, can I not save you, Mr. Carton? Can I not recall you— forgive me again!—to a better course? Can I in no way repay your confidence? I know this is a confidence," she modestly said, after a little hesitation, and in earnest tears, "I know you would say this to no one else. Can I turn it to no good account for yourself, Mr. Carton?"

He shook his head.

"To none. No, Miss Manette, to none. If you will hear me through a very little more, all you can ever do for me is done. I wish you to know that you have been the last dream of my soul. In my degradation I have not been so degraded but that the sight of you with your father, and of this home made such a home by you, has stirred old shadows that I thought had died out of me. Since I knew you, I have been troubled by a remorse that I thought would never reproach me again, and have heard whispers from old voices impelling me upward, that I thought were silent for ever. I have had unformed ideas of striving afresh, beginning anew, shaking off sloth and sensuality, and fighting out the abandoned fight. A dream, all a dream, that ends in nothing, and leaves the sleeper where he lay down, but I wish you to know that you inspired it."

"Will nothing of it remain? O Mr. Carton, think again! Try again!"

"No, Miss Manette; all through it, I have known myself to be quite undeserving. And yet I have had the weakness, and have still the weakness, to wish you to know with what a sudden mastery you kindled me, heap of ashes that I am, into fire—a fire, however, inseparable in its nature from myself, quickening nothing, lighting nothing, doing no service, idly burning away."

"Since it is my misfortune, Mr. Carton, to have made you more unhappy than you were before you knew me—"

"Don't say that, Miss Manette, for you would have reclaimed me, if anything could. you will not be the cause of my becoming worse."

"Since the state of your mind that you describe, is, at all events, attributable to some influence of mine—this is what I mean, if I can make it plain—can I use no influence to serve you? Have I no power for good, with you, at all?"

"The utmost good that I am capable of now, Miss Manette, I have come here to realise. Let me carry through the rest of my misdirected life, the remembrance that I opened my heart to you, last of all the world; and that there was something left in me at this time which you could deplore and pity."

"Which I entreated you to believe, again and again, most fervently, with all my heart, was capable of better things, Mr. Carton!"

"Entreat me to believe it no more, Miss Manette. I have proved myself, and I know better. I distress you; I draw fast to an end. Will you let me believe, when I recall this day, that the last confidence of my life was reposed in your pure and innocent breast, and that it lies there alone, and will be shared by no one?"

"If that will be a consolation to you, yes."

"Not even by the dearest one ever to be known to you?"

"Mr. Carton," she answered, after an agitated pause, "the secret is yours, not mine; and I promise to respect it."

"Thank you. And again, God bless you."

He put her hand to his lips, and moved towards the door.

"Be under no apprehension, Miss Manette, of my ever resuming this conversation by so much as a passing word. I will never refer to it again. If I were dead, that could not be surer than it is henceforth. In the hour of my death, I shall hold sacred the one good remembrance— and shall thank and bless you for it—that my last avowal of myself was made to you, and that my name, and faults, and miseries were gently carried in your heart. May it otherwise be light and happy!"

He was so unlike what he had ever shown himself to be, and it was so sad to think how much he had thrown away, and how much he every day kept down and perverted, that Lucie Manette wept mournfully for him as he stood looking back at her.

"Be comforted!" he said, "I am not worth such feeling, Miss Manette. An hour or two hence, and the low companions and low habits that I scorn but yield to, will render me less worth such tears as those, than any wretch who creeps along the streets. Be comforted! But, within myself, I shall always be, towards you, what I am now, though outwardly I shall be what you have heretofore seen me. The last supplication but one I make to you, is, that you will believe this of me."

"I will, Mr. Carton."

"My last supplication of all, is this; and with it, I will relieve you of a visitor with whom I well know you have nothing in unison, and between whom and you there is an impassable space. It is useless to say it, I know, but it rises out of my soul. For you, and for any dear to you, I would do anything. If my career were of that better kind that there was any opportunity or capacity of sacrifice in it, I would embrace any sacrifice for you and for those dear to you. Try to hold me in your mind, at some quiet times, as ardent and sincere in this one thing. The time will come, the time will not be long in coming, when new ties will be formed about you—ties that will bind you yet more tenderly and strongly to the home you so adorn—the dearest ties that will ever grace and gladden you. O Miss Manette, when the little picture of a happy father's face looks up in yours, when you see your own bright beauty springing up anew at your feet, think now and then that there is a man who would give his life, to keep a life you love beside you!"

He said, "Farewell!" said a last "God bless you!" and left her.

CHAPTER 32

The Grindstone

Tellson's Bank, established in the Saint Germain Quarter of Paris, was in a wing of a large house, approached by a courtyard and shut off from the street by a high wall and a strong gate. The house belonged to a great nobleman who had lived in it until he made a flight from the troubles, in his own cook's dress, and got across the borders. A mere beast of the chase flying from hunters, he was still in his metempsychosis no other than the same Monseigneur, the preparation of whose chocolate for whose lips had once occupied three strong men besides the cook in question.

Monseigneur gone, and the three strong men absolving themselves from the sin of having drawn his high wages, by being more than ready and willing to cut his throat on the altar of the dawning Republic one and indivisible of Liberty, Equality, Fraternity, or Death, Monseigneur's house had been first sequestrated, and then confiscated. For, all things moved so fast, and decree followed decree with that fierce precipitation, that now upon the third night of the autumn month of September, patriot emissaries of the law were in possession of Monseigneur's house, and had marked it with the tri-colour, and were drinking brandy in its state apartments.

A place of business in London like Tellson's place of business in Paris, would soon have driven the House out of its mind and into the Gazette. For, what would staid British responsibility and respectability have said to orange-trees in boxes in a Bank courtyard, and even to a Cupid over the counter? Yet such things were. Tellson's had whitewashed the Cupid, but he was still to be seen on the ceiling, in the coolest linen, aiming (as he very often does) at money from morning to night. Bankruptcy must inevitably have come of this young Pagan, in Lombard-street, London, and also of a curtained alcove in the rear of the immortal boy, and also of a looking-glass let into the wall, and also of clerks not at all old, who danced in public on the slightest provocation. Yet, a French Tellson's could get on with these things exceedingly well, and, as long as the times held together, no man had taken fright at them, and drawn out his money.

What money would be drawn out of Tellson's henceforth, and what would lie there, lost and forgotten; what plate and jewels would tarnish in Tellson's hiding-places, while the depositors rusted in prisons, and when they should have violently perished; how many accounts with Tellson's never to be balanced in this world, must be carried over into the next; no man could have said, that night, any more than Mr. Jarvis Lorry could, though he thought heavily of these questions. He sat by a newly-lighted wood fire (the blighted and unfruitful year was prematurely cold), and on his honest and courageous face there was a deeper shade than the pendent lamp could throw, or any object in the room distortedly reflect—a shade of horror.

He occupied rooms in the Bank, in his fidelity to the House of which he had grown to be a part, lie strong root-ivy. it chanced that they derived a kind of security from the patriotic occupation of the main building, but the true-hearted old gentleman never calculated about that. All such circumstances were indifferent to him, so that he did his duty. On the opposite side of the courtyard, under a colonnade, was extensive standin—for carriages—where, indeed, some carriages of Monseigneur yet stood. Against two of the pillars were fastened two great flaring flambeaux, and in the light of these, standing out in the open air, was a large grindstone: a roughly mounted thing which appeared to have hurriedly been brought there from some neighbouring smithy, or other workshop. Rising and looking out of window at these harmless objects, Mr. Lorry shivered, and retired to his seat by the fire. He had opened, not only the glass window, but the lattice blind outside it, and he had closed both again, and he shivered through his frame.

From the streets beyond the high wall and the strong gate, there came the usual night hum of the city, with now and then an indescribable ring in it, weird and unearthly, as if some unwonted sounds of a terrible nature were going up to Heaven.

"Thank God," said Mr. Lorry, clasping his hands, "that no one near and dear to me is in this dreadful town to-night. May He have mercy on all who are in danger!"

Soon afterwards, the bell at the great gate sounded, and he thought, "They have come back!" and sat listening. But, there was no loud irruption into the courtyard, as he had expected, and he heard the gate clash again, and all was quiet.

The nervousness and dread that were upon him inspired that vague uneasiness respecting the Bank, which a great change would naturally awaken, with such feelings roused. It was well guarded, and he got up to go among the trusty people who were watching it, when his door suddenly opened, and two figures rushed in, at sight of which he fell back in amazement.

Lucie and her father! Lucie with her arms stretched out to him, and with that old look of earnestness so concentrated and intensified, that it seemed as though it had been stamped upon her face expressly to give force and power to it in this one passage of her life.

"What is this?" cried Mr. Lorry, breathless and confused. "What is the matter? Lucie! Manette! What has happened? What has brought you here? What is it?"

With the look fixed upon him, in her paleness and wildness, she panted out in his arms, imploringly, "O my dear friend! My husband!"

"Your husband, Lucie?"

"Charles."

"What of Charles?"

"Here.

"Here, in Paris?"

"Has been here some days—three or four—I don't know how many— I can't collect my thoughts. An errand of generosity brought him here unknown to us; he was stopped at the barrier, and sent to prison."

The old man uttered an irrepressible cry. Almost at the same moment, the beg of the great gate rang again, and a loud noise of feet and voices came pouring into the courtyard.

"What is that noise?" said the Doctor, turning towards the window.

"Don't look!" cried Mr. Lorry. "Don't look out! Manette, for your life, don't touch the blind!"

The Doctor turned, with his hand upon the fastening of the window, and said, with a cool, bold smile:

"My dear friend, I have a charmed life in this city. I have been a Bastille prisoner. There is no patriot in Paris—in Paris? In France—who, knowing me to have been a prisoner in the Bastille, would touch me, except to overwhelm me with embraces, or carry me in triumph. My old pain has given me a power that has brought us through the barrier, and gained us news of Charles there, and brought us here. I knew it would be so; I knew I could help Charles out of all danger; I told Lucie so.—What is that noise?" His hand was again upon the window.

"Don't look!" cried Mr. Lorry, absolutely desperate. "No, Lucie, my dear, nor you!" He got his arm round her, and held her. "Don't be so terrified, my love. I solemnly swear to you that I know of no harm having happened to Charles; that I had no suspicion even of his being in this fatal place. What prison is he in?"

"La Force!"

"La Force! Lucie, my child, if ever you were brave and serviceable in your life—and you were always both—you will compose yourself now, to do exactly as I bid you; for more depends upon it than you can think, or I can say. There is no help for you in any action on your part to-night; you cannot possibly stir out. I say this, because what I must bid you to do for Charles's sake, is the hardest thing to do of all. You must instantly be obedient, still, and quiet. You must let me put you in a room at the back here. You must leave your father and me alone for two minutes, and as there are Life and Death in the world you must not delay."

"I will be submissive to you. I see in your face that you know I can do nothing else than this. I know you are true."

The old man kissed her, and hurried her into his room, and turned the key; then, came hurrying back to the Doctor, and opened the window and partly opened the blind, and put his hand upon the Doctor's arm, and looked out with him into the courtyard.

Looked out upon a throng of men and women: not enough in number, or near enough, to fill the courtyard: not more than forty or fifty in all. The people in possession of the house had let them in at the gate, and they had rushed in to work at the grindstone; it had evidently been set up there for their purpose, as in a convenient and retired spot.

But, such awful workers, and such awful work!

The grindstone had a double handle, and, turning at it madly were two men, whose faces, as their long hair Rapped back when the whirlings of the grindstone brought their faces up, were more horrible and cruel than the visages of the wildest savages in their most barbarous disguise. False eyebrows and false moustaches were stuck upon them, and their hideous countenances were all bloody and sweaty, and all awry with howling, and all staring and glaring with beastly excitement and want of sleep. As these ruffians turned and turned, their matted locks now flung forward over their eyes, now flung backward over their necks, some women held wine to their mouths that they might drink; and what with dropping blood, and what with dropping wine, and what with the stream of sparks struck out of the stone, all their wicked atmosphere seemed gore and fire. The eye could not detect one creature in the group free from the smear of blood. Shouldering one another to get next at the sharpening-stone, were men stripped to the waist, with the stain all over their limbs and bodies; men in all sorts of rags, with the stain upon those rags; men devilishly set off with spoils of women's lace and silk and ribbon, with the stain dyeing those trifles through and through. Hatchets, knives, bayonets, swords, all brought to be sharpened, were all red with it. Some of the hacked swords were tied to the wrists of those who carried them, with strips of linen and fragments of dress: ligatures various in kind, but all deep of the one colour. And as the frantic wielders of these weapons snatched them from the stream of sparks and tore away into the streets, the same red hue was red in their frenzied eyes;—eyes which any unbrutalised beholder would have given twenty years of life, to petrify with a well-directed gun.

All this was seen in a moment, as the vision of a drowning man, or of any human creature at any very great pass, could see a world if it were there. They drew back from the window, and the Doctor looked for explanation in his friend's ashy face.

"They are," Mr. Lorry whispered the words, glancing fearfully round at the locked room, "murdering the prisoners. If you are sure of what you say; if you really have the power you think you have—as I believe you have—make yourself known to these devils, and get taken to La Force. It may be too late, I don't know, but let it not be a minute later!"

Doctor Manette pressed his hand, hastened bareheaded out of the room, and was in the courtyard when Mr. Lorry regained the blind.

His streaming white hair, his remarkable face, and the impetuous confidence of his manner, as he put the weapons aside like water, carried him in an instant to the heart of the concourse at the stone. For a few moments there was a pause, and a hurry, and a murmur, and the unintelligible sound of his voice; and then Mr. Lorry saw him, surrounded by all, and in the midst of a line of twenty men long, all linked shoulder to shoulder, and hand to shoulder, hurried out with cries of—"Live the Bastille prisoner! Help for the Bastille prisoner's kindred in La Force! Room for the Bastille prisoner in front there! Save the prisoner Evremonde at La Force!" and a thousand answering shouts.

He closed the lattice again with a fluttering heart, closed the window and the curtain, hastened to Lucie, and told her that her father was assisted by the people, and gone in search of her husband. He found her child and Miss Pross with her; but, it never occurred to him to be surprised by their appearance until a long time afterwards, when he sat watching them in such quiet as the night knew.

Lucie had, by that time, fallen into a stupor on the floor at his feet, clinging to his hand. Miss Pross had laid the child down on his own bed, and her head had gradually fallen on the pillow beside her pretty charge. O the long, long night, with the moans of the poor wife! And O the long, long night, with no return of her father and no tidings!

Twice more in the darkness the bell at the great gate sounded, and the irruption was repeated, and the grindstone whirled and spluttered. "What is it?" cried Lucie, affrighted. "Hush! The soldiers' swords are sharpened there," said Mr. Lorry. "The place is national property now, and used as a kind of armoury, my love."

Twice more in all; but, the last spell of work was feeble and fitful. Soon afterwards the day began to dawn, and he softly detached himself from the clasping hand, and cautiously looked out again. A man, so besmeared that he might have been a sorely wounded soldier creeping back to consciousness on a field of slain, was rising from the pavement by the side of the grindstone, and looking about him with a vacant air. Shortly, this worn-out murderer descried in the imperfect light one of the carriages of Monseigneur, and, staggering to that gorgeous vehicle, climbed in at the door, and shut himself up to take his rest on its dainty cushions.

The great grindstone, Earth, had turned when Mr. Lorry looked out again, and the sun was red on the courtyard. But, the lesser grindstone stood alone there in the calm morning air, with a red upon it that the sun had never given, and would never take away.

CHAPTER I

The Period

It was the best of times, it was the worst of times, it was the age of wisdom, it was the age of foolishness, it was the epoch of belief, it was the epoch of incredulity, it was the season of Light, it was the season of Darkness, it was the spring of hope, it was the winter of despair, we had everything before us, we had nothing before us, we were all going direct to Heaven, we were all going direct the other way—in short, the period was so far like the present period, that some of its noisiest authorities insisted on its being received, for good or for evil, in the superlative degree of comparison only.

There were a king with a large jaw and a queen with a plain face, on the throne of England; there were a king with a large jaw and a queen with a fair face, on the throne of France. In both countries it was clearer than crystal to the lords of the State preserves of loaves and fishes, that things in general were settled for ever.

It was the year of Our Lord one thousand seven hundred and seventy-five. Spiritual revelations were conceded to England at that favoured period, as at this. Mrs. Southcott had recently attained her five-and-twentieth blessed birthday, of whom a prophetic private in the Life Guards had heralded the sublime appearance by announcing that arrangements were made for the swallowing up of London and Westminster. Even the Cock-lane ghost had been laid only a round dozen of years, after rapping out its messages, as the spirits of this very year last past (supernaturally deficient in originality) rapped out theirs. Mere messages in the earthly order of events had lately come to the English Crown and People, from a congress of British subjects in America: which, strange to relate, have proved more important to the human race than any communications yet received through any of the chickens of the Cock-lane brood.

France, less favoured on the whole as to matters spiritual than her sister of the shield and trident, rolled with exceeding smoothness down hill, making paper money and spending it. Under the guidance of her Christian pastors, she entertained herself, besides, with such humane achievements as sentencing a youth to have his hands cut off, his tongue torn out with pincers, and his body burned alive, because he had not kneeled down in the rain to do honour to a dirty procession of monks which passed within his view, at a distance of some fifty or sixty yards. It is likely enough that, rooted in the woods of France and Norway, there were growing trees, when that sufferer was put to death, already marked by the Woodman, Fate, to come down and be sawn into boards, to make a certain movable framework with a sack and a knife in it, terrible in history. It is likely enough that in the rough outhouses of some tillers of the heavy lands adjacent to Paris, there were sheltered from the weather that very day, rude carts, bespattered with rustic mire, snuffed about by pigs, and roosted in by poultry, which the Farmer, Death, had already set apart to be his tumbrils of the Revolution. But that Woodman and that Farmer, though they work unceasingly, work silently, and no one heard them as they went about with muffled tread: the rather, forasmuch as to entertain any suspicion that they were awake, was to be atheistical and traitorous.

In England, there was scarcely an amount of order and protection to justify much national boasting. Daring burglaries by armed men, and highway robberies, took place in the capital itself every night; families were publicly cautioned not to go out of town without removing their furniture to upholsterers' warehouses for security; the highwayman in the dark was a City tradesman in the light, and, being recognised and challenged by his fellow- tradesman whom he stopped in his character of "the Captain," gallantly shot him through the head and rode away; the mall was waylaid by seven robbers, and the guard shot three dead, and then got shot dead himself by the other four, "in consequence of the failure of his ammunition:" after which the mall was robbed in peace; that magnificent potentate, the Lord Mayor of London, was made to stand and deliver on Turnham Green, by one highwayman, who despoiled the illustrious creature in sight of all his retinue; prisoners in London gaols fought battles with their turnkeys, and the majesty of the law fired blunderbusses in among them, loaded with rounds of shot and ball; thieves snipped off diamond crosses from the necks of noble lords at Court drawing-rooms; musketeers went into St. Giles's, to search for contraband goods, and the mob fired on the musketeers, and the musketeers fired on the mob, and nobody thought any of these occurrences much out of the common way. In the midst of them, the hangman, ever busy and ever worse than useless, was in constant requisition; now, stringing up long rows of miscellaneous criminals; now, hanging a housebreaker on Saturday who had been taken on Tuesday; now, burning people in the hand at Newgate by the dozen, and now burning pamphlets at the door of Westminster Hall; to-day, taking the life of an atrocious murderer, and to-morrow of a wretched pilferer who had robbed a farmer's boy of sixpence……..

CHAPTER 8

A Sight

"You know the Old Bailey, well, no doubt?" said one of the oldest of clerks to Jerry the messenger.

"Ye-es, sir," returned Jerry, in something of a dogged manner. "I DO know the Bailey."

"Just so. And you know Mr. Lorry."

"I know Mr. Lorry, sir, much better than I know the Bailey. Much better," said Jerry, not unlike a reluctant witness at the establishment in question, "than I, as a honest tradesman, wish to know the Bailey."

"Very well. Find the door where the witnesses go in, and show the door-keeper this note for Mr. Lorry. He will then let you in."

"Into the court, sir?"

"Into the court."

Mr. Cruncher's eyes seemed to get a little closer to one another, and to interchange the inquiry, "What do you think of this?"

"Am I to wait in the court, sir?" he asked, as the result of that conference.

"I am going to tell you. The door-keeper will pass the note to Mr. Lorry, and do you make any gesture that will attract Mr. Lorry's attention, and show him where you stand. Then what you have to do, is, to remain there until he wants you."

"Is that all, sir?"

"That's all. He wishes to have a messenger at hand. This is to tell him you are there."

As the ancient clerk deliberately folded and superscribed the note, Mr. Cruncher, after surveying him in silence until he came to the blotting-paper stage, remarked:

"I suppose they'll be trying Forgeries this morning?"

"Treason!"

"That's quartering," said Jerry. "Barbarous!"

"It is the law," remarked the ancient clerk, turning his surprised spectacles upon him. "It is the law."

"It's hard in the law to spile a man, I think. Ifs hard enough to kill him, but it's wery hard to spile him, sir."

CHAPTER 26

A Plea

When the newly-married pair came home, the first person who appeared, to offer his congratulations, was Sydney Carton. They had not been at home many hours, when he presented himself. He was not improved in habits, or in looks, or in manner; but there was a certain rugged air of fidelity about him, which was new to the observation of Charles Darnay.

He watched his opportunity of taking Darnay aside into a window, and of speaking to him when no one overheard.

"Mr. Darnay," said Carton, "I wish we might be friends."

"We are already friends, I hope."

"You are good enough to say so, as a fashion of speech; but, I don't mean any fashion of speech. Indeed, when I say I wish we might be friends, I scarcely mean quite that, either."

Charles Darnay—as was natural—asked him, in all good-humour and good-fellowship, what he did mean?

"Upon my life," said Carton, smiling, "I find that easier to comprehend in my own mind, than to convey to yours. However, let me try. You remember a certain famous occasion when I was more drunk than— than usual?"

"I remember a certain famous occasion when you forced me to confess that you had been drinking."

"I remember it too. The curse of those occasions is heavy upon me, for I always remember them. I hope it may be taken into account one day, when all days are at an end for me! Don't be alarmed; I am not going to preach."

"I am not at all alarmed. Earnestness in you, is anything but alarming to me."

"Ah!" said Carton, with a careless wave of his hand, as if he waved that away. "On the drunken occasion in question (one of a large number, as you know), I was insufferable about liking you, and not liking you. I wish you would forget it."

"I forgot it long ago."

"Fashion of speech again! But, Mr. Darnay, oblivion is not so easy to me, as you represent it to be to you. I have by no means forgotten it, and a light answer does not help me to forget it."

"If it was a light answer," returned Darnay, "I beg your forgiveness for it. I had no other object than to turn a slight thing, which, to my surprise, seems to trouble you too much, aside. I declare to you, on the faith of a gentleman, that I have long dismissed it from my mind. Good Heaven, what was there to dismiss! Have I had nothing more important to remember, in the great service you rendered me that day?"

"As to the great service," said Carton, "I am bound to avow to you, when you speak of it in that way, that it was mere professional claptrap, I don't know that I cared what became of you, when I rendered it.—Mind! I say when I rendered it; I am speaking of the past."

"You make light of the obligation," returned Darnay, "but I will not quarrel with YOUR light answer."

"Genuine truth, Mr. Darnay, trust me! I have gone aside from my purpose; I was speaking about our being friends. Now, you know me; you know I am incapable of all the higher and better flights of men. If you doubt it, ask Stryver, and he'll tell you so."

"I prefer to form my own opinion, without the aid of his."

"Well! At any rate you know me as a dissolute dog, who has never done any good, and never will."

"I don't know that you `never will.'"

"But I do, and you must take my word for it. Well! If you could endure to have such a worthless fellow, and a fellow of such indifferent reputation, coming and going at odd times, I should ask that I might be permitted to come and go as a privileged person here; that I might be regarded as an useless (and I would add, if it were not for the resemblance I detected between you and me, an unornamental) piece of furniture, tolerated for its old service, and taken no notice of. I doubt if I should abuse the permission. It is a hundred to one if I should avail myself of it four times in a year. It would satisfy me, I dare say, to know that I had it."........

CHAPTER 32

The Grindstone

Tellson's Bank, established in the Saint Germain Quarter of Paris, was in a wing of a large house, approached by a courtyard and shut off from the street by a high wall and a strong gate. The house belonged to a great nobleman who had lived in it until he made a flight from the troubles, in his own cook's dress, and got across the borders. A mere beast of the chase flying from hunters, he was still in his metempsychosis no other than the same Monseigneur, the preparation of whose chocolate for whose lips had once occupied three strong men besides the cook in question.

Monseigneur gone, and the three strong men absolving themselves from the sin of having drawn his high wages, by being more than ready and willing to cut his throat on the altar of the dawning Republic one and indivisible of Liberty, Equality, Fraternity, or Death, Monseigneur's house had been first sequestrated, and then confiscated. For, all things moved so fast, and decree followed decree with that fierce precipitation, that now upon the third night of the autumn month of September, patriot emissaries of the law were in possession of Monseigneur's house, and had marked it with the tri-colour, and were drinking brandy in its state apartments.

A place of business in London like Tellson's place of business in Paris, would soon have driven the House out of its mind and into the Gazette. For, what would staid British responsibility and respectability have said to orange-trees in boxes in a Bank courtyard, and even to a Cupid over the counter? Yet such things were. Tellson's had whitewashed the Cupid, but he was still to be seen on the ceiling, in the coolest linen, aiming (as he very often does) at money from morning to night. Bankruptcy must inevitably have come of this young Pagan, in Lombard-street, London, and also of a curtained alcove in the rear of the immortal boy, and also of a looking-glass let into the wall, and also of clerks not at all old, who danced in public on the slightest provocation. Yet, a French Tellson's could get on with these things exceedingly well, and, as long as the times held together, no man had taken fright at them, and drawn out his money.

What money would be drawn out of Tellson's henceforth, and what would lie there, lost and forgotten; what plate and jewels would tarnish in Tellson's hiding-places, while the depositors rusted in prisons, and when they should have violently perished; how many accounts with Tellson's never to be balanced in this world, must be carried over into the next; no man could have said, that night, any more than Mr. Jarvis Lorry could, though he thought heavily of these questions. He sat by a newly-lighted wood fire (the blighted and unfruitful year was prematurely cold), and on his honest and courageous face there was a deeper shade than the pendent lamp could throw, or any object in the room distortedly reflect—a shade of horror.

He occupied rooms in the Bank, in his fidelity to the House of which he had grown to be a part, lie strong root-ivy. it chanced that they derived a kind of security from the patriotic occupation of the main building, but the true-hearted old gentleman never calculated about that. All such circumstances were indifferent to him, so that he did his duty. On the opposite side of the courtyard, under a colonnade, was extensive standin—for carriages—where, indeed, some carriages of Monseigneur yet stood. Against two of the pillars were fastened two great flaring flambeaux, and in the light of these, standing out in the open air, was a large grindstone: a roughly mounted thing which appeared to have hurriedly been brought there from some neighbouring smithy, or other workshop. Rising and looking out of window at these harmless objects, Mr. Lorry shivered, and retired to his seat by the fire. He had opened, not only the glass window, but the lattice blind outside it, and he had closed both again, and he shivered through his frame.

From the streets beyond the high wall and the strong gate, there came the usual night hum of the city, with now and then an indescribable ring in it, weird and unearthly, as if some unwonted sounds of a terrible nature were going up to Heaven.........

CHAPTER 45

The Footsteps Die Out For Ever

Along the Paris streets, the death-carts rumble, hollow and harsh. Six tumbrils carry the day's wine to La Guillotine. All the devouring and insatiate Monsters imagined since imagination could record itself, are fused in the one realisation, Guillotine. And yet there is not in France, with its rich variety of soil and climate, a blade, a leaf, a root, a sprig, a peppercorn, which will grow to maturity under conditions more certain than those that have produced this horror. Crush humanity out of shape once more, under similar hammers, and it will twist itself into the same tortured forms. Sow the same seed of rapacious license and oppression over again, and it will surely yield the same fruit according to its kind.

Six tumbrils roll along the streets. Change these back again to what they were, thou powerful enchanter, Time, and they shall be seen to be the carriages of absolute monarchs, the equipages of feudal nobles, the toilettes of flaring Jezebels, the churches that are not my father's house but dens of thieves, the huts of millions of starving peasants! No; the great magician who majestically works out the appointed order of the Creator, never reverses his transformations. "If thou be changed into this shape by the will of God," say the seers to the enchanted, in the wise Arabian stories, "then remain so! But, if thou wear this form through mere passing conjuration, then resume thy former aspect!" Changeless and hopeless, the tumbrils roll along.

As the sombre wheels of the six carts go round, they seem to plough up a long crooked furrow among the populace in the streets. Ridges of faces are thrown to this side and to that, and the ploughs go steadily onward. So used are the regular inhabitants of the houses to the spectacle, that in many windows there are no people, and in some the occupation of the hands is not so much as suspended, while the eyes survey the faces in the tumbrils. Here and there, the inmate has visitors to see the sight; then he points his finger, with something of the complacency of a curator or authorised exponent, to this cart and to this, and seems to tell who sat here yesterday, and who there the day before.

Of the riders in the tumbrils, some observe these things, and all things on their last roadside, with an impassive stare; others, with a lingering interest in the ways of life and men. Some, seated with drooping heads, are sunk in silent despair; again, there are some so heedful of their looks that they cast upon the multitude such glances as they have seen in theatres, and in pictures. Several close their eyes, and think, or try to get their straying thoughts together. Only one, and he a miserable creature, of a crazed aspect, is so shattered and made drunk by horror, that he sings, and tries to dance. Not one of the whole number appeals by look or gesture, to the pity of the people.

There is a guard of sundry horsemen riding abreast of the tumbrils, and faces are often turned up to some of them, and they are asked some question. It would seem to be always the same question, for, it is always followed by a press of people towards the third cart. The horsemen abreast of that cart, frequently point out one man in it with their swords. The leading curiosity is, to know which is he; he stands at the back of the tumbril with his head bent down, to converse with a mere girl who sits on the side of the cart, and holds his hand.

He has no curiosity or care for the scene about him, and always speaks to the girl. Here and there in the long street of St. Honoure, cries are raised against him. If they move him at all, it is only to a quiet smile, as he shakes his hair a little more loosely about his face. He cannot easily touch his face, his arms being bound.

On the steps of a church, awaiting the coming-up of the tumbrils, stands the Spy and prison-sheep. He looks into the first of them: not there. He looks into the second: not there. He already asks himself, "Has he sacrificed me?" when his face clears, as he looks into the third.

"Which is Evremonde?" says a man behind him.

"That. At the back there."

"With his hand in the girl's?"

"Yes."

The man cries, "Down, Evremonde! To the Guillotine all aristocrats! Down, Evremonde!"

"Hush, hush!" the Spy entreats him, timidly.

"And why not, citizen?"

"He is going to pay the forfeit: it will be paid in five minutes more. Let him be at peace."

But the man continuing to exclaim, "Down, Evremonde!" the face of Evremonde is for a moment turned towards him. Evremonde then sees the Spy, and looks attentively at him, and goes his way.

The clocks are on the stroke of three, and the furrow ploughed among the populace is turning round, to come on into the place of execution, and end. The ridges thrown to this side and to that, now crumble in and close behind the last plough as it passes on, for all are following to the Guillotine. In front of it, seated in chairs, as in a garden of public diversion, are a number of women, busily knitting. On one of the foremost chairs, stands The Vengeance, looking about for her friend.

"Therese!" she cries, in her shrill tones. "Who has seen her? Therese Defarge!"

"She never missed before," says a knitting-woman of the sisterhood.

"No; nor will she miss now," cries The Vengeance, petulantly. "Therese."

"Louder," the woman recommends.

Ay! Louder, Vengeance, much louder, and still she will scarcely hear thee. Louder yet, Vengeance, with a little oath or so added, and yet it will hardly bring her. Send other women up and down to seek her, lingering somewhere; and yet, although the messengers have done dread deeds, it is questionable whether of their own wills they will go far enough to find her!

"Bad Fortune!" cries The Vengeance, stamping her foot in the chair, "and here are the tumbrils! And Evremonde will be despatched in a wink, and she not here! See her knitting in my hand, and her empty chair ready for her. I cry with vexation and disappointment!"

As The Vengeance descends from her elevation to do it, the tumbrils begin to discharge their loads. The ministers of Sainte Guillotine are robed and ready. Crash!—A head is held up, and the knitting- women who scarcely lifted their eyes to look at it a moment ago when it could think and speak, count One.

The second tumbril empties and moves on; the third comes up. Crash! —And the knitting-women, never faltering or pausing in their Work, count Two.

The supposed Evremonde descends, and the seamstress is lifted out next after him. He has not relinquished her patient hand in getting out, but still holds it as he promised. He gently places her with her back to the crashing engine that constantly whirrs up and falls, and she looks into his face and thanks him.

"But for you, dear stranger, I should not be so composed, for I am naturally a poor little thing, faint of heart; nor should

I have been able to raise my thoughts to Him who was put to death, that we might have hope and comfort here to-day. I think you were sent to me by Heaven."

"Or you to me," says Sydney Carton. "Keep your eyes upon me, dear child, and mind no other object."

"I mind nothing while I hold your hand. I shall mind nothing when I let it go, if they are rapid."

"They will be rapid. Fear not!"

The two stand in the fast-thinning throng of victims, but they speak as if they were alone. Eye to eye, voice to voice, hand to hand, heart to heart, these two children of the Universal Mother, else so wide apart and differing, have come together on the dark highway, to repair home together, and to rest in her bosom.

"Brave and generous friend, will you let me ask you one last question? I am very ignorant, and it troubles me—just a little."

"Tell me what it is."

"I have a cousin, an only relative and an orphan, like myself, whom I love very dearly. She is five years younger than I, and she lives in a farmer's house in the south country. Poverty parted us, and she knows nothing of my fate—for I cannot write—and if I could, how should I tell her! It is better as it is."

"Yes, yes: better as it is."

"What I have been thinking as we came along, and what I am still thinking now, as I look into your kind strong face which gives me so much support, is this:—If the Republic really does good to the poor, and they come to be less hungry, and in all ways to suffer less, she may live a long time: she may even live to be old."

"What then, my gentle sister?"

"Do you think:" the uncomplaining eyes in which there is so much endurance, fill with tears, and the lips part a little more and tremble: "that it will seem long to me, while I wait for her in the better land where I trust both you and I will be mercifully sheltered?"

"It cannot be, my child; there is no Time there, and no trouble there."

"You comfort me so much! I am so ignorant. Am I to kiss you now? Is the moment come?"

"Yes."

She kisses his lips; he kisses hers; they solemnly bless each other. The spare hand does not tremble as he releases it; nothing worse than a sweet, bright constancy is in the patient face. She goes next before him—is gone; the knitting-women count Twenty-Two.

"I am the Resurrection and the Life, saith the Lord: he that believeth in me, though he were dead, yet shall he live: and whosoever liveth and believeth in me shall never die."

The murmuring of many voices, the upturning of many faces, the pressing on of many footsteps in the outskirts of the crowd, so that it swells forward in a mass, like one great heave of water, all flashes away. Twenty-Three.

They said of him, about the city that night, that it was the peacefullest man's face ever beheld there. Many added that he looked sublime and prophetic.

One of the most remarkable sufferers by the same axe—a woman-had asked at the foot of the same scaffold, not long before, to be allowed to write down the thoughts that were inspiring her. If he had given any utterance to his, and they were prophetic, they would have been these:

"I see Barsad, and Cly, Defarge, The Vengeance, the Juryman, the Judge, long ranks of the new oppressors who have risen on the destruction of the old, perishing by this retributive instrument, before it shall cease out of its present use. I see a beautiful city and a brilliant people rising from this abyss, and, in their struggles to be truly free, in their triumphs and defeats, through long years to come, I see the evil of this time and of the previous time of which this is the natural birth, gradually making expiation for itself and wearing out.

"I see the lives for which I lay down my life, peaceful, useful, prosperous and happy, in that England which I shall see no more. I see Her with a child upon her bosom, who bears my name. I see her father, aged and bent, but otherwise restored, and faithful to all men in his healing office, and at peace. I see the good old man, so long their friend, in ten years' time enriching them with all he has, and passing tranquilly to his reward.

"I see that I hold a sanctuary in their hearts, and in the hearts of their descendants, generations hence. I see her, an old woman, weeping for me on the anniversary of this day. I see her and her husband, their course done, lying side by side in their last earthly bed, and I know that each was not more honoured and held sacred in the other's soul, than I was in the souls of both.

"I see that child who lay upon her bosom and who bore my name, a man winning his way up in that path of life which once was mine. I see him winning it so well, that my name is made illustrious there by the light of his. I see the blots I threw upon it, faded away. I see him, fore-most of just judges and honoured men, bringing a boy of my name, with a forehead that I know and golden hair, to this place— then fair to look upon, with not a trace of this day's disfigurement —and I hear him tell the child my story, with a tender and a faltering voice.

"It is a far, far better thing that I do, than I have ever done; it is a far, far better rest that I go to than I have ever known."

And There Are Many More Chapters Which Should Be Read By Students.

Bibliography

A Tale of Two Cities: *Dickens's Revolutionary Novel.* Boston: Twain Publishers, 1991.

Beckwith, Charles, ed. *Twentieth Century Interpretations of* A TALE OF TWO CITIES. Englewood Cliffs, New Jersey: Prentice-Hall, 1972.

Bloom, Harold. *Charles Dickens's* A TALE OF TWO CITIES. New York: Chelsea House Publishers, 1987.

Collins, Philip, ed. Dickens: The Critical Heritage. London: The Chaucer Press, 1971. Good for learning what critics from 1859 to present have said about Dickens.

Costell, Michael, ed. *Critical Essays on Charles Dickens's* A TALE OF TWO CITIES. New York: G.K. Hall, 1998.

Dickens, Charles. *A Tale of Two Cities.* New York: Barnes and Noble Books, 1993.

Evans, B. Ifor. *A Short History of English Literature.* Baltimore, Md., Penguin Books, 1940. Brief and not especially helpful panorama of English literature from *Beowulf* to Joyce.

Fielding, K. J. *Charles Dickens: A Critical Introduction*. New: York: David McKay Company, Inc., 1958. Chapter Ten is especially good concerning the background of Dickens and *Tale.*

Glancy, Ruth. A Tale of Two Cities: *An Annotated Bibliography.* New York: Garland, 1993.

Goldberg, Michael. *Carlyle and Dickens.* Athens, Ga.: University of Georgia Press, 1972. Chapter Seven is excellent analysis of *Tale* and Carlyle's *The French Revolution.*

Holmes, Mabel Dodge, ed. Dickens's *A Tale of Two Cities,* abridged version. New York: Globe Book Company, 1941.

Karl, Frederick R. *A Reader's Guide to the Nineteenth-Century British Novel.* New York: The Noonday Press, 1964. Chapter Five gives excellent overview of Dickens, but dismisses *Tale* in few sentences.

Marzials, Frank T. *Life of Charles Dickens.* London: Walter Scott, 1887.

Murray, Brian. *Charles Dickens.* New York: Continuum, 1994.

Newlin, George. *Understanding* A TALE OF TWO CITIES: *A Student Casebook to Issues, Sources, and Historical Documents.* Westport, Connecticut: Greenwood Press, 1998.

Price, Martin. *To the Palace of Wisdom.* New York: Doubleday, 1964. Not very helpful book on Burke's writing.

Priestly, J.B. *Charles Dickens: A Pictorial Biography.* London: Thames and Hudson, 1961.

Sanders, Andrew. *The Companion to* A TALE OF TWO CITIES. London: Unwin Hyman, 1988.

Swisher, Clarice, ed. *Readings on Charles Dickens.* San Diego, California: Greenhaven, 1998.

The Modern Library 1950. Probably best book for a critical introduction to Dickens and the novel.

The New Encyclopedia Britannica, Volume 17. Chicago: The University of Chicago, 1992.

Wagenknecht, Edward ed. Dickens's *A Tale of Two Cities.* New York: Random House,

Yarwood, Doreen. European Costumes; 4000 Years of Fashion. London: B. T. Tatsford Ltd., 1975. Drawings used to show modes of dress. Not as good as the Lauer book, but it has fair coverage of Europe's fashion during the eighteenth century. Pp. 177-213 are useful.

Youngham, Edith Carol, ed. Dickens', A Tale of Two Cities, abridged version. New York: Harcourt, Brace & World, Inc., 1950. Has excellent background of eighteenth-century Paris. Students should enjoy this.

